Conversational Design

Improving participation and decision-making in public organizations

I0112673

Michael Arnold Mages

BIS Publishers

BIS Publishers

Timorplein 46

1094 CC Amsterdam

The Netherlands

T +31 (0)20 515 02 30

bis@bispublishers.com

www.bispublishers.com

ISBN 978-90-636-9732-7

A thank you to all who supported this work.

A project of this scope cannot be completed by the effort of one person.

First, I would like to thank people who were additionally part of bringing this book to completion. Aure Schrock, editor for their criticality and frank and careful feedback, Melissa Neely, designer for her striking graphic narrative, and Harm van Kessel at BIS, whose voluminous patience and forbearance made this project possible.

Too many students to name have contributed to this work, volunteered to act as facilitators for community meetings, transcribed surveys, collated data, and challenged my ideas with their perspectives. Thank you to the students of Carnegie Mellon University and Northeastern University. Most recently, Northeastern doctoral students Chenfei Yu and Maria Fernanda Ramirez Cifuentes have argued interpretations, developed new applications for these approaches, and enriched my academic life.

I'd like to thank former mentors from Carnegie Mellon University: Jonathan Chapman, Dan Lockton, and Cameron Tonkinwise, who all provided critical guidance and feedback at different points in the early development of this work. Jonathan and Dan lent their astute critical eyes to the many of the arguments and provided collegial emotional support throughout the initial development of these approaches. I am forever grateful to Cameron for his unwavering criticality, and creative suggestions for resources, activities, approaches and interventions in firsts years of this project.

Some of the work described was completed in partnership with Carnegie Mellon University's Program for Deliberative Democracy, under the leadership and guidance of Robert Cavalier. Robert provided his experience, and our collaborations, discussions, and arguments were a valuable formative component of this work. Robert also lent encouragement and support in founding the Art of Democracy.

ACKNOWLEDGEMENTS · A THANK YOU TO ALL WHO SUPPORTED THIS WORK.

The Carnegie Mellon University Center for Diversity & Inclusion supported other aspects of this research. M. Shernell Smith offered the opportunity to work with the student orientation leadership team, which resulted in many valuable insights.

Work with WQED, the Heinz Endowments, and the Environmental Charter School was created in the context of commercial relationships with those organizations as clients. In those contexts I was working as a designer and founding partner of the Art of Democracy, a start-up spun out of the CMU Program for Deliberative Democracy. I would like to thank Selena Schmidt and Tim Dawson, who were my collaborators on these projects.

Much of this work would not have been possible without the support of the City of Pittsburgh. The municipal government was a key collaborator throughout this process, offering resources, connections to potential collaborators, and a *raison d'être*. Mayor Bill Peduto, Alex Pazuchanics, Grant Ervin, and Ray Gastil generously opened the processes of their citizen engagement activities to me. Most significantly, Sally Stadelman played perhaps the largest role, and her generous sharing of her expertise, perspective, and intellectual curiosity, as well as her fruitful involvement in nearly every project with the City of Pittsburgh was invaluable.

The City of Boston also provided more recent ground to test these ideas. Special thanks go to Renato Castelo and Cynthia Lin, Yusufi Vali, Farah Elhadidy and Kristin McSwain.

At Northeastern University, where I have spent the past years has been a rich environment for risk-taking and expansion of these ideas in new contexts. Of the many colleagues who have helped me, I'd like to especially thank Dietmar Offenhuber for his courage, mentorship and guidance, my Center for Design colleagues including Miso Kim and Paolo Ciuccarelli for their unwavering support and encouragement, the entire team of Community Data Theater practitioners, especially Dani Snyder-Young. Kim Lucas negotiated critical bridges between Northeastern University and the City of Boston. Kristian Kloeckl provided support developing this book proposal. I'd like to especially thank Estefania Ciliotta Chehade, whose work as a student, and continued work as a colleague has inspired new perspectives and approaches in my own work.

The Dean's Office of the College of Arts, Media, & Design supported this work through a variety of grants, as well as providing connections to research opportunities.

My parents, Al and Susan listened to my complaints about the writing process with patience.

Last and most significantly, I would like to thank Tarissa, my spouse, and my daughters Emily, Camille, Lillian, and Josephine. Without their support, sacrifices, kindness, and forbearance throughout these years, this project would not have been realized. This book is dedicated to them.

CONVERSATIONAL DESIGN
TABLE OF CONTENTS

INTRODUCTION
Why Do We Need Conversation?

CHAPTER 1
Designing a Surfacing Conversation

CHAPTER 5
Planning a Conversation

CHAPTER 6
How Things Support a Conversation

CHAPTER 9
Conclusion

FIGURES

Why Do We Need Conversation?

A STORY ABOUT EQUIPOISE

There's a peculiar word used by medical practitioners who research decision-making: equipoise.

Equipoise is a state in which a choice in treatment is to be made among a set of treatment options, where the balance of outcomes and treatment effectiveness cannot be clearly quantified by the physician. Beyond medical practice where the term is used, equipoise can describe more mundane decision-making situations.

A group of neighbors might come together to discuss redesigning a traffic corridor road. The decisions that they make in the basement of the local community and cultural center will have far-reaching effects on the neighborhood —deciding where bus stops will be and where "curb cuts" will be allowed to provide access to parking in front of businesses. A group of residents might come

1

together to talk about policies that create more affordable housing in their community. Similar to the example above, these policies decide what kind of housing will be built and where, and will have long-term and far-reaching effects on the character and value of the neighborhood. A group of parents and school administrators might come together to discuss where school catchment boundary lines will be drawn. These boundary lines have implications that extend over years and shape the lives of the many young people who are routed to different elementary, middle, and high school experiences.

Equipoise is a state in which a choice in treatment is to be made among a set of treatment options, where the balance of outcomes and treatment effectiveness cannot be clearly quantified by the physician.

Contained in these conversations is a deeper activity than merely choosing between alternatives. They take place in the context of a dynamic and evolving social and historical frame that has developed over hundreds of years—and continues to change and evolve. The distinctions that make some alternatives more desirable than others are not absolute. Conversation is often how these kinds of decisions get made. Conversations with a physician, a loved one, a friend, or a trusted advisor are how people collaboratively deliberate or make sense of complex situations. Conversations are the medium through which people make commitments to one another. They are the primary modality and the path to healing for most patients engaged in psychotherapy. Conversational technologies pervade our everyday experience. During waking hours, little more than a minute goes by that we do not receive an electronic request for conversation. In short, conversation is how we humans open our lifeworlds to each other—the foundation of how we do things together.

When designers design a thing, beyond designing form, function, and meaning, they create a set of potentials for conversations to be had with, through, or facilitated by that thing. Yet the role that these things play in conversation is often neglected or ignored by the designers, often to the detriment of the conversational participants.

Throughout the following chapters, we will unpack the complexities of these deceptively simple conversations and how design plays a role in steering these conversations.

CONVERSATIONS ARE FUNDAMENTAL TO HUMAN EXPERIENCE

What Conversational Design is Not

Before we get too deeply into this discussion, let's take a moment to also discuss what we will and *will not* be talking about in this book. It is essential that a conversation begin with goodwill on both sides. Therefore, this book will not discuss conversations from the point of view of deception or coercion. Imbalances exist in many conversations, but the goal of the engagements presented here is to rectify some of these difficulties, not create situations where participants are placed on an uneven field. Of course, design can be used to exacerbate imbalance. Consider the classic scene in Frank Capra's 1946 film *It's a Wonderful Life,* in which George Bailey is engaged by Mr. Potter in a negotiation conversation and finds the chair he is offered is much lower in height than Mr. Potter's. Unlike the winners and losers of debate or negotiation, problem-solving is difficult enough without deliberately damaging the conversational field by design.

We will also not discuss conversations that force people to take a particular path. A wealth of writing already exists on persuasion, advertising, and the conversations of the sales process. There may even be medical conversations in which a physician is convinced that they know the "right path" for their patient. We will instead focus on sense-making, developing a shared understanding, and surfacing all parties' expertise and lived experience in relation to the problem.

The conversations in this book are also not negotiations—where two parties engage and attempt to come to an agreement that balances conflicting interests. Negotiation is organized around a zero-sum game that creates winners and losers. The conversations that we will engage with in this book are informed by constructive engagement from both parties aiming to collaboratively find solutions for difficult problems. In other words, I assume that the actors in the conversation are oriented toward doing something together.

The role things play in conversation is often neglected

In this book, I argue that things play a greater role in shaping conversations than is often believed. For academic practitioners, this sentence opens a "can of worms" because it requires defining the seemingly innocuous word *thing*. To prevent people from abruptly closing the book in frustration, I will offer a brief definition here. I'll also spend the rest of the book unpacking the implications of thingness in conversation. Things are at once a set of assembled materials and a highly variable set of social relations that occur around and through a thing. A thing might be an object like a table or chair, or a set of processes put in place by a city government or a resident. Things are composed of both material stuff, and socially constructed perspectives that, like a comet's tail, cling to materiality, making it visible and meaningful to people.

A few examples might make this definition clearer. A table and chairs that support conversation are clearly things composed of metal, wood, and plastic. The chairs are also composed of a social perspective that views them as suitable for sitting on. Most people see a chair and think something like "Ah! I can sit there!" They develop assumptions about whether the chair will be comfortable or not. Other things might have a different balance of social perspectives and materials. The space where we are playing frisbee in the park might not have precise boundaries, but it is understood by social perspectives that define who is playing and who should avoid walking through the area. I'd argue that the space of playing frisbee is more social than material, even though there is grass, air, and a frisbee that each might be identified as a material part of the game. But the space of frisbee play is no less a thing than the chair.

This book will help designers to think more broadly about the impact of their design—to consider how the things they design shape social situations. Designers who are working in civic contexts will better understand the unique ways the things that they design function. For example, things in political processes act in a different way. Sometimes they compress information. A report carries the intents, values, and beliefs of thousands of citizens into the polity, for example. Other things frame an issue for participants, inviting them to participate. Sometimes they serve as a record of one person's political intent.

This book offers a unique perspective on conversational design. It helps designers see the things they make in a way they never have before. This book will show you how to shape conversations through designing these combinations of social and physical. In it, I'll draw from cases that I have engaged with over the past decade to discuss how things structure, facilitate, and contextualize our conversations.

Structuring

Things can organize a conversation. They can tell participants when it is their turn to speak, reveal the current topic of conversation, or indicate how long each part of the conversation will last. One obvious example is the use of a meeting agenda for organizing the topics that need to be discussed. Agendas communicate what will happen in a meeting and enforce the sequence of conversations. Other things like agendas actively structure conversations. Some meetings begin with "ground rules" or have a specific title indicating possible actions within the meeting. For example, no employee would expect to have an in-depth conversation about their team's past performance in a "Project Kick-off" meeting, although the same people might be in both meetings. Throughout this book, we will discuss many things (like agendas and titles, but also models and room arrangements) that help structure the conversation, some more social, some more material.

Facilitating

Things can facilitate conversation. If you have ever been to a dinner party with a long rectangular table, you may remember the challenge of being able to converse only with the two people seated on either side of you. Side-by-side seating at a dinner party, meeting, or theater can discourage whole-group conversation. Seating can encourage conversation in a more egalitarian way if placed in a circle. A physician's consultation room can be set up with a computer monitor on a swinging arm, so both patient and doctor can look at digital health records together. Or the computer monitor might act as a blockade that the physician and patient must look around or over to discuss treatment options. Difficult topics can be approached using model making, or "manipulatables." Sand tray therapy uses a set of small figurines as delegates for concepts or actors when people need to talk about a difficult topic. Somewhat different than things that structure, things that facilitate offer to smooth the path, making the desired actions easier, more pleasant, or more engaging.

Contextualizing

Things can provide important context in a conversation. Until digital 3D renderings dominated the practice, architects built scale models of proposed buildings or additions out of cardboard. A toy version of a building, (a maquette) serves several important purposes. It shows the scale of various parts in relation to one another and the scale of the completed building in relation to the site. A maquette can be produced cheaply, relative to the completed solution, which allows the architect and client to "play" together with the proposed intervention. More subtly, a maquette organizes people in a circle to discuss the proposed approach. When people come to discuss the building, the maquette invites people to gather around it. Everyone is looking in, seeing it from a different angle. If the architect were to present the building with a slide presentation or a video, this mode of presentation would organize the group into an "audience" likely in a darkened room, in rows of chairs. If the architect were merely to describe the building with words or showed only elevation drawings, the client might fail to see important contextual cues. They might miss how the rooms connect to one another, where windows might be placed, or have little understanding of what the infinite possibilities of views of the building are.

Conversations are how humans do things together

The etymology of the word conversation shows it descends from the Latin *conversārī,* meaning both to "turn oneself about" and "to live with."[1] Alternate definitions of conversation include ideas of spiritual intimacy, sexual intimacy, cohabitation, and business dealings.[2]

Considering these past and current understandings, conversation has been bound up with the idea of being, intimacy, exchange, and congress with other humans. However, these different intimacies have faded, leaving an idea of conversation solely focused on the idea of talk.

Cybernetician and polymath Gordon Pask (1928–1996) was deeply interested in conversation throughout his life. For Pask, conversations were how people learn about and come to know the world. Pask had a nuanced and subtle understanding of conversation through the lens of learning and memory. While Pask made many models to describe the various aspects of conversation through learning, the most foundational aspect—of how conversation works through memory—was never visualized.

---

1   "converse, v." *OED Online.* Oxford University Press, March 2015. Web. 10 May 2015.
2   "conversation, n." *OED Online.* Oxford University Press, March 2015. Web. 10 May 2015.

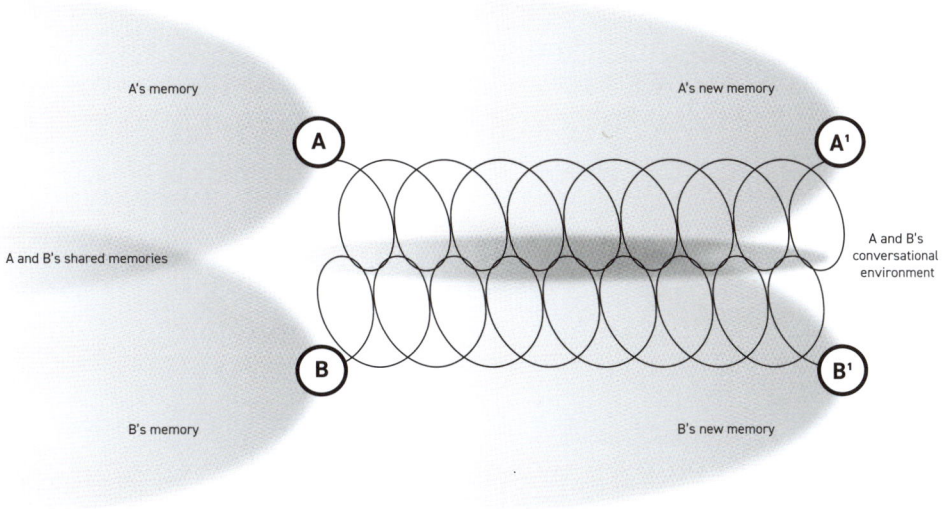

Figure 1: Model of conversation and memory after Gordon Pask

To aid in envisioning how conversations work, this proposed diagram is derived from Pask's (1987) descriptions of conversation. Figure 1 depicts a conversation between two actors: A and B. While a conversation may occur between multiple actors, our idealized version shows only two for the sake of graphic simplicity. In conversation, a kind of evolution—or to put it more staidly, learning—takes place. Through that learning, the participants become different individuals. The memories generated by the conversation are incorporated into their brain matter as neurochemical signatures—effectively changing these human organisms into something new.

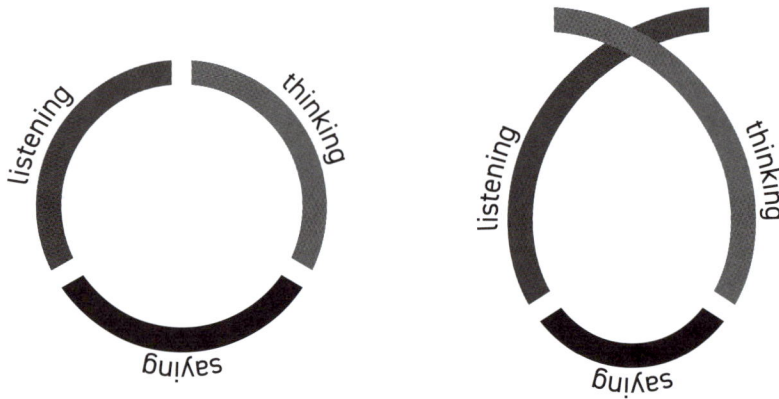

Figure 2: The principal conversational actions

Additionally, participants in conversations construct shared memories. Communication in a conversation is less like passing messages back and forth (imagine shooting message cylinders back and forth through pneumatic tubes) and more like the two participants becoming entwined and entangled with one another. Each participant discloses a bit of self to the other. Through that process, they each grow and change as a person.

The model above proposes that the conversation takes place in a conversational environment composed of physical things and personal history (as experienced through memory). In our idealized conversation (shown in Figure 1 by a series of turns), but also in any functional conversation, A and B must come to the conversation with a degree of shared memory. At the very least, the shared memory must include a mutual agreement to the meaning of the vocabulary of the conversation. In many more cases, A and B's shared memory will include an understanding of the context of the conversation, a shared culture, and shared values and beliefs. It is better yet if A and B both recognize that the other actor is not a singular being but part of a network of beings that are affected by the outcome of the conversation. The conversation, experienced in-action, exists only in memory. In this model, each loop is composed of moments of listening, thinking, and saying. In any conversation, those aspects are slightly out of phase for each participant: at any point each participant will be at a slightly different point in the loop (ideally, listening while the other person is talking).

This book considers how to design the environment for each conversation. The conversational environment consists of the images, spaces, and objects that surround the conversation. In the context of the deliberative democracy projects that I have worked on, the environment of the conversation event is thought of in a rather delimited sense, similar to the way people theorized as participants are divorced from their existence as people. For instance, Burkhalter, Gastil, and Kelshaw (2002) define the behavioral elements of face-to-face deliberative conversation as:

> (a) a process that involves the careful weighing of information and views, (b) an egalitarian process with adequate speaking opportunities and attentive listening by participants, and (c) dialogue that bridges differences among participants' diverse ways of speaking and knowing. (p. 418)

Further, Burkhalter et al. claim that participants must evaluate solutions and reach decisions (though decisions need not be shared among participants); and group members must attempt to consider and understand what each individual says, and give each participant's views mutual respect.

These behavioral, deliberative approaches fail to recognize that to model conversation as principally words and thoughts is to leave the material world behind. Little is said of bodies unless they are deliberative bodies; the places of deliberation or the tangible components of the interaction receive short shrift if they are considered at all.

In the case of deliberative democracy protocols, the material elements might consist of the invitation, email, or social media post that informs someone about the meeting; the images and text framed as a pedagogical slideshow; the briefing document that contains complementary information in greater detail; and the survey instrument that collects participants' feedback. To go further, the material environment consists of folding tables and chairs, the church basements or dusty union halls, or the community rooms at the local recreation center. The material environment may even include the surrounding neighborhood, with its layers of physical infrastructure and the natural environment.

The book *Democracy in Motion* (2012) contains a section promisingly called "Process and Design." Rather than using the term "design" to indicate the material focus more familiar to design practitioners, the section focuses predominantly on the processes of defining issues and designing deliberative events. Engagement with material processes within or outside of the event is either not addressed or addressed only in the context of running an effective deliberative event. Equally important is the ability of event creators to richly engage with the culture of the organization that convenes the event and the culture of the communities that convene to share their situated knowledge and experience.

To understand the context of community conversations more fully and effectively design in those situations, a practitioner needs to re-read the material environment where conversations are constituted. The environment consists of objects, but also includes the history of the issue and how it manifests in the affected communities, all of which participants must make sense of.

Sense-making

Conversations are, at their core, a sense-making activity. If you imagine a conversation where sense-making is happening, you would hear people talking together to unpack their understanding of an issue. People might be sharing facts, definitions, opinions, or narratives. People might be agreeing about some of the definitions, perhaps challenging, or even disputing them. People engaged in sense-making would be gathering information, gaining an understanding from the information, and then using that understanding to do something.

Problem-solving

More specific than sense-making, problem-solving is an activity that often requires conversation. Donald Schön went so far as to refer to design—a discipline that is quite engaged with problems and their solutions—as a "reflective conversation with the materials of the situation" (Schön, 1983). In complicated contemporary situations, it often takes a conversation just to agree upon what the problem is. Problem-solving is an important act for conversation and a special kind of sense-making, as it requires a couple or group of stakeholders to gather information, gain an understanding, and agree on what the problem is. Urban planner Horst Rittel wrote about a special class of problems—wicked problems—where the difficulty lies in merely agreeing on what the problem is.

Wicked problems showed up early in the career of facilitator Adam Kahane, where he facilitated conversation among a group of people to propose scenarios, not solutions, for the future of South Africa. Rather than try to solve the variety of intractable problems, moving forward by attaining agreement on what the possible futures might be was a valued outcome. In more mundane problem-solving situations, a conversation as problem-solving might follow the sequence of first defining the problem, proposing and evaluating approaches to the problem, implementing an approach, and evaluating the outcomes.

Coordinating work

Another role for conversations that will be addressed in this book is their role in coordinating work. Conversations coordinating work typically contain nameable statements. Some are as simple as a request, negotiation, and promise. Request: "Tom, can you take a look at this article draft for me?" Offer: "When do you need it back? Is Tuesday OK?" Acceptance: "Tuesday is fine." Promise: "OK, I can do that." Oftentimes, the coordinating work is significantly more complex and requires many conversations that stretch across days, weeks, or even years.

Yet when we coordinate work, the essential element of this coordination is trust-building. The request → promise couplet, if fulfilled, is the foundation of collaborative relationships. The design of conversations coordinating work has been the basis of research for researchers such as Pelle Ehn, who initiated the Scandinavian movement of Computer-Supported Cooperative Work. Throughout his work Ehn has emphasized the importance of collaborative dialog and participatory decision-making in organizational settings, advocating for inclusive processes that support the dignity of the worker (participant) and delegate power to workers to co-create their own work environments. The research and writing of Franciso Flores, Terry Winograd, and Lucy Suchman have included discussions of commitment-making in professional and interpersonal life. While these thinkers were occasionally at odds, coordinating complex work is of ongoing interest and a central theme, and throughout this book we will return to and evolve lines of thinking initiated by this group.

How things work in conversations

In all the conversational examples above, things can be marshaled to guide people to have better conversations. Things can get models "out there" so participants can play with them, adjust specifics, and reposition or substitute parts of a model. In emotional conversations, things can act as delegates to represent concepts, actions, or beings that may be difficult to discuss directly. Things can guide participants to understand the different capacities of the conversation—what agency is possible from it, what its rules are, and even productive ways to break the rules.

We will spend the rest of the book recounting the variety of possible material interventions that may improve a conversation. But let's begin with just one example that has proved so valuable that it has become a nearly ubiquitous stand-in for creative thinking in business and design.

My own computer monitor is surrounded by Post-its. Some contain a fragment of an idea that I one day hope to develop into an article, while others serve as memory aids—containing a list of budget indexes that my various university purchases need to be reported against, a question I need to bring up in a future meeting, or a reminder to ask how a friend's project is going. One contains a little motivational phrase spoken in a meeting with my department chair and mentor: "Get your voice out there!" Some contain central questions that I try to answer every time I write "Why should anyone care about this specific situation?"

Post-it notes are a ubiquitous tool for designers. In the Cambridge office of the design firm IDEO, Post-it notes cover the wall floor-to-ceiling in the back hallway. Post-its are not just incidental tools in the creative process serving their principal function but can be found on doors and even in the bathroom. Post-its have a central function as reminders or prompts, referential to whatever they happen to be stuck to. They act as a representative of a network node when a group of designers are developing models, or as a company division, or a feature of a new product, or carry a particular user's goals. But beyond this more conventional use, IDEO's Post-its transcend spatial boundaries, trespassing into many places where Post-its should not go. They speak to you from kitchen cabinets, doors, windows, and bathroom surfaces. The Post-its at the IDEO office are more than leftovers from the creative process, but an active conversation reflecting office culture. Here the Post-its are—in their tactile immediacy and collaborative affordance—more than just representatives of the abstract-made-physical. They epitomize the culture of conversation, collective creativity, and innovation that IDEO hopes to foster.

In short, the complexities of how the Post-it functions, the intelligence it contains, and the spirit that is imbued in each of these colorful squares of adhesive paper manifest as a visual tapestry of ideas, insights, and iterations, reflecting the dynamic interchange with a designer and his community. These Post-its engage the attentive person in conversation, shaping outcomes, perspectives and actions. Not to go too far down the road of the animistic perspective, but these Post-its are active creatures in our environment organizing our thinking into bite-sized 3"× 3" units that can be manipulated and rearranged, shaping outcomes, perspectives, and actions in collaboration with designers and their communities.

The conversational terrain

Dialog

The essence of dialog is that it is co-produced. What does that mean? Think about two singers singing a duet together. You'll hear a pleasant duet if the two singers are attentive to the ongoing singing by listening and responding to each other. It's not enough that both singers are singing notes and words at the same time. They must be actively engaged in their own sound-making while listening attentively to the sound of the other. In other words, through active and attentive engagement, or co-production, the singers are in dialog.

David Bohm literally wrote the book on dialog. For Bohm, dialog is a co-produced system of committed engagement between people. Strongly relational, dialog goes further than the shared meaning-making in a dialectic or the progressive steps toward agreement in a negotiation. However, dialog is also the pathway toward a relationship that extends beyond the literal meaning of spoken words or performed actions.

Deliberation

Deliberative events surface opinions and feelings on an issue that exists within the group of participating attendees. Bruno Latour refers to this as the "matter of concern." Such events are the site of co-producing the conversations between participants, as well as generating a deeper engagement with the matters of concern that the people participating face. Considering the deliberative event as a form of service, the outputs have a character that is at once rational and relational, informed by their situated expertise and lived experiences.

Deliberation is how participants dig deeper into their own understanding of a matter of concern. Through this process, they consider their own perspectives in light of alternatives, informed by hearing about the lived experiences of other participants. Deliberation is a process of careful consideration that relies upon *phronesis*, or the practical wisdom of participants.

Hannah Arendt, in her imaginative and influential work *The Human Condition* described deliberation as a fundamental cornerstone of considered political action. Arendt envisioned meaningful deliberative spaces where a community could come together to engage on matters of common concern. In *Inclusion and Democracy,* Iris Marion Young offered a framework for a communicative democracy in which deliberative spaces are accessible and equitable. They challenge dominant power structures by fostering genuine dialog across social and economic divides.

Planning

> In preparing for battle I have always found that plans are
> useless, but planning is indispensable. —Dwight Eisenhower[3]

Much of this book approaches conversation as a tool for planning. The insightful reader will notice that we did not refer to plans here, as these are "frozen" concepts of how specific actions will manifest. Plans might result from conversational designs, but they should not be considered as the most positive (or only!) endpoint. Rather, the designs we will discuss involve supporting a group of interested people working through a problem they are implicated in. Perhaps in an ideal world, actions might always ensue from these conversations, but the reality is that any given conversation might simply be an inflection point on a longer journey to subsequent actions or conversations.

High stakes

The matter of *stakes* figures prominently in this book. A conversation about where we might go to lunch together or what color we might choose to paint our bathroom are examples of low-stakes conversations. All that is at risk is a mildly negative experience or the possibility of a positive one. High stakes means that something quite significant is at play. In this book, we will discuss high-stakes conversations from the perspective of the content that is under discussion. There may be other aspects of a conversation that contribute to it being fraught. Difficult contemporary social relationships between participants, a history of negative interactions, or feelings of shame around a topic can all contribute to a difficult situation. The definition of high stakes I will use in this book encompasses an *expert* and a *client* attempting to engage in planning where the situation is imminent, the topic is of consequence to the client, and there exists a significant imbalance of knowledge, experience, and emotion regarding the conversation topic.

3   Richard Nixon, *Six Crises* (1962); attributed to Dwight Eisenhower

Getting to know conversations

I've written this book to share expertise I've developed by conducting over 100 community meetings and workshops over the past ten years. I've conducted countless prototyping sessions with city and community partners and reflected on the process, both as a practitioner and academic. With work like this, it is a bit difficult for a designer to claim authorship over what happens in the community conversation they designed. So much of value that comes from this work involves bringing together diverse voices, and each voice shapes the discourse and contributes their own perspective. Yet authorship over the design work itself is more clear, involving thinking rigorously beforehand, anticipating challenges, and orienting participants towards positive outcomes. Like much design work, the designer sets the stage, but the actual work of the conversation is performed by other people. Facilitators, moderators, participants, greeters, invited experts, caterers and custodial staff must all play their separate roles in civic conversation events. In other words, for this work to be effective, it must be *co-produced* and requires the engagement and ongoing coordination and attentiveness of people playing various roles to create.

Learning from the success of a method can come from either a smooth and seamless execution or from disgruntled or recalcitrant participants. Participants might linger long after the event is over, making plans to see each other again or continue the conversation in a nearby pub. But for the designer, being aware of the signs of failed conversations or missed connections is just as important. Watching carefully for signs of enthusiasm, engagement, and productivity is just as important as engaging with boredom, indifference, and indolence. While there is a strong temptation to interpret participant reactions as "helpful," a more neutral state of observation treats all participant actions as data for analysis. The methods and approaches shared here have been tested in community meetings, but that also is no guarantee of success. Understanding that conversation really lives in the performance rather than the words is a challenge for designers because they are so often focused on perfecting an object.

The first community meetings I worked with were also the first Capital Budget hearings done in a deliberative democracy format. It was hard to tell if expectations from Pittsburgh City government were high or if our enthusiasm for the project overwhelmed the business-as-usual city staffers. In consultation with a team of researchers from Carnegie Mellon's Center for Deliberative Democracy and City of Pittsburgh staff, we spent weeks developing the new meeting format. We argued about whether we needed an additional five minutes for the presentation at the beginning of the meeting and agonized over word choices in our question prompts. The day of the first meeting, we researchers led a pair of student volunteers up a steep hillside to the Magee Recreation Center to wait for our moderators. Then we waited for residents to find their way back to the Greenfield community room. Immediately, problems of design became apparent. While the location was suitable for nearby neighbors who were mostly walking to the meeting, the building was on busy, steep, and winding Greenfield Road, with no parking. Instead of arriving eager, bright-eyed, and ready to engage in deliberation, most residents were coming from work, providing childcare, or were neighborhood-dwelling senior citizens who walked from their nearby homes. They didn't look like a model of eager, thoughtful, deliberative democrats.

Thinking about all the things that we had to write and make, we left little time in our planning to think about how the participants were going to feel, and what the participants were going to do.

These first few arresting minutes helped me realize that over the past weeks, in the hours spent refining the meeting structure and carefully crafting the words and graphics, we had actually paid insufficient attention to the participants' experience of the design. Thinking about all the things that we had to write and make, we left little time in our planning to think about how the participants were going to feel, and what the participants were going to do. While we planned a neighborhood door-knocking campaign in the days leading up to the event, we spent little time discussing what factors would motivate participants to attend.

The next three years we worked with the City of Pittsburgh, the Heinz Endowments, the Obama White House program My Brother's Keeper, and the US Veteran's Administration program MyVA Communities to fill in some of these gaps. We learned the types of conversations people wanted to have and factors that motivated civic participation. We learned how to translate data collated through civic participation into the polity in ways that made it actionable by policymakers. As a result, our ongoing efforts have contributed to a deeper comprehension of these dynamics, empowering us to foster more meaningful civic engagement and facilitate informed policy decisions based on community input.

Throughout this process, contemporary record-keeping built the knowledge base I draw from in this book. Meetings with stakeholders were documented, with detailed notes in-action and reflective notes after meetings that captured insights, perspectives, and decisions gleaned from collaborative discussion. Additionally, I visually documented participatory sessions, including photos of physical spaces and active sessions. This data provided rich contextual cues for better understanding participant experiences. Further, artifacts produced by the participants were collected or photographed while in-use. These broad yet detailed data helped form a picture of deliberative engagements. They also offered valuable insights into the co-creation of knowledge and the transformative and "thing-full" participatory design processes.

This book is informed by approaches that I have developed over years of direct engagement with communities. It offers practical approaches for designers and professionals who want to shape their plans and material environments to facilitate better conversations. The ongoing project that is this research explores concepts crucial for effective civic participation, including civic empowerment, inclusivity, and community agency. The layers of data that lie hidden in our various communities can be given the opportunity to surface through the dynamics and mechanisms of contemporary civic engagement initiatives. By investigating social and communicative constructs, this book defines, analyzes, and highlights things as designable, fundamental elements of effective civic discourse. By reflecting on the implications of disenfranchisement, social segregation, and our economic interdependence, my research paves a path for design: to anticipate the challenges of fostering community self-determination and agency in relation to government conveners.

Community deliberative forum for the City of Pittsburgh Affordable Housing Task Force, April 5, 2016, held at the Hill House Association. Photo by the author, courtesy City of Pittsburgh

OUTLINE OF CHAPTERS

THE FIRST SECTION

The rest of this book is divided into two sections, a division that reflects contemporary thinking on the relationship between words and things. The first section—encompassing the first four chapters—introduces four types of conversation that are commonly encountered in designing participatory practices. These types of conversations represent flexible models that can be applied in a variety of situations. Chapter one—Designing a surfacing conversation—explores designing for the layers of conversations aimed at surfacing information and ideas. It discusses how things can act as memory aids, record complex relationships, and offer access to hidden data and perspectives. With a focus on the action of planning rather than plans, chapter two discusses challenges in conversations for strategizing and decision-making. We will discuss ways to weigh different options and map arguments that reveal the landscape of a decision space. Turning to the challenge of interpersonal dynamics in conversation, chapter three offers approaches for designing around sensitive topics. In it, I show designers how to help participants navigate discomfort, think about social identity, and engage in reflective thinking with others. The first section of the book culminates with chapter four—"Designing a High-stakes Conversation"—which aims to address some of the complexities of surfacing, decision-making, and challenging emotional dynamics in one conversation.

THE SECOND SECTION

In the second part of the book, we shift our focus to the broader contexts of conversation design, discussing a variety of goals and tactical interventions that may happen at different points in the arc of any of the conversations discussed in section 1. Chapter five, "Planning a Conversation," offers a roadmap for preparation, underscoring the importance of laying a solid foundation for fruitful dialogue. Drawing from understandings developed in service design practice, we explore the planning and design of conversational facilitators through the lens of service-dominant logic. Chapter six discusses using things to scaffold the conversation in-action. It also discusses the importance of the holding environment—the layered space where the conversation will take place. Drawing from game design, chapter six details a variety of practical game-like approaches, concluding with opportunities to open the door for *play*, even in the context of serious subject matter. Chapter seven explores strategies for cultivating genuine engagement and inclusivity in conversations, with the goal that all voices, not just the loudest, are equitably heard and valued. This chapter explores the role of the body in conversation, the significance of bodied relations, physical presence, and nonverbal cues enhance interaction. We will discuss creating environments that encourage active listening and the power of intentional disclosure in building trust and transparency within conversations, promoting the open sharing (and acknowledging) of thoughts and feelings.

Chapter eight discusses the compression problems inherent in working with the data produced by conversations—complex, qualitative, temporal, situated—to avoid loss of valuable knowledge. We will also discuss strategies for design, facilitation, and data collection that collect what the participants deem the most important data. A section on "reporting out" discusses tactics for communicating findings and outcomes to relevant stakeholders as well as returning data to the community in a way that facilitates transparency and accountability. In the concluding chapter, I reflect on the potent influence of design within conversational and participatory contexts, recognizing its capacity to shape interactions and outcomes. We discuss some of the overarching ethical challenges of shaping the conversational environment and consider how committing to designing participatory processes essentially alters the balance of power in design practice.

Towards the beginning of this chapter, we discussed the foundational role of design for conversation in shaping collective action and collaborative endeavors—how we "do things" together. This book remains committed to supporting the designer's perspective by recognizing the pivotal role of design in mediating and facilitating conversational interactions within diverse socio-cultural contexts. However, from the vantage point of a North American design scholar whose professional endeavors have predominantly unfolded within urban landscapes spanning Colorado, Pennsylvania, and Massachusetts, it is important to acknowledge the situatedness of these perspectives and the need for a nuanced understanding of and engagement with local approaches. Embracing the complexities of design practice, theory, and application, I will also support my arguments with cases that are drawn not only from my practice but acknowledge that this activity has had significant support in other parts of the globe. Through the following pages, I hope to unravel some of the complexities of this work and offer tools and techniques that foster agency and open access to the shared wisdom of people as together we attempt to address the needs, values, and priorities of our cosmopolitan communities.

THE SECOND SECTION

1

Designing a Surfacing Conversation

WHAT IS A SURFACING CONVERSATION?

During our time in Pittsburgh, we lived on the South Side Slopes. Houses were built on the steep sides of the hills facing the Monongahela River, accessible only by concrete and steel stairways or narrow roads. Most of these narrow houses were two stories with a large garret third story at the top. Each structure sat on a basement below ground on the uphill side of the house and above ground on the downhill side of the house. Most homes on the Slopes had 1 or 2 rooms per story, and a door that led directly from the ground level into the basement. The neighborhoods were filled with tiny vertical buildings only 3 or 4 feet apart. In the basement of each house was a "Pittsburgh bathroom" or a toilet and shower in a corner of the basement on the side away from the furnace.

This neighborhood was originally home to the working-class families of Pittsburgh. On the South Side Slopes, most men who lived in these homes when they were built worked in the steel mills and refineries that lined the nearby river.

Nearby, the Hot Metal Bridge was named so because in the days when steel production was the driver of the Pittsburgh economy, train cars shuttled all day long across the river. They carried crucibles filled with molten iron on one side of the bridge and returned empty to be refilled on the other side. The South Side Slopes were full of latent knowledge. Spartan basement bathrooms were the preferred place for soot-covered and sweaty steel workers returning home to bathe after work. The Hot Metal Bridge eventually became a traffic, bike, and pedestrian bridge, even as pilings from steel and coal piers still line the riverbanks. Venerable neighborhood residents know these material histories and can share the story of these historical markers and what was there before. Having a conversation can surface their knowledge about a particular problem or community need—what I call a *surfacing conversation*.

When designing for the surfacing conversation, the designer's goal is to show people how their knowledge and lived experience are relevant to the problem at hand.

A surfacing conversation in a civic context is not simply eliciting the interesting stories and hidden histories of the community. While this may be enjoyable and of use to community historians, in a civic context, we typically wish to surface knowledge in relation to a particular problem. The principal challenge of hosting an effective surfacing conversation is helping participants know how their deep knowledge is relevant to the challenge we face. When designing for the surfacing conversation, the designer's goal is to show people how their knowledge and lived experience are relevant to the problem at hand.

WQED, Pittsburgh's PBS affiliate station, sponsored the production of a three-show series called THINK!, which aimed "to bring people together to talk about the issues that divide us." For these three shows, we convened stakeholders to find the most challenging aspects of issues. Next, we designed and hosted community conversations to elicit deep insights from the community. The third episode was titled "Poverty in Western Pennsylvania." Through story-sharing sessions with community members, we learned about feelings of dissociation. A less affluent group living in poverty would distinguish itself from another living in similar circumstances. Inspired by these community-focused conversations, the project producer, Gregory Scott Williams Jr., sought out the stories of residents who spoke to the learned shame that accompanied the experience of living in poverty. In the resulting show, these rich narratives were encapsulated by the personal story of Kim El, an after-school site manager, writer, and playwright. As a child, she lived across the street from the public housing projects, and then later in the public housing projects. El told of her grandfather's negative perception of the people who lived in the projects and how it profoundly influenced her own self-image in later life.

The stories of community residents guided us toward El's powerful stories. They were brought to light through open-ended questions in story-sharing sessions and associative mapping exercises that opened conversations about related topics. Multigenerational art activities at a food distribution event were particularly successful at starting conversations. While children waited for adults to complete the food distribution circuit colored on paper and were watched by volunteers, the adult participants wrote statements on pieces of fabric. The adults then wove their statements together into a large textile using a standing loom. This activity invited people to share their stories with each other, and many continued talking as they made their way through the food distribution event.

What Are You Surfacing?

Profound knowledge sits latent within communities. The surfacing conversation aims to unlock that knowledge and apply it to a challenge being faced by the community. The expression "using local knowledge to solve local problems" lies at the heart of the surfacing conversation, and we seek to unlock that knowledge with a conversation. Economist Frederick Hayek wrote of latent knowledge in 1945, writing about "how valuable an asset in all walks of life is knowledge of people, of local conditions, and of special circumstances." (p. 522) Those specificities are elicited by the surfacing conversation. The surfacing conversation identifies solutions informed by lived experiences and contextual understanding.

At Carnegie Mellon in Pittsburgh, Pennsylvania, the Remaking Cities Institute was working with a group of communities along Route 51. The Institute was leading a project to install "smart" traffic signals that would actively monitor and dynamically adjust traffic signal times and synchronize them to reduce traffic congestion. A key piece of this project was understanding the local knowledge of traffic patterns—the popular destinations, dangerous intersections, and neighborhood-level workarounds only learned after several months of residence. Because "smart" signalization impacts not only private traffic but also commercial vehicles and public transit, feedback was also sought from people who used public transit and Pittsburgh Regional Transit representatives. As Hayek presaged, these local conditions and special circumstances informed a solution to the problem of re-signaling this complicated transportation corridor.

Not all communities are geographically located. Some might be, for example, communities of affinity during a particular time in people's lives. For example, a community might be composed of new parents caring for an infant for the first time, or middle-aged adults who are caring for geriatric parents. In each case, the group has similar experiences and faces similar challenges. These residents might have collective knowledge about how to deal with public health challenges, where to offer advice for aging-in-place in your community, or how to implement resource-sharing so that parent networks can provide free or low-cost childcare. Other such temporary communities exist and can be addressed by civic conversations. The community of residents who have recently moved to a city is often targeted by companies—for example, those that sell home repair supplies or furniture—that are seeking new customers. That same community of new residents might also be targeted by civic organizations to surface specific knowledge related to becoming a new resident.

The first step for a good quality surfacing conversation is to identify and convene members of the community or communities where the specific knowledge exists. Surfacing conversations begin with broad, inclusive, open-ended questions that elicit knowledge from diverse perspectives. Once the need becomes clear, participants are often very willing to share their knowledge and lived experience with other members of the community and civic organizational staff. Further approaches can be drawn from focus group techniques, including the use of an easy ice-breaker question at the beginning "What brought you to this meeting?" and a closing question at the end "Is there anything that someone wished to say about this issue that we haven't covered?" or "Is there anyone who hasn't yet had a chance to speak, and would like to share some closing thoughts?"

Not all goals or topics are good candidates for a surfacing conversation. If the aim is to convince a community group to adopt a particular policy or accept a particular development, a surfacing conversation may not be appropriate. It does not aim to advocate for a policy position or convince people something is "good for them." Instead, it surfaces latent knowledge held by a community. Complex technical questions are not a good fit for a surfacing conversation. Participants typically come to technical conversations between other obligations and cannot dedicate copious amounts of time to gain fluency with unfamiliar contexts. Surfacing conversations work best when the answer to a question lies in the everyday lived experience of the people you are convening. In this case, people only need to be shown how their lived experience is relevant to the problem at hand. In this situation, the people convened are truly subject matter experts in the latent knowledge of that community.

The Common Challenges of The Surfacing Conversation

In surfacing conversations, two significant challenges often arise: working with people with dignity and helping them envision the unknown. Addressing these challenges is crucial for ensuring the surfacing conversation is respectful and effective. The first challenge is designing to ensure the conversation is respectful and empowering and avoid making participants feel exploited or merely used for information. Strategies like maintaining inclusive facilitation, reciprocity, and transparency are essential. For instance, community-led design workshops can transform participants into co-creators rather than treating them as mere informants. The second challenge involves encouraging participants to think beyond their current knowledge and experiences. Techniques drawn from creative visualization, scenario planning, and role-playing can help participants imagine future possibilities. One example is designers using generated videos of walk-throughs of potential future construction projects to help people envision the buildings currently whose designs are under consideration. By structuring conversations with these strategies, surfacing conversations can become more inclusive and productive, leading to meaningful outcomes.

As previously stated, you bring people together to have a surfacing conversation because they have a particular expertise. Their lived experience of a problem space offers direct access to valuable information available nowhere else. If we begin work with this assumption, it follows that the people coming to the surfacing conversation should be treated as experts. Success in a surfacing conversation flows from treating the participants with dignity and respect to ensure that the conversation design is empowering and uplifting rather than exploitative and extractive. One might think of the tables of participants as groups of distinguished faculty from nearby universities or teams of high-powered consultants from a respected firm. Think of what your organization would do for a similar meeting and use that as a guide for designing the surfacing conversation. The trappings of hospitality that are completely appropriate for a panel of visiting experts are also appropriate for participant experts coming to a community meeting to share their knowledge. Changing the language used internally for these events may also be necessary. You might describe the event as "hosting a panel of resident experts" rather than "having a resident feedback session." These techniques may inspire a different attitude towards the event among residents.

Facilitating with Dignity

The weaving board mentioned in the introductory paragraphs of this chapter is a good model for facilitating with dignity. At that event, participants were invited to be co-creators of a tapestry of ideas that represented the community's accumulated knowledge. Not all meetings need such a poetic tool. However, organizers can carry a similar attitude through their activities. You might give participants Post-it notes and markers and ask them to write short ideas and arrange them together with other participants' ideas. Organizers could request that participants sketch or write stories on butcher paper on the walls. You could also supply collage materials and ask participants to create arrangements that depict a set of complex relationships that exist in their community. These simple yet powerful techniques open up the flow of stories and ideas.

Inclusivity is crucial to ensure that all stories are heard and valued by the group. Negative self-talk should be avoided and countered when it emerges. For example, a participant sharing their story after drawing a diagram might say, "I don't want to show my drawing because it isn't very good." The facilitator could counter this negativity by saying, "I saw it when you were working on it and found it insightful. I hoped to hear what you were going to say about it!" Participants thinking that their stories are typical or uninteresting can also be pre-empted by facilitators sincerely stating the importance of stories from the community at the beginning of the sharing session. Thanking participants for their stories in a public and sincere fashion encourages other participants to share and sets up a dynamic of gratitude for knowledge-sharing from the conveners to the participants. Before ending a session, facilitators might ask, "Is there anyone who hasn't shared who wants to?" while making eye contact with people who haven't yet publicly shared. Gentle encouragement to share can often prompt a reluctant participant to share. Avoid coercive "calling out" of participants personally. Instead, "call in" people by modeling gratitude and respect for shared knowledge.

Reciprocity is another principle to adhere to when designing surfacing conversations. Facilitators should be provided the tools to share outcomes and benefits with participants in the meeting immediately. Meeting organizers should prepare to provide outcomes and benefits of the conversation over a longer-term cycle. For the purposes of data collection, organizers may wish to have stories recorded on paper and collected by the facilitators. However, for the purposes of a successful meeting, the agenda should include an opportunity for the public to share and appreciate those stories. With the consent of participants to have their images recorded, it is possible to photograph and project the contributions of participants onto the same screen that was used for an introductory presentation, for instance. Including participant contributions in a collective artwork or shared model may also satisfy this principle in meetings. Further, organizers should be prepared to collect participant data from the meeting not only to add them to the group's mailing list but to share the meeting results. Part of reciprocity is communicating the results compellingly to the people who generated the data. A thank-you note, along with a link to any reporting of the meeting conversation or an update, extends the reciprocity of the meeting. Evidence or reporting of the value of the data that participants shared exists in slide presentations, report-outs to city councils, and documentary evidence, which informs later work. These can all be shared with participants to demonstrate their value and gratitude for their contributions.

Facilitating with Transparency

Last, transparency is a key design principle for surfacing conversations. Being clear about the purpose of the conversation, what data will be collected, and how the data will be used fosters a trustful relationship between conveners and participants. Clarity in recruitment materials, meeting materials, and follow-up materials should be strived for. Transparency plays a significant role, especially in public conversations. In internal conversations convened by the City of Boston Mayor's Office, the mayor hoped to improve communication and coordination between the Mayor's Office, cabinet leaders, and city department managers, like heads of Parks and Recreation and Facilities Management. The conversation began with the Mayor's office sharing a story of an attempted policy change that resulted in failed coordination and an uneven response by a particular department. In this retelling, the missed connection even caused tension between that department and the Mayor's Office. The Mayor's Office was open and transparent about the purpose of this conversation—to improve communication and coordination—and frank about a previous failure known to the community. They acknowledged feelings among city staff, common in situations where one party feels excluded or railroaded. In this way, the Mayor's Office fostered an environment of problem-solving and collaboration that improved participants' engagement and conversations.

This meeting included an agenda design that answered the question, "Why are we doing this?" and spoke to the question, "What will happen because of this conversation?" The suggested approaches and specific proposals for improvement were then considered for implementation by the Mayor's Office at a future Cabinet and Department Head meeting. By giving cabinet heads and department managers a set of examples of specific models that could be implemented to consider and discuss in the meeting, the Mayor's Office avoided overpromising solutions that could not be implemented. It freed participants to focus on what would provide valuable coordination, and to suggest tools that they might use daily in their departments.

Frankness and transparency created an atmosphere where cabinet heads and department managers felt empowered to share challenges and be honest about what would work in the context of their department workflows. Solutions already familiar to participants, like "policy memos," had broad support and were easily implemented, but also received frank criticisms that revealed the challenges those methods faced. Participants said that, "we need to cut down on the volume of daily memos to reduce frivolous reporting," and "distinguish between important and urgent matters to avoid confusion and miscommunication." For the Mayor's office, admitting to being party to a failed implementation was risky, it was also an interpretation of events familiar to the community of cabinet heads and managers. Being transparent about problems rather than glossing over them set up an environment where a request for help and problem-solving from the community was well-received. Participants left feeling that their voices were heard, and that these community forums could be a way to explore other issues facing the city staff.

Accessing Local Knowledge

Participants can also use their local knowledge to project beyond their current knowledge and experiences. Often, this approach is necessary when implementing a new project or service. Like the planning conversations that will be discussed in chapter 2, this approach asks people to imagine possible futures. However, unlike that approach, in a surfacing conversation we are mainly interested in the application of local knowledge and perspectives. Designers are interested in seeing if an approach might be congruent with the values, beliefs, and environment of the neighborhood.

Working with the Rockefeller Foundation's 100 Resilient Cities initiative for the City of Pittsburgh's resilience planning efforts, we aimed to uncover local knowledge and neighborhood resources at the street, neighborhood, and city levels. The discussion convened residents to talk about how their communities might cope with different shocks and stresses, which formed the basis of the approach through which our design team aimed to surface community knowledge. Using scenario-based prompts, we asked residents to discuss the strengths and weaknesses of their neighborhood in relation to these possible future situations.

Acute *shocks* are sudden, large-scale disasters that disrupt city services and threaten residents. They include environmental events like storms and heat waves, economic crises such as industry collapse and bank failure, and social emergencies like disease outbreaks and food shortages. In Pittsburgh, residents experienced severe flooding during Hurricane Ivan in 2011, extreme cold during the 2014 Polar Vortex, and the collapse of the steel industry in the 1980s.

Chronic *stresses* are long-term issues that overwhelm city resources and erode residents' well-being. They include environmental stresses such as poor air and water quality, economic challenges like poverty and unemployment, and social issues such as violence and a struggling education system. Pittsburgh has been dealing with the consequences of its industrial history, including poor air and water quality. While the city has made improvements, the Environmental Protection Agency still considers the Pittsburgh area a "nonattainment area" —a geographic area that consistently fails to meet national standards for air and water quality.

A city becomes more resilient by addressing both acute shocks, such as fires, disease outbreaks, and terrorist attacks, and chronic stresses, such as inefficient transportation, crime, and poverty. Attention to both allows a city to respond better to adverse events and deliver basic functions effectively in both good times and bad.

Scenarios were a key method that supported this approach. In these sessions, participants were supplied with real examples from Pittsburgh's recent history. They heard about the impacts of climate change, the transportation of flammable and toxic materials by rail, and landslides and other subsidence in area communities. Confronted with these examples, residents thought through the likelihood of different shocks and considered the impact that each might have on their community. Residents also explored the stresses that affected their communities. Racial and economic disparities, aging infrastructure, and environmental degradation from decades of industrial and mining activity were discussed. Residents shared information about the severity of those stresses and how they manifested in their neighborhoods. Residents also shared information about the strengths and weaknesses of their neighborhoods, sharing positive data about social cohesion, like what it's like to live on a street where neighbors know and trust one another. Residents discussed strengths, like neighbors who served as social catalysts for a particular street, and weaknesses they had observed, such as rusting bridges and damaged streets and sidewalks.

One fear expressed by residents when discussing neighborhood strengths or coping with shocks and stresses was the fear of being left "on their own." Concerns about insufficient support from local authorities, inadequate resources, and a lack of community cohesion led some to think the initiative aimed to help local governments avoid responsibility during sudden shocks. Discussing such challenging matters while asking residents to share their community knowledge while considering uncertain futures can be intimidating! Addressing these concerns involves fostering stronger community networks, ensuring effective communication, and assuring that all neighborhoods will receive the necessary support during times of crisis.

Using Role-play

Carefully considered role-play can also be used with civic participants. The meeting might be designed to include a section that includes role-play. With civic participants, role-play need not be childish or cartoonish but can ask participants to assume the perspective of other actors within the city. In a resilience planning session, for instance, participants might be asked to speak as the inanimate objects or systems that are part of the city. Assuming the persona of roads or bridges, the business sector, trees, wildlife, or the river might offer opportunities for participants to step out of the mindset they brought to the issue under discussion. Role-playing as residents, the city's bureaucracy, or a large educational institution can allow participants to apply their knowledge and lived experience from another perspective.

However, care must be taken to avoid problematic role-play. Role-playing can sometimes unintentionally reinforce stereotypes or marginalize certain groups, leading to discomfort or harm. What will be embodied through role-play should be carefully considered by meeting designers beforehand to prevent injuring the dignity of people who may or may not be in the room. It is crucial to set clear guidelines and provide context to ensure the exercise is respectful and inclusive. Facilitators should be prepared to intervene if the role-play veers into problematic territory and debrief participants afterward to address any concerns that arise. Thoughtful planning and sensitivity can make role-play a powerful tool for civic engagement and resilience planning, fostering empathy, and deepening mutual understanding among participants.

One role-play technique that can be used successfully in surfacing conversations that aim to engage participants is Edward de Bono's *Six Thinking Hats* (1999). Drawn from ancient Greek theories of knowledge, de Bono suggests that people who apply existing knowledge to new problems might adopt these ancient knowledge models to structure their approaches. Addressing challenging new areas with de Bono's approach does require a bit of trust on the part of participants. A facilitator asks each participant to role-play thinking by wearing a particular "thinking hat." Each "hat" represents a particular thinking style. The white hat is concerned with facts and quantifiable measurements, while the red hat sees the world through an emotional lens. The black hat's darkness focuses on the weaknesses or negative aspects of any approach, and the yellow hat orients towards "sunny" positive thinking, hope, and optimism. The green hat orients towards creative ideas, and the blue hat is the organizing force in the conversation—the facilitator.

Using de Bono's technique, different participants agree to "wear" one of the thinking hats for part of the session. While that participant is in a particular role, they contribute only the type of thinking designated to the particular "hat." The blue hat is worn by the facilitator or organizer of the meeting, and they do not typically trade hats with other participants. Using de Bono's technique, a meeting might consist of several rounds, where participants don different hats. Alternatively, the "blue hat" facilitator might share a list of the different thinking hat types. They could call for the entire group to put on the green hat and generate more creative approaches. They might follow that round with a yellow hat round that looks for the hopeful implications of those creative solutions. A black hat round might attempt to identify problems with these proposals, concluding with a red hat round where people discuss the feelings engendered by these different approaches.

The game-like qualities of scenario planning and role-play enable access to a powerful, yet tacitly understood concept in civic conversations: ludic space. As de Bono says, the artificiality of role-play is its strength. The play space of role-play creates an opportunity to transgress social or cultural boundaries or personal restrictions that might keep participants from the full power of their knowledge and experience. Ludic space in civic conversations refers to a playful and imaginative environment where participants can explore different perspectives and ideas through creative methods like role-playing, storytelling, and scenarios. A game-like approach encourages open dialogue, fosters collaboration, and helps uncover innovative solutions to civic issues. A "normal" civic meeting is already a kind of ludic space. The old model of "each participant has 3 minutes at the microphone" is an artificial performance situation. However, role-play, scenarios, and storytelling tap into actions that people know and understand how to do. They provide powerful opportunities for surfacing participant knowledge in ways that are comfortable and familiar.

CONCLUSION

Surfacing conversations are directed toward problems that face communities and must be addressed by government or organizational staff. Surfacing conversations work to unlock latent community knowledge, and offer residents the opportunity to share stories, knowledge, and wisdom developed over years of deep association with a place and culture. These conversations can be a deeply respectful and empowering endeavor. For residents, feeling heard by organizations that seem like a powerful monolith offers a view into processes that many do not participate in or even regularly see. Further, the chance for residents to get together and share knowledge plays a crucial role in community infrastructuring, or the making of new friends and acquaintances among residents. This infrastructuring leads to stronger, more resilient communities.

Throughout this chapter, I have emphasized the need to design with respect and honor for residents' contributions, to empower and uplift them. Thinking through meeting designs to ensure that the process that helps residents share is time well spent. Opportunities for residents to create new associations through these meetings can create an underlying positive feeling toward the convening organization. Tools and techniques discussed in this chapter have included storytelling, scenario consideration, and role-play. Any of these can be supported with structured visualization methods that allow participants to realize the value of their own knowledge and how that knowledge applies to the problem at hand. Whether it is a simple issue like understanding traffic patterns at a problematic corner or a complex one like addressing resilience planning for a city or region, the surfacing conversation offers a powerful approach to gain access to the latent knowledge of a community.

Community deliberative forum for the City of Pittsburgh 100 Resilient Cities initiative, sponsored by the Rockefeller Foundation, Nov 19, 2015, held at East Liberty Presbyterian Church. Photo by the author, courtesy City of Pittsburgh

runoff

creates

flooding

destroys

2

Designing a Planning Conversation

Imagine that we want to take a trip to the beach together. The first time we are going to the beach together, we'd like it to be an enjoyable experience. We will need to have a conversation in which we define the parameters for the trip. Do we need to talk about our goals or are the goals implied by the nature of the trip? Is it obvious we will swim because we will be at the beach? Perhaps one person's idea of a fun day is sitting on the sand enjoying the sun and waves, and the other's is ranging through tidal pools and collecting seashells. Talking about goals would probably be a good idea! Do we need to talk about the scope of the trip—how long we will be gone and what day we'll be going? Do we need to talk about tasks to prepare? Do we need to talk about responsibilities? Who will drive? Who will bring chairs, an umbrella, towels, food, or drinks? Discussing what we need to plan, what commitments will be made, what timelines will be agreed to, is the essence of the planning conversation.

Perhaps this seems overly complicated, but our civic planning conversations are even more complex. Uniting a group of people to work together to accomplish a goal is a complicated task. Among friends, much of the planning conversation is often assumed. On our trip to the beach, if we are friends, we know each other. We likely know something about the other person's goals, capacities, and what they are likely to be able to contribute. If we are friends, we already have established a history of trustful behavior. For our hypothetical beach trip, much of the planning can be assumed from contextual clues. However, for conversations with unfamiliar actors—as is common in civic conversations—most planning must be made explicit for participants. The planning conversation is where those agreements are articulated and made visible.

Defining success in civic projects is more complicated than the simple binary of success vs. failure. Success is often *bracketed*, meaning that a policy that succeeds for one group might be neutral or even harmful to other groups. Success might not even be evenly distributed among a group. Zoning changes that allow the construction of high-density luxury condominiums may, for instance, well-serve developers and be an economic engine that supports construction and material sales in the region. However, they may also have profoundly negative consequences on the neighborhood in which such a development is placed. Economist Herbert Simon's often quoted as having said: "Everyone designs who devises courses of action aimed at changing existing situations into preferred ones." However, this aphorism leaves out this essential question: *For whom?* A planning conversation aims to understand how the success or failure of an initiative might be distributed across groups. The goal of the planning conversation is to foster change that maximizes access to opportunity for the broadest population and minimizes harm. The planning conversation is an opportunity to ensure that all voices are heard.

What is a Planning Conversation?

Bringing a group together to have a conversation about planning future action happens across all professional and creative disciplines. They are held within families and social groups, within government and groups of policymakers, and between residents and municipal governments. When you think back to the beginnings of society, coordination of work is at the core of social organization. Planning conversations have a broader scope than just having a conversation about the current challenges before the city planning department. A planning conversation convenes a group to coordinate commitments and actions toward a collective goal. Hosting a planning conversation implies that an organization is willing to commit to co-working on a problem with the groups that participate in the conversation. Scholars have devoted their careers to studying these necessary coordinating activities.

Pelle Ehn began his career examining how the tools and practices of design can be opened to participation by non-experts (Ehn, 1988). Drawing from the writings of Rob Kling, and many others who examined the democratic sociality of early efforts in collaborative computing, Ehn pointed out that the tools of design are particularly suited to organizing conversations in complex, conflicting, and pluralistic social settings. Ehn's participatory design perspective began with the ethic that those affected by a design should guide the development of the design. This ethic still applies today in our civic conversations.

Scope planning and commitment-making are key components that should be considered by the designers, particularly in collaborative efforts between residents and the government. Often, the main types of conversations between residents and the government are thought of as surfacing conversations discussed in Chapter 1, in which policymakers try to gauge resident preferences and values. However, in larger and more complex projects, civic leaders or heads of prominent nonprofits might need to engage a broad group of community members to plan initiatives collaboratively. Initiatives that entail planning might include projects with multiple stages that engage different groups of stakeholders, require coordination between groups, or involve one group making changes and a network that responds to them. Contemporary civic life has more complex needs for ongoing feedback between policymakers and residents than voting can sustain.

Many familiar efforts need thoughtful planning and ongoing resident engagement. Leaders wish to create more affordable housing for people without harming or displacing residents. They could be interested in "smart city" initiatives like robotic signalization of major traffic corridors or implementation of public Wi-Fi networks. Other civic necessities include public health campaigns and community policing strategies to improve health, safety, and well-being in a community. For these kinds of complex efforts to be successful and meet the broad needs of communities (rather than those of extractive business interests), they need commitment-making and commitment-keeping between residents and government. Planning conversations form the foundation of trust necessary for successful projects.

Scope Planning, or "What are we going to do?"

Planning conversations require clearly defining objectives and desired outcomes of civic projects or initiatives. Deciding upon these objectives is at the center of the planning conversation. Often, objectives are determined by policymakers, and residents are consulted to see how palatable those objectives might be or what kind of messaging might make those objectives more appealing to a public constituency. Bringing together a community to collaborate on setting objectives and scope opens opportunities for full resident participation in the planning process. Improving public health outcomes, supporting community development, improving public infrastructure, and changing policy affect all members of a community. Making these objectives clear can be challenging.

When residents work with civic entities toward these long-term objectives, the intermediate steps can tend to benefit participants who consciously or unintentionally steer outcomes toward their own interests. Participation in public processes remains a luxury only afforded by those with a surplus of resources. The ongoing challenge of planning initiatives is to actively broaden participation and input, especially as regards setting objectives for change. Clear objectives for a project or initiative set the bounds of a project and determine what material elements it might require. For complex challenges, a whole set of conversations might orient around deciding upon meaningful objectives for a community. Clear objectives can also drive participation, even when the objective of the planning conversation is to set objectives for later work. Ultimately it is essential that, through planning conversations, these long-term objectives become *community property*, so that they remain a guiding star, outlasting capricious political environments.

In 2014, the Obama Administration sponsored a nationwide initiative, My Brother's Keeper (MBK), to improve outcomes for men and boys of color. As a part of the team who both facilitated and developed the supporting materials for these conversations, our objective was to develop a playbook—a document that defined the objectives and approaches of the community in Southwestern Pennsylvania. We employed a double-loop approach for planning within a difficult problem space. Engaging the community in setting the objectives requires more commitment of time and resources but is also key to community ownership. The opportunity to contribute to the development of this playbook was widely shared among the leaders in the community and drove interest and attendance from community members.

As is the case with many of these initiatives, a significant amount of background work was necessary to develop a plan appropriate for a community. This conversation began on October 31, 2014, when Allegheny County and the City of Pittsburgh hosted an "MBK Summit." The summit engaged more than 100 leaders from ten sectors, including service and community centers, healthcare, faith-based organizations, philanthropy, education, government, corporate, law enforcement, workforce, and advocacy.

Building on the work initiated at the summit, a sixteen-member MBK Committee was formed in February 2015. This committee included representatives from academia, city and county government, clergy, community groups, local school systems, and police. The MBK Committee was tasked with creating an "MBK Playbook" to identify actions, strategies, and effective means to support the success of all young people in the region, particularly young men and boys of color.

Over the following months, the MBK Committee members collected data and information to understand the challenges faced by young people and to identify existing resources already addressing these challenges.

Upon reviewing the six goals proposed by the White House, the MBK Committee focused on three core areas: education, workforce, and police and community relations. The results of this work were captured in a report titled "I am My Brother's Keeper." This report provided a foundation for the region's MBK Playbook. At the MBK Deliberative Community Forums, participants were asked to draw on their own knowledge of the challenges young people of Pittsburgh faced and consider how they would address these challenges.

To do this, we hosted two levels of conversations. The first level engaged community activists, leaders in social good organizations, and other non-governmental organizations. Fearing that "experts" may dominate community conversations, people in leadership positions or other positions of community responsibility first spoke together. Not only did this provide a forum for a new kind of engagement, but these community leaders also became engaged. They were key to successfully recruiting participants for the second level, which was focused on the community. The second level of the conversation was a broadly constituted group of residents who self-selected to attend based on their interests. Predominantly members of the Black community in Pittsburgh, this broader group examined the work of the first level to ensure that objectives and milestones were legible to the community, mattered to them, and nothing was missed.

Although the group of community leaders met first, both groups began with the same information that was developed at the MBK Summit. These two groups worked together to develop a livability index that would track progress toward the six goals and could be noticed in the community as indicators of progress. They aimed for the indicators to be measurable and noticeable so that they could be understood by specialists and non-specialists alike. Participants in both conversations identified outcomes that were meaningful and highly visible to the community—what one participant called "what young men of color see, hear, and feel in their neighborhood." For the education area, factors included the rate of absenteeism in schools, the rate of suspensions in schools, and environmental conditions surrounding neighborhood schools. They aimed to track these factors through surveys of school students and indirectly through metrics like the availability of high-quality early childhood programs, third-grade reading levels, and changes in achievement levels on state-run Algebra I Keystone Exams. Participants at both levels also agreed that socio-economic factors played a significant role in all the goals and developed a list of socio-economic factors, which included the percentage of households with income less than $20,000, as well as highly visible community assets such as sports fields, green spaces, public art, and playgrounds.

Here are the three key areas, six goals, and actions that we brought forward for the community conversation:

Core Area: Education		Actions
Goal #1	All our children enter school prepared cognitively, physically, socially, and emotionally	**Continue the focus of early childhood including play and literacy by:** · Increasing the percentage of quality preschools with a rating of 3–4 Keystone Stars · Expanding access to technology at early childhood centers **Support healthy initiatives by:** · Expanding enrollment in Women Infant and Children (WIC) programs · Ensuring all children are immunized · Expanding healthy meals to children involved in after school programs
Goal #2	All our children read at grade level by third grade	**Improve data-sharing by:** · Offering independent evaluation to assist schools and agencies to increase school attendance · Mobilize community partners to implement the "Be There" program in all 43 Allegheny County school districts **Highlight the importance of literacy by:** · Increasing distribution of age-appropriate books at all 110 summer food locations · Expanding the number of "Little Free Libraries"
Goal #3	All our young people graduate from high school prepared for college or career	**Support programs that engage and inspire students by:** · Forming "Students in Action" teams to solve problems and expand youth input and "voice" · Piloting "Smart Horizons," a high school degree certification and workforce readiness program, to increase the number of residents obtaining a high school diploma · Recruiting more mentors of color for our young men of color to increase the number of youth that feel "cared for" · Recruiting foster families for teens, particularly teens of color, in the communities where they live to reduce congregate care and ensure neighborhood and school stability

Core Area: Workforce		Actions
Goal #4	All our youth complete post-secondary education or training	**Provide support (financial and social) to increase completion of post-secondary education and training by:** · Increasing the percentage of students that receive the Promise Scholarship · Creating a support system for students of color in college that increases their ability to afford, be admitted and graduate **Expand internet access by:** · Developing an analysis and map of free Wi-Fi hotspots · Increasing public locations for wireless internet accessibility in communities
Goal #5	All our youth who have graduated from college or a training program are employed	**Encourage private and non-profit investment in workforce development by:** · Expanding the number of youth served by the Summer Youth Employment Program (SYEP) especially in jobs related to science, technology, engineering, and math (STEM) **Increase financial status and standard of living by:** · Expanding financially literacy, including understanding of banking and mortgage systems **Respond to the workforce needs of the region by:** · Expanding enrollment in Career and Technical Education (CTE) · Increasing the number of youth acquiring "digital badges" in related competencies **Promote small businesses by:** · Supporting existing small-business mentorship programs to connect established companies with smaller businesses, newer businesses, or potential clients to provide guidance for starting a new venture. · Promoting and supporting local E-commerce, including developing tutoring and mentorships aimed at small-business owners.

Core Area: Police and Community Relations		Actions
Goal #6	All our youth are safe from violent crime and receiving the second chances they deserve	**Create a more positive relationship between police and community by:** • Tapping the talents of Faith-based communities to engage with Violence Prevention programs • Creating a youth advisory council that develops proactive strategies that reflects the priorities of youth • Hosting quarterly conversations with local leaders and youth as a means to build trust and community healing • Increasing the numbers of police of color in the police force **Ensure safe routes to school and safe places when students are not in school by:** • Identifying safe routes with crossing guards trained to serve as "keepers" **Promote the attitude that a young man of color can have a second chance by:** • Increasing the numbers of employers that hire ex-offenders • Increasing the participation in jail collaborative and reentry services for men of color involved in the criminal justice system

As we worked through these different goals and actions, participants deliberated on key questions: Based on your knowledge and experience, how well do you think the actions the MBK Committee identified will help us address the challenges facing young people in our region? This question asked participants to apply their expertise and lived experience to the challenges faced when creating infrastructure to support youth. This approach shifts the conversation to where people have expertise. It treats the group not as people who need to be educated to contribute but as a valuable community of experts who contribute to the conversation from the basis of their wisdom.

Finally, the MBK community forums ended with the question: What actions do you imagine you could take, as an individual within your community or through the groups of which you are a member, to advance the goals identified by the MBK Committee? This question emphasized participants' agency and the community solidarity they experienced through churches, schools, and other community organizations. It offered an opportunity for people to speak to their own values and beliefs. Some residents who attended took the opportunity of this conversational moment to speak to how their own commitments and values related to the MBK initiatives.

Who is Going to do it? (Commitment-making)

The My Brother's Keeper playbook also accomplished a second key task: setting milestones for progress. After these initial conversations that set objectives and determined milestones, the playbook was circulated throughout the community. It was printed, placed on the MBK website, and shared on internet-based discussion groups to enable the nonprofit community to commit resources to achieving its outlined objectives. The process of committing resources to these objectives was a decentralized process in which different organizations pledged what their means would allow.

The MBK project exemplifies how the planning conversation enables commitments to be made. With the MBK, that mechanism was the development of the MBK Playbook and the subsequent reports generated by MBK and shared with participants and the community. By naming MBK and organizing community leaders around it, energy was created surrounding this initiative. This energy helped to solidify commitment through the conversation in two ways.

First, government and community leaders held a forum in which they could visibly make commitments to the community. As a part of the MBK initiatives, the Mayor created a "Blue Ribbon Panel on Early Education" and a "Child Care Subcommittee" to examine and understand the needs of childcare providers in city neighborhoods. Learning initiatives associated with MBK were initiated, including digital media education through the Carnegie Library network, digital multi-media and gaming in a regional school district, and The Together Project for technology and literacy in a predominantly Black suburb. Another learning initiative that started through MBK was the Mandarian Chinese Teleconferencing program in a different majority-minority school district. Local business owners committed to hiring citizens returning to the community after incarceration. A major endowment committed to funding priorities defined in the MBK Playbook. The city government committed to maintaining engagement with the MBK process. County government committed leadership and resources to MBK initiatives. Many local church leaders committed to encouraging their congregants to continue participating in MBK initiatives. Of course, these initiatives and the many others that were initiated by community "Keepers" could have happened independently and would still have served the community. However, having these initiatives as a part of the network of commitment-making that grew out of these planning conversations made them visible as a web of coordinated efforts to support a community in need.

Second, community leaders could speak about MBK more easily to their communities. Communities knew there was a concerted effort to "make something happen" for communities of color in Pittsburgh. Through this mechanism, community members themselves could make personal commitments to the process and organize their own efforts and labor to achieve the shared goals these conversations established. While these personal commitments were less documented and celebrated than the commitment-making of government entities, organizations, and school districts, they truly made these initiatives effective.

As a mechanism to track progress, these commitments were recorded in the MBK Playbook as goals. Their progress was tracked through regular reports and community updates. Throughout this process, progress was driven by the making of regular updates to the community. That is, MBK organizers checked in with the "Keepers" for progress updates. The regular reporting served as a tool for accountability for all involved.

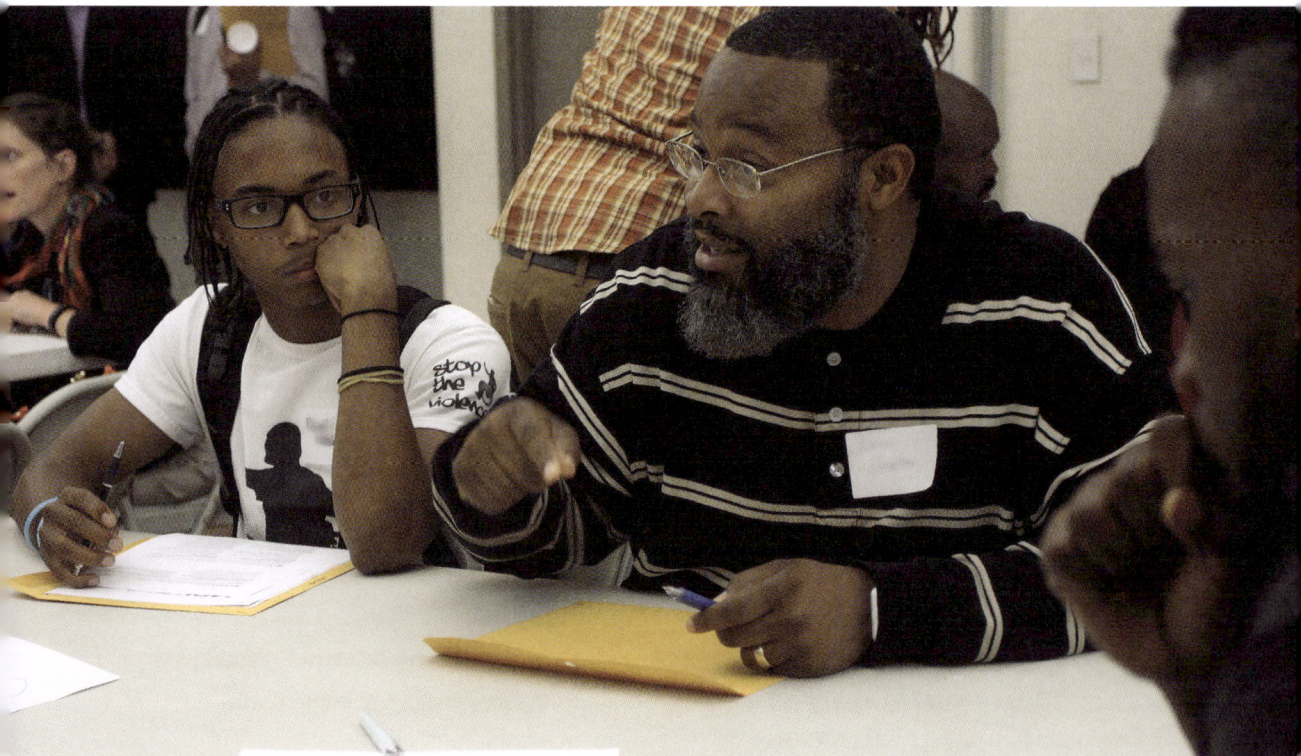

The City of Pittsburgh embraced President Obama's call to action for My Brother's Keeper. This community conversation was one of 4 that were held, and hosted over 160 residents at the Kingsley Center in Pittsburgh on Sept 22, 2015. Photo by the author, courtesy City of Pittsburgh

HOW DESIGNERS SURMOUNT THE COMMON CHALLENGES OF THE PLANNING CONVERSATION

In a civic context, groups having a planning conversation can be composed of actors each with interests related to a matter of concern that might be the subject of the conversation. Residents will come to a planning conversation because they see some alignment between their interests and the subject matter. Dan Hill, in his book *Dark Matter and Trojan Horses*, writes about Alfred Hitchcock's use of the "MacGuffin" in cinema and applies it in a design context. In Hitchcock's more action-oriented movies, the MacGuffin was the thing in the movie that all the characters chased. In the movie *The Maltese Falcon*, the falcon statue was pursued by characters, thereby advancing the plot. Translated to a design context as pertains to community-based action, the MacGuffin, Hill says, is an organizing force that drives action in a community conversation. One example Hill uses is an innovatively designed building that the community desires, which, to construct, requires governmental officials to remedy problems in outdated policies that prohibit more sustainable or energy-efficient buildings. The My Brother's Keeper program served as such a motivational device. The additional power and gravity lent by the Office of the US Presidency heightened the desirability of engaging in this conversation. The planning conversation, executed well, accumulates its own energy and encourages community actors and individuals to become a part of it.

Aligning goals and expectations across actors is a key reason for having the planning conversation in complicated civic spaces. Holding the planning conversation helps ensure that residents, community leaders, municipal staff, and officials are all working toward the same objectives. This fosters a sense of unity and purpose and offers the opportunity for elected officials to be seen doing work that reflects the will of the community residents. In most cases, these goals and expectations are well constructed by thoughtful preparation and collaborative co-working across scales and functional areas. My Brother's Keeper, after being initiated by the Obama White House, was picked up by a coalition of actors that included community leaders and elected officials within Pittsburgh city government. The developmental work was examined and deliberated upon by a broader group of community leaders, including business leaders, clergy, academic researchers, and nonprofit organization leaders, as well as community residents.

Planning conversations thus build consensus among diverse stakeholders. Consensus is a powerful tool. It can give a community a sense of purpose and agency as they see fellow community members and leaders working towards the goals that they believe in. But consensus also has a potentially negative side. In these projects, consensus can appear to leave minority viewpoints behind and exclude those whose unique needs might not be broadly shared. Consensus can also be harder to achieve in a diverse community conversation. Community actors with varied goals might be unwilling or even unable to set aside those goals for the sake of consensus. One example of this effect might be the consensus that has gradually developed within the US Public Health community that COVID-19 is no longer a significant public health threat in 2024. While it may be the case that COVID-19 isn't a mortal threat for many people, this consensus has damaged the lives of disabled people.

One case for consensus-building in a planning process can be taken from the case of the Mothers Against Drunk Drivers (MADD) organization, discussed by Charles Spinosa in *Disclosing New Worlds* (1997). The women organizing MADD created a platform for consensus with some agreement on a principal point—engaging in the practice of full responsibility for drinking—but were flexible about the reasons why people might agree with that practice. The MBK conversations oriented towards the ethic of scaffolding the practice of creating better lives for men and boys of color but accepted multiple routes to stakeholders arriving at that consensus. Thus, reasons and backgrounds can be flexible and locally adaptable to each community of interest.

Designers play a crucial role in navigating the complexities of planning conversations, helping participants understand the scope of their agency and reshaping that scope as necessary. In the planning conversation, it can be challenging for participants to know what the scope of their power is. Is this conversation just a "brainstorming" session, where participants contribute ideas that may or may not be realized, or is this a moment where participants have a chance to shape goals or outcomes? Through the things they make, designers must clearly communicate the purpose and potential impact of the conversation to manage expectations and foster a sense of genuine involvement. They need to establish a highly visible process, outlining how participant input will be used and ensuring that contributions are not only heard but also integrated into the planning outcomes and reflected back to the participants. This clarity helps build trust among participants, as they understand that their voices matter and their input has real influence.

Trust

Trust is a foundational part of the collaborative process in planning conversations. These conversations require investment and risk-taking from all participants. Trust is essential for risks to be taken when building programs, infrastructure, or services. Because conveners have limited opportunities to build trust with participants at a single event, trust must evolve over time. Robert Solomon and Fernando Flores (2001) present trust as an emotional skill that can be fluently achieved. Distinguishing authentic trust from other forms—like simple trust (non-reflective trust) or "blind trust" that a child might have for their parents—authentic trust is built from a history of successful interactions. It is a characteristic of the self rather than the other. Let's look at some examples of how trust might be built.

The City of Boston has a robust system for addressing simple municipal problems like potholes, broken streetlights, clogged storm drains, and overflowing trash cans. Like the nationwide emergency phone line system 911, people in Boston can call 311 for municipal problems. When calling, residents are directed to a pool of city service representatives who will record the problematic issue and send a notice to the relevant city department. As someone highly interested in civic action, I often use the 311 phone line and app to report potholes on the road. When reporting issues like potholes, overflowing public trash cans, graffiti in public parks, and broken benches at transit stops calling 311 reliably dispatches city workers who repair or remediate issues. The communication pattern leading to successful repairs encourages a strong feeling of trust between myself and the 311 system. I have expanded my use of and reliance on this system by downloading the Boston 311 app. I use it as an example of low-level civic action in classes, and I also evangelize its use to my students when they complain about city maintenance issues.

However, the 311 system does not create trust when reporting *larger* problems. An intersection on Huntington Avenue near my campus, at the cross street of Belvedere, has a severely rippled pavement surface. The uneven surface presents a hazard, and drivers often swerve in their lanes to go around the worst sections. It is a hazardous area, as pedestrians are often crossing the intersection here as well. I have periodically reported this problematic intersection. However, because repairing this large area of pavement requires marshalling more resources than just sending out the public works "pothole" team, the scope of the problem is not a good fit for the purview of 311 reporting. No one ever comes to repair it. This neglect has breached my trust in the 311 system—at least as regards larger-scale issues.

The pattern of results from my use of the system has taught me to trust the system for small issues like potholes. However, I have also learned to distrust the system for larger-scale problems like the rippled street surface at a major intersection.

Similarly, people whose only civic interaction is receiving municipal water bills or experiencing surveillance from police will learn to develop a relationship with the city that reflects those interactions. They often feel at odds with the city government. They see city government in a role of enforcing laws and regulations and demanding payment for services rather than being a collaborator. Designing planning conversations where residents play a role serves a more complex set of ends than just gathering public opinion for use in policy decisions. These conversations enact new relationships with residents and promote communication between and among residents and city staff. Through an effectively designed planning conversation, residents feel welcomed to contribute, like they are an important part of contributing to the authoring and execution of larger projects within civic life. Which indeed, they are!

Making the plan and agreement visible

Design plays an essential role in sharing the results of the planning conversation back with the broader community. Design is the medium by which commitments are made visible to the community. Philosophers J.L. Austin and Paul Grice (followed by John Searle) developed the concept of "speech acts." Speech acts are performative statements that change the quality of a relationship between people. One example might be the interpersonal statement: "I forgive you." This statement absolves an emotional or material debt between two individuals. The performative statement alters the relationship between the two people simply or profoundly, depending upon the debt cleared. While a full accounting of the nuances of speech acts is not possible here, one kind of speech act is particularly important in planning conversations.

The type of speech act that most matters to planning conversations is that of, as Searle puts it, the "commissive," or the promise. United States readers may be familiar with the childhood experience of the *Pledge of Allegiance*, where schoolchildren would daily recite "I pledge allegiance to the Flag of the United States of America..." This pledge is more than empty words being recited by sleepy-eyed elementary school students at 8:00 am. The pledge is a group performance of a commitment to the state. As discussed earlier in this chapter, in the example of the My Brother's Keeper program, the planning conversation involves securing pledges or commitments from actors at governmental, mid-level, and grassroots levels. Design's power in this conversation goes beyond crafting the statement of the commitment. Design's power lies in making those commitments publicly visible to the large group that is a party to the planning conversation.

Like the exchange of rings at a wedding ceremony, design creates material forms of commitment that are both a reminder to an organization of a pledge given and a visible public statement of that pledge. Consider the small lock icon on an internet web browser when using a secured connection. The symbol does not, in and of itself, provide any functionality or force. Rather, the lock icon on the web browser is a mere symbol that tells a customer that the site's owners have architected their technology so that internet transactions will be secure. It is a promise from the website owners and developers to the customers that says: "We will not let your data be compromised in this process."

Different methods than wedding rings and pictures of locks are more appropriate for civic projects. The planning conversations of the My Brother's Keeper project included diagrams of important information discovered, timelines of past and future events, and visible lists of commitments made by "Keepers"—government, nonprofit, and private entities. The My Brother's Keeper project named the different entities and listed, in clear language, the commitment they had made. For example, the MBK website and the accompanying reports included text on "Private Sector Partnerships to Support Literacy: Grow Up Great by PNC Bank," a program which offered financial support to local philanthropies that promote and advance early childhood education initiatives and others that equip young children for school.

The project has continued through 2024, with new energy and attention from the current mayor. The MBK website remains an important resource for the Pittsburgh community. As a visible source of the history of the project, including commitments made and fulfilled, the site acts as an agent, documenting the history of trustful commitments and their realizations between government, organizations, and community members.

CONCLUSION

In civic spaces, planning conversations are frequent. Keeping the planning process open to authoring by the community members is an important duty for public organizations. To remain a broadly inclusive process, the key components of scope planning and commitment-making should be done in partnership with residents. Prioritization of planning tasks, validation of the value of tasks in the community, and the mechanism by which tasks are committed can successfully be done by delegating power to the community residents. Teams of mid-level experts can work productively to prepare plan elements so they are clear and actionable, which further facilitates resident participation. In these processes, trust is essential. Design alone cannot prevent leaders or organizations from acting in bad faith. On the positive side, design can materialize commitment-making and surface promises of resources and effort from organizations.

When designing for the surfacing conversation, the designer's goal is to show people how their knowledge and lived experience are relevant to the problem at hand.

Effective design for planning conversations and their outcomes are at the core of achieving broad-based success for civic projects and fostering ongoing collaboration between residents and municipal government.

Enhancing collaboration through planning conversations involves creating structured dialogues where stakeholders can align their goals, make commitments, and track progress collectively. The MBK project illustrates how planning conversations can be effectively utilized to achieve these objectives. By developing the MBK Playbook and subsequent reporting documents, the project set clear milestones and objectives that were circulated throughout the community, ensuring widespread understanding and engagement. The decentralized process of resource commitment allowed organizations to pledge support, fostering a sense of collective responsibility and action.

In civic settings, similar planning conversations can enhance collaboration by providing forums in which stakeholders, including government officials, community leaders, nonprofit organizations, and residents can come together to discuss and commit to common goals. These conversations build trust and transparency through visible commitments and regular progress updates. For instance, government and community leaders might establish panels or committees to address specific issues, such as education or public safety, and initiate learning and development projects. A key element of successful planning initiatives is ensuring an ongoing communication cycle among stakeholders. This cycle of communication shouldn't end when the community conversations are completed. Planning is an ongoing effort that is co-produced by all the members of a community seeking to coordinate to develop new initiatives. By creating a network of coordinated efforts, these initiatives become part of a larger, cohesive strategy to address community needs. Additionally, the visibility of these efforts generates momentum and encourages broader community participation, ensuring that the benefits of these initiatives are felt at the grassroots level.

A panel of community leaders responds to participants' questions as part of President Obama's call to action, My Brother's Keeper. This community conversation was held at Ebeneezer Baptist Church in Pittsburgh on Sept 22, 2015. Photo by the author, courtesy City of Pittsburgh.

3

Upland Interceptor   2 lanes   "New" Median w/ left-turn pocket   2 lanes   Multi-use Trail   Drains to creek   Riparian Zone   Re-nature the creek corridor

CHAPTER 3

Designing a Difficult Conversation

WHAT IS A DIFFICULT CONVERSATION?

A difficult conversation has a heightened emotional tone. On an everyday basis, many conversations might instill you with fear or anxiety. These types of conversations go beyond the typical emotional level that you might have. Conversations in civic spaces about social identities such as race, ethnicity, religion, and sexual identity are often considered difficult conversations. However, certain conversations can be difficult for some and not others. Having a conversation among co-workers about where to go to lunch as a group might be assumed to be "easy" for most participants. It is easy to fall into an overly broad assumption that we all approach the world in the same ways. However, for a co-worker with severe food allergies, the mere idea of going to an unfamiliar restaurant induces unpleasant feelings. The model of the difficult conversation developed by researchers Stone, Patton, and Heen (2010) identifies these conversations based on participants' heightened feelings of vulnerability, caring, or interpersonal emotions. The insightful Stone model was created to address interpersonal dynamics. In other words, difficulty in conversation can also be a property of groups. I will use their model as a framework and then describe how it can be applied in civic or group contexts. We will also discuss naming the conversation at the outset to help resolve unproductive conflict and create a shared understanding of the topics and emotional stakes involved.

Conversation Under Threat

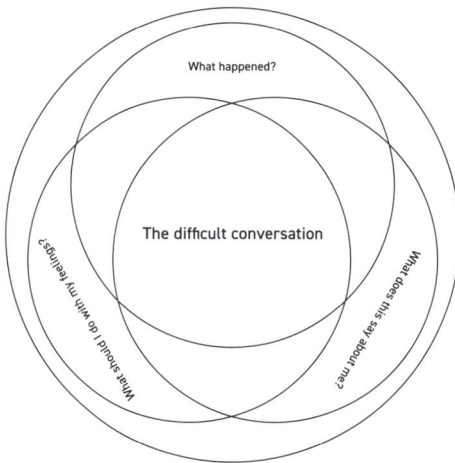

Figure 3: Each difficult conversation contains three conversations that happen simultaneously. Stone, Patton and Heen describe this model in interpersonal relationships. It also occurs in civic life.

The Stone model identifies three layers in a difficult conversation. Let's consider the three layers of the conversation and how they work in civic spaces. The most apparent layer is the discussion about *what should happen* or *what we might do together*—also known as the matter of concern. The question of "what happened?" gets to the essential facts of the matter. While it might seem that this question is straightforward, people can and often do disagree on factual matters. The matter of concern is most often simply the topic or context of the meeting. Capital budget meetings, participatory budget sessions, urban corridor redevelopment meetings, re-zoning discussions—any of these typical civic events could elicit matters of concern from residents. They might be concerned about: How should we spend the city's money? How ought we redesign this major street? What kind of policies will support more affordable housing in our city? How will this affect my street? As staffers who have attended public meetings as government representatives well know, these seemingly straightforward questions can be contested among residents. If we were only dealing with this first layer, the conversation might be a feisty exchange of points of view, but it might never become difficult. The true challenge of the difficult conversation lies in the other layers.

A difficult conversation includes a second layer of feelings related to the matter of concern. This layer is laden with affect—the emotional engagement entangled with the conversation about the matter of concern. Most residents don't come to community meetings in a relentless yet optimistic quest for the best of all possible worlds. They are also not a jury of peers, carefully selected for neutrality. Residents attend because they care deeply about a matter of concern related to the meeting topic and the implications for their neighborhood. The group of residents that attend a community conversation is not a political scientist's representative ideal sampling but a group of highly motivated individuals. Almost by default, residents assuming this posture of care entails strong feelings. Personal values get folks out of their homes and into folding chairs in the basement meeting room of a local city building or senior center on a Thursday night at 7 PM to discuss zoning policy. This kind of self-selection guarantees that participants will have strong feelings about the matter of concern, satisfying the second layer of the difficult conversation model.

The third layer concerns the support or threat to a participant's identity or sense of self. In this layer we can find participants' morals, values, and beliefs that they hold in relation to their social identity or group membership. This third layer of the conversation is most apparent when the matter of concern entails discussing race, religion, gender identity, or other classes protected under discrimination laws. However, threats to a participant's social identity can also occur when the identity of participants does not seem obviously related to the matter of concern.

One simple way to notice if a participant might be experiencing a threat to their sense of self is if they feel compelled to state aspects of a visible or non-visible identity. They might say: "I'm a father of three children and a daycare provider," or, "I'm an EMT and a mother," or, "I was born in Boston and grew up in the 1980s." When participants want to reveal an aspect of their social identity—or offer their *bona fides*—it may indicate that they are noticing their identity more in relation to the matter of concern. While what constitutes a threat to identity may be unique to every individual, but it is an essential component of what makes a conversation difficult.

Pittsburgh participated in the Rockefeller Foundation's 100 Resilient Cities challenge, to help cities build resilience to the challenges of the coming century. Here, residents deliberated on how the city might support neighborhoods to meet these challenges. Nov 19, 2015. East Liberty Presbyterian Church. Photo by the author, courtesy City of Pittsburgh.

WHY ARE YOU HAVING A DIFFICULT CONVERSATION?

It is hard to consistently predict when you might be facilitating a difficult conversation. Aspects of difficulty might emerge from what seemed to be a noncontroversial topic. There are, however, some reliable factors that might augur when a difficult conversation might be at hand. Thinking through the possible threats that a conversation might produce can be a way to predict if a conversation might take a difficult turn. For instance, a group of community conversations convened with the support of the Heinz Endowments for the US Veteran's Administration program, MyVA Communities. They sought to improve services for veterans in Southwestern Pennsylvania. They spent time considering the support that veterans might need, providing a practical perspective on a topic that can evoke strong emotions or pose a threat to identity, such as achieving a successful and fulfilling job placement after leaving the service.

Veterans may struggle to articulate the value of skills that they developed in the military to civilian employers. As a result, many veterans end up underemployed. It is not difficult to understand why transitioning from a highly skilled, high-reliability position in military life to a less challenging position in civilian life might threaten one's self-image as a competent and reliable person. In a room of veterans talking about support services, it is quite likely that they are struggling with these kinds of emotions. Veterans who have been in dangerous situations struggle to cope with the intense feelings of post-traumatic stress, depression, or anxiety. While there are far fewer veterans experiencing this challenge than the quite common challenge of translating military skills to civilian paradigms, in a meeting that convenes a group of 50 veterans, one or two may likely struggle with these more profound mental health challenges. Similarly, people attending a meeting to discuss affordable housing may be living in poverty currently and may experience feelings of shame or inadequacy.

While it is beyond the scope of public meetings to provide group therapy to attendees, a nuanced and sensitive design can acknowledge the difficulty in a conversational topic by giving permission for participants to break the "code of silence" and voice their difficult feelings. It may even be productive and validating to hear that difficult feelings are commonly experienced by members of a group convened for a meeting. As discussed in the introductory chapter, strong emotions are not something to forbid or avoid in civic conversations. However, the conversation design should be prepared to understand that emotions are relevant data being shared by participants.

HOW TO DESIGN FOR THE DIFFICULT CONVERSATION

Navigating the complexities of difficult conversations requires effective planning and a thoughtful approach. Building on the Stone model's three layers—factual matters, emotional engagement, and identity concerns—this section will present practical tactics designers can use to address the inherent challenges of interactions between layers in difficult conversations. By considering each layer, it is possible to facilitate understanding, empathy, and productive dialogue. The following strategies will help designers foster an environment where participants feel heard, respected, and capable of contributing meaningfully to the conversation.

Conflict in difficult conversations can be productive or unproductive. Productive conflict fosters a deeper understanding and uncovers underlying issues that may have been overlooked. Productive conflict may challenge participants' or organizers' assumptions related to a matter of concern. By contrast, unproductive conflict escalates tensions and hinders progress. Unproductive conflict includes such behaviors as poisoning collective sources of conversation and thought by manipulating facts, holding back true information, or giving false information. Unproductive conflict may include verbal attacks on the character or identity of other participants, including attempts to exclude them based on their personal characteristics.

The three layers of the difficult conversation model chart clear paths forward for designers and suggest key challenges designers can surmount. Through the application of some practical approaches and techniques that facilitate difficult conversations, they can guide participants towards more engaged and valuable experiences.

In the outermost layer of the conversation—the layer that deals with the facts of the matter—unproductive conflict over factual or historical matters can sometimes be resolved by preparing documentation of commonly agreed-upon facts for the group. Conveners can avoid arguments over factual matters by preparing the conversation by drawing from informational sources that are mutually respected and presenting factual information using language that acknowledges the values and beliefs of a plurality of viewpoints.

The factual component of difficult conversations can be supported through material scaffolds. A pedagogical frame at the beginning can guide common discussion topics for all participants. Common language and a set of facts that are assented to by the group enable conversation and alleviate the burden of difficult conversations. Common elements that designers are familiar with preparing can be valuable. For example, they can prepare briefing documents to give a general overview of complex material. Designers can also construct information visualizations that present information in a way that makes it easier to understand the important systemic or social relationships of complex systems.

Designers should carefully consider the neutrality of language in supporting materials because participants are often sensitive to such nuances. However, it is difficult for materials to be neutral, meaning neutrality might even be an impossible aspiration. Designers might create materials that better incorporate viewpoints from two or more dominant narratives that relate to the matter of concern. For example, a civic conversation hosted by the League of Women Voters (LWV) aimed to understand people's personal perspectives regarding possibilities for sensible gun regulation in their community.

While residents of other countries might think of guns in civil society as a uniquely "American problem," I would encourage readers from other cultures to avoid getting distracted by the particulars of this issue. While this conversation might be local to the United States, each culture has seemingly intractable issues. I'd offer that the underlying design process to enable difficult conversations might be used as a template and inspire opportunity-finding in a broader range of contexts than the Midwestern United States.

Naming the conversation can also help resolve unproductive conflict. In the case of a community conversation on gun legislation, our design team conducted preliminary research to prepare to host this conversation. In collaboration with volunteers from the LWV, our team interviewed representatives from two foundational partners that were secured for this initiative: The National Alliance for Mental Illness and The Center for Victims— a Pittsburgh community-based nonprofit organization that provides services for victims of all crime in Pennsylvania. The Center also supports one-on-one conversations with responsible gun owners and gun safety trainers. Informed by these conversations, we titled the forums "Living with Guns in a Free Society." We aimed for this title to be legible and welcoming to gun rights advocates and those who supported legislation restricting or banning guns. To recruit a diverse group of people and invite a broader conversation, the title needed to reflect the competing aspects of dominant narratives about guns.

Beyond crafting a welcoming title, choosing a productive agenda in a difficult conversation is also "design work." It is not enough to merely create an agenda that attempts to incorporate the dominant narratives regarding the matter of concern. The work to be done at the meeting should be productively completed by the diverse groups attending. Choosing to deliberate on the hardest, most intransigent aspects of an issue is not a productive use of anyone's time. Convening a community to spend hours in a stagnant conversation helps no one. Within an issue, there are, however, broad swaths of agreement among people who might seem to hold irreconcilable, diametrically opposed viewpoints.

For the community conversation about Living with Guns in a Free Society, our design team began with the supposition that in a country with well over 300 million guns, there would not be a practical policy or law enforcement option that would rid our civil society of all guns. We also assumed that there was broad practical agreement; the best policy or law enforcement approach would not be to ensure that guns were freely available to anyone throughout our civil society. People can agree that the two extremes—no guns for anyone and guns free for everyone—are unreasonable positions. Our assumptions were further supported by our stakeholder representatives. From that agreement, we continued to ask ourselves: where might further agreement lie?

Our techniques opened space for a nuanced discussion about a controversial issue for US residents. Among our stakeholders, preventing firearms-related suicide was seen as a goal everyone could agree upon. The painful truth is that most people who die from a gun die by suicide. It is a significant problem in US society, and it merits deliberation. This is a point where diverse participants could have a nuanced discussion. How might we implement policies that would support programs or services to prevent firearms-related suicides? For this topic, we used a two-part rubric to proceed from a place of agreement to explore this issue further:

1. The truth we don't discuss
2. The myth we need to counter

In a difficult conversation, asking these questions charts a path towards areas of basic agreement—the foundation of initiating a conversation.

There were numerous factual truths that went undiscussed. For a long time, most gun-related deaths in the US have been the result of suicide (Centers for Disease Control and Prevention, n.d.; DeSilver, 2013). Guns work together with the under-provisioning of care for mental health challenges by the US healthcare system to create a profoundly negative outcome. While there are other avenues for suicide, self-inflicted death by firearm is the most used, quickest, and most lethal method. Gun availability is also a significant risk for suicide, and the number of guns in a community correlates to suicides among residents (Hemenway & Miller, 2013;

Miller & Hemenway, 1999). The myth that emerges amid this discussion is that people with mental health difficulties are more likely to be violent. This is not the case, as people with mental health difficulties are no more or less violent than anyone else.

Second, we learned from our stakeholders that there was a strong desire on all sides to prevent injury or death from gun accidents or misuse. Gun safety was another topic around which there was broad agreement. As suicide is universally regarded as a negative, gun safety was universally regarded as desirable. How might we implement policies that could improve gun safety? Gun safety methods of interest to the broad community include child-safe gun locks and limiting access to guns for people in distress or with a record of domestic abuse.

> *Engagement is better than silence, as it fosters collaboration and approaches to improve the current situation.*

Finally, everyone could agree that private gun ownership has an invisible cost that must be subsidized by all taxpayers. The question of what a reasonable dollar figure that residents are willing to pay in taxes to subsidize private gun ownership by a minority of individuals was determined to be a possible question for discussion. Direct costs included socialized costs of emergency medical treatment for victims of gun violence who do not have the means to pay for care. Direct costs also include the cost of policing guns through permitting legal guns and cataloging, storing, and disposing of guns used in crimes. Indirect costs include the purchase of security or protective equipment intended to defend against guns. They include bulletproof vests or other personal protective equipment for police, powerful weapons needed by police to compete in an "arms race" with criminals, armored vehicles, and bulletproof glass in public buildings. The necessity of all these expenses is debatable in urban areas in the United States with relatively low crime rates. However, one cannot blame public servants for wanting to avoid death or serious injury while performing their jobs. Our research team regarded this last question—the question of the public costs of private gun ownership and who bears them—as the most potentially volatile and where tempers might flare. However, these three issues were designed to encourage productive discussion.

We can take several lessons from this example of a difficult conversation. Engagement is better than silence. That is, engaging the viewpoints of difference creates an emergent place where collaboration might be fostered, and approaches to improving the current situation might emerge. Difficult conversations in civic space can thus begin by considering the various layers that such conversations must traverse. The factual, feelings, and identity layers each have important considerations that can be engaged with through design action.

Beginning from a place of factual agreement is one opportunity for considering how a conversation might be framed and what issues might be discussed. Framing it as a "problem-finding" or "problem-solving" conversation for the community offers a concrete space where people might work together. The problems that are the subject of the difficult conversation are not personal problems or owned by only one interest group. Difficult problems are always shared by a community.

It is difficult to design a difficult conversation to de-escalate feelings of jeopardized identity among the participants. Social identity is a complicated thing. Even psychological researchers cannot agree on a unified definition or definitively describe how it is constituted. Some facets of social identity are highly durable, while others are changeable. People who thought of themselves as members of one group may still do so as they age or change their perspective and identify with a new group. Social identity can be asserted by an individual or assigned to someone in a culture based on their outward appearance. There is no surefire way to understand all the ways a matter of concern might support or threaten a participant's social identity. However, well-meaning designers can think through and help prepare participants for the challenges that a difficult conversation might present. Reframing a difficult conversation as problem-solving also influences other layers of the difficult conversation. If the group can orient toward problem-solving together rather than becoming overcome by emotion or feeling the need to justify or defend aspects of their social identity, the conversation can be generative and orient the participants toward mutual learning and collaborative discovery.

Leaning on the Things that Surround the Conversation

Things can be designed to absorb some of the emotional labor for participants and conveners. That is, labor that might be absorbed by people can rather be delegated to the things present in the conversational space. Consider how the Boston-area social good organization, the Louis D. Brown Peace Institute (visited 2023-o5-17), implements this approach in workshop sessions to support the surviving family members of victims of violence. Their services are open to all who have experienced loss because of violence—family members of victims as well as family members of incarcerated loved ones. The institute uses a method they call "Peace Play in Urban Settings," which they adapted from a method developed by clinical psychologist Gisela Schubach DeDomenico (Schadler & De Domenico, 2012). Inside an unassuming brick building that was formerly a residence, the walls of several rooms are covered on all sides with shelves that hold well over a thousand miniatures—small figural statuettes, cake decorations, and children's toys. Organized by categories such as insects, sea creatures, household & leisure, and trees, these miniatures are at the center of a process developed to support participants engaging in a difficult inner conversation. Peace Play conversations access powerful feelings that can open the door to healing.

While there is not enough space in this book to do justice to the richness of the process here, Peace Play in Urban Settings taps into a complex process of emotional delegation using a deceptively simple method. People who have experienced grief visit the institute and receive a short introduction in which they are given a pie or cake pan with a layer of sand. Next, they tour the rooms of miniatures and select any miniatures that, as the facilitator says, "speak to them." After moving the sand in the tray to a participant's preference, each participant arranges the selected miniatures in the tray in a way that is meaningful to them. People are invited to, if they choose, share the reasons for their choices and tell a story embodied by their arranged miniatures in the sand. Experiencing this myself with a group of colleagues provided some access to the compelling power of this method. By delegating different aspects of one's thoughts and feelings to these miniatures, arranging them in the sand allowed me to reflect on each feeling, thought, family member, and institution they represented.

To consider the Peace Play in Urban Settings process as developed by the Louis D. Brown Peace Institute, we can extrapolate a general principle for design from this approach. When dealing with the second layer of the difficult conversation—the feelings layer—delegation of the difficult feelings to objects can be a powerful tactic to move those feelings "outside of the body" and onto an object. The objects can be moved around, considered, and reconfigured, offering an opportunity for reflective engagement with difficult feelings. A similar tactic in design has been used by the author to confront the challenges of the third layer of the difficult conversation—social identity. In a workshop setting where questions of social identity may be at play, a warm-up activity asks participants to draw parts of their social identity that they are willing to share. Their actions create an opportunity to reveal the parts of someone's identity that may not be immediately apparent to others in a casual meeting. Taking time to draw symbols or representations helps participants exemplify aspects of identity, visible and non-visible, assigned and assumed. Then, disclosing their chosen narrative with fellow participants creates a space for participants to reveal their identity in a way that supports their dignity and their ability to openly share their unique personal perspectives.

CONCLUSION

Difficult conversations can test the best work of designers and facilitators. However, when done well, they open a path to deeper understanding across differences. In this chapter, I have shown how the three layers of the difficult conversation—the factual, feelings, and identity layers—can be designed. In this way, difficult conversations invite designers to facilitate people coming together to address difficult topics. By considering the use of inclusive titling, neutral language, and thinking about the aspects of the discussion that are best for the community of participants to be convened, designers can shape conversations, so people contribute their best responses.

Finding a base of agreement from which to work and hosting the conversations that are most possible might seem to fall to critiques of "incrementalism." This familiar critique is that civic conversations seek areas of overlap within which to build agreement and alleviate the difficulty of participation by only delivering solutions that are palliative in nature. While these critiques might be valid, it is not possible to ignore human beings' common resistance to change. An audacious vision for long-term change might be held by activists, policymakers, or other community leaders. The goal of designing a difficult civic conversation is to instigate conversation on an issue. Talking together is infinitely better than no progress or, worse, regressing.

CHAPTER 4

What is a High-Stakes Conversation?

So far, we have discussed how conversations surface latent data or ideas that exist within a community. These data and ideas help groups plan and make commitments to one another, and navigate the fraught challenges faced when a person's own identity or sense of self becomes threatened in a conversation. Consider the following conversation situations:

> A community organizer and a local resident group have a conversation to determine whether it is better to proceed with a neighborhood improvement project using limited funding and resources or wait with the hope that additional support and resources might become available before the neighborhood's issues worsen. The organizer explains the potential benefits and drawbacks of moving forward with the current plan, highlighting how it could address some immediate needs but may not fully meet the community's long-term goals. On the other hand, waiting for more funding could result in a more comprehensive solution but carries the risk that more funding may never come, and of further decline in the neighborhood's conditions.

A group of residents and government officials have a conversation to determine how to renovate a section of their neighborhood that is in jeopardy of periodic flooding, combined sewer overflow, and rife with derelict buildings.

A doctor and a prospective liver transplant patient have a conversation to determine whether it is better to accept a suboptimal organ for transplant or wait with the hope that a better match might appear before the patient's health deteriorates.

A design strategist and their client have a conversation to determine how the client can reorient their business toward producing more sustainable products and services.

A financial advisor and their client have a conversation to determine whether to transfer the client's retirement savings from a low-risk, low-margin investment to a higher-risk investment with a potentially better rate of return.

These situations are examples of what I call high-stakes conversations, which have several aspects in common. Drawing from post-normal science (Funtowicz & Ravetz, 2003), a viewpoint that sees policymaking, science, and technology as a set of interrelated systems, embedded in societal and natural contexts. Post-normal science responds to the current crisis in science as applied within the public sphere, taking a broader perspective regarding the distinctions of "values" and "facts," and reorienting discussions of absolute "truth" toward "quality" of evidence. Post-normal science emphasizes a common language to discuss science- and policy-related decision-making but acknowledges the broad-based existence of many possible "normals" that might exist across diverse communities and environments. I define high-stakes conversations by five main characteristics, on top of those present in all conversations. This model has been shaped through my work designing civic and public conversations up to the present day, as well as participating in many other less formal conversations in client meetings, the design classroom, and the design studio. The characteristics of high-stakes conversations are:

1. There is **no "right" answer.**

2. The dialog centers around making an **imminent** decision.

3. Groups of participants are characterized by **imbalance.**

   > Participants typically have an imbalance of knowledge and/or agency relating to the conversation domain (expert vs client).

   > Participants have an imbalanced level of experience in having the conversation (routine vs singular).

   > Participants have an imbalanced level of investment in the outcome (policymaker vs resident).

4. The dialog centers around making a **consequential decision.**

5. Once a decision is made, it is **irrevocable**, or very difficult or costly to revoke.

No right answer

In high-stakes conversations, there is frequently no "right" answer. That is, the fit of any answer is highly subjective and may involve deliberating about several suboptimal approaches. This framing of no "right" answer or talking about options being suboptimal might sound like a defeatist position. You might even say "well, if there is no 'right' answer, I could just pick a choice at random." People might be tempted to take this somewhat nihilistic position in the face of a challenge that has no "right" answer. But "right" is in quotation marks for a reason. No "right" answer simply means that there is no universal "right" answer for everyone. There might, however, be an optimal answer, or even a better answer for you personally. There might also be a better answer for your community.

High-stakes conversations confront the problem of a group of participants needing to choose between different alternatives. When a single choice must be made by a group, there are two discussions that need to happen. The first discussion is having the group consider what the different aspects of the solution are. You might call these the different aspects the *variables* or *factors* of the problem under consideration. In the case of an affordable housing discussion, these variables might include housing density, parking minimums, transit accessibility, income levels, housing prices, construction costs, demographic trends. All these variables likely have a reasonable range that might be considered. But affordable housing is not a scientific certainty, existing in a system that can be isolated from other influencing factors. Further, from a purely social perspective, it is likely impossible to achieve an optimal configuration for all interested stakeholders.

Economist Herbert Simon advances the model of *satisficing* (a portmanteau of the words satisfy and suffice) to make decisions in situations with no "right" answer (Simon, 1996). When you are making decisions in a satisficing way (or employing what Simon calls bounded rationality), you might be confronted with too many different variables to evaluate. Simon acknowledges that in situations where the number of variables informing a decision is sufficiently large, the search for the perfect solution requires an unreasonable expenditure of energy. Simply put, when a problem gets too complex, any reasonable human would quit searching and "make do" before finding the perfect solution. Urban planner Horst Rittel[4] similarly describes the problem of unbounded expenditure of energy as having *no stopping rule*, an aspect of a special class of problems that Rittel called wicked

---

4 Herbert Simon and Horst Rittel worked on these problems at a similar point in time. Simon does not cite Rittel, nor does Rittel cite Simon, as they seemed unaware of one another's work.

problems. These are intractable problems encountered in urban planning and other social scenarios (Rittel & Webber, 1973). In cases of satisficing, the stopping rule in a search for a solution becomes the first satisfactory solution reached. It is Simon's contention that an optimal decision is not possible in complex scenarios.

To address when a solution might be satisfactory, we are left with, as Simon further describes, various degrees of satisfaction and dissatisfaction, summed up as an *aspiration level,* describes a sufficiently significant degree of satisfaction coupled with a sufficiently insignificant degree of dissatisfaction. Unfortunately, human experience does not submit neatly to metrics applied through binary distinctions like satisfaction and dissatisfaction, nor can we tidily assign a scalar value to the aspiration level of a human experience. Yet, the lack of a right answer is a key contributory factor to a high-stakes conversation. For our example of a growing city facing an affordable housing crisis, a successful result could be defined as one that supports long-term housing stability for residents, while also feeding a viable financial model that supports the building and maintenance of the affordable units and the supporting city infrastructure. The combination of policy variables doesn't need to be "right" or create a situation where everyone is well satisfied, it just needs to be "good enough." Thinking about our policy conversations as optimizing for a calculated satisfaction, is less valuable in the real world than having the conversation that explores the values that shape the overall system.

Another aspect of no "right" answer can be drawn from the writings of Rittel. In a high-stakes conversation, each actor, expert, and client operates from the *deontic premise*, or the personal statement of what ought to be (Rittel, 1972). For Rittel, each person in the conversation acts according to their concept of what a successful solution would be, in the actual sense, but also in the moral and ethical sense. However, in the high-stakes conversation, the deontic premise may be difficult for the actors to apply, even when the potential for real-world outcomes is well understood. When considering, for example, planning policy to create more affordable housing in an urban area, there are many possible interventions, each with a range of effectiveness and attendant drawbacks. The deontic premise that "people ought to be able to stay in their homes" may conflict with the functional obsolescence of dilapidated structures, the use of toxic materials in old construction, or gaps between household incomes and the ability to pay the costs of maintaining existing housing. Complex and competing factors warrant a conversation to seek approaches that can lay the groundwork for transformative approaches, rather than accepting incremental improvements on the status quo.

Imminence

High-stakes conversations often center around a decision or problem that must be addressed within a limited time frame. Imminence creates an additional force in conversations, an element to consider while designing them. This experience of time pressure may exert a coercive force upon the actor who must make a decision. Imminence has two components: the decision is temporally proximate (you're "up against it") and must be made.

Gary Klein, over years of studying people making decisions under extreme time pressure — firefighters, emergency room physicians, military commanders — developed the model of recognition-primed decision-making. Klein found that over years of experience of making decisions under time pressure, people develop and apply a set of intuitive *heuristics*, or a felt sense of what might be the right path in each situation. When people are pressed for time and must decide quickly, Klein says, they decide what to do by intuitively recognizing aspects in the current situation that they have experienced before. Yet, high-stakes conversations don't have precisely the same imminence experienced in emergency rooms or at fire scenes. The situations that are the subject of high-stakes conversations offer the opportunity to be reflective, offer the opportunity for consideration of options.

One approach to imminence in high-stakes conversations is the comparison of scenarios by participants. Rather than trying to enumerate all the aspects of a decision to be made and consider each separately, a different meeting design might offer two or three scenarios to explore. Meeting participants can examine the different scenarios as relevant or not relevant to their own situation, exploring potential outcomes and impacts, discussing what might be positive or negative possibilities from each.

Imbalance

Imbalance is a key characteristic of high-stakes conversations. Imbalance occurs in myriad ways and influences the nature and content of the discourse. While high-stakes conversations can occur in nearly any knowledge domain, they rarely occur where both participants have deep knowledge of and experience with the domain of the conversation. Frequently, these conversations have a high degree of imbalance of understanding of the knowledge domain: a patient and a doctor in a health care domain, a client and a lawyer in a contract domain, or a client and a financial advisor in an investment planning domain. Unlike Rittel's wicked problems, a symmetry of ignorance (Rittel, 1972) is not a factor in a high-stakes conversation in the same sense as it is in a wicked problem. In a high-stakes conversation, typically the domain of the problem is known, and perhaps even well understood. Experts can be found, but in a high-stakes conversation, knowing the way forward is befuddling because there are many potential forward paths, with none being clearly optimal.

Frequently paired with the knowledge imbalance as discussed above, there is also an inverse difference between knowledge and level of investment in the conversation for the two parties. That is, the person with high investment in the outcome has low domain knowledge, but the actor with high domain knowledge comes to the conversation with lower investment.

In the high-stakes conversation, agency is also of importance and can be coupled with imbalances. To understand the role of agency in a high-stakes conversation, let us examine some archetypal examples. Consider a conversation between a police officer and a citizen she has stopped for a traffic violation. This dynamic may fulfill many of the above criteria for a high-stakes conversation. In the traffic stop, there is no answer that is "right," in the sense that there are many possible outcomes. Imminence, consequence, and irrevocability are all factors, and the degree of imbalance between the two participants is significant. In this scenario, the police officer has most of the characteristics of the expert, and the citizen has those of the client. However, in the police-citizen conversation, the officer (the expert) possesses agency. Armed with weapons and the authority of the state, to a far greater extent, the police officer can determine the outcome of the conversation by making the most consequential decisions. The police-suspect conversation is even more coercive, as mutuality does not exist. In this book, I examine high-stakes conversations where the burden (or privilege) of agency lies with the client.

Consider the doctor-patient conversation. It may appear that the doctor only has agency, but it is the patient who has the decision-making ability. In the doctor-patient relationship, the doctor suggests, requests, or insists, yet it is ultimately the patient who acts. In a lawyer-client conversation, the relationship is perhaps clearer. The client provides decision, direction, support, and information, and the lawyer acts as a knowledgeable proxy for the client. Designers take a quite different role with their clients. Commonly, the designer is assigned an objective and is given a wide latitude with which to pursue that objective. A designer may act at the behest of the client but may pursue explorations that they trust the client to understand and approve.

The economic theory of agency was developed from initial research on the Principal-Agent (P-A) problem, which can manifest in any expert-client relationship. The P-A problem occurs when there are two actors in a principal-agent relationship. As defined by Stephen Ross, "one, designated as the agent, acts for, on behalf of, or as representative for the other, designated the principal, in a particular domain of decision problems" (Ross, 1973). The problem arises when the principal delegates an agent to act in their best interests, yet the agent is conflicted. They either act in their own best interest or in a way that reflects a degraded sense of the principal's interest. Because the stakes are high for the principal and low (or nonexistent) for the agent, one would think that the agent would have no difficulty acting in the principal's best interest. However, in real world situations, the doctor-patient relationship has been compromised by the payment structure for physicians. The model of fee-for-service in the medical industry monetarily incentivizes the physician to advocate for the patient consuming more services. Real estate agents frequently suffer from the same conflicted interest. The real estate agent is remunerated when the sale of the real estate is completed. This incentivizes the agent to complete the sale and sublimate (or disregard) the interest of the principal they are representing in favor of sale completion. Elected officials, who are similarly delegated agents, are sometimes found to act in their own interest (working to secure funding for getting reelected) rather than in the interest of the constituents. Carefully considering what compensation might exist for the expert needs to be explored in the design of a high-stakes conversation situation.

The following table delineates the different characteristics of the imbalance associated with high-stakes conversations.

	Expert	Client
Pressure of Imminence	L	H
Experience of Consequence	L	H
Imbalance of Knowledge	H	L
Imbalance of Experience	H	L
Imbalance of Emotion	L	H

Table 1: Characteristics of the imbalance associated with high-stakes conversations

In a high-stakes conversation, these imbalances can never be fully ameliorated by design. For designers, the goal is not to get rid of the imbalances, (an impossible task) but to either make them visible or frame the conversation based on the knowledge and wisdom of the expert and client.

Consequence & Irrevocability

High-stakes conversations have consequences, meaning that the conversation deals with a subject that has significant meaning to the client. A high-stakes conversation may result in a decision or agreement that triggers a chain of events that leads to an outcome that is irrevocable, or difficult or costly to revoke. (For example, when choosing an exit from a burning building, each step towards a given exit increases the relative distance from every other exit.) Though, I do not consider all conversations of consequence and irrevocability to be high-stakes, and not all conversations of consequence are irrevocable.

High-stakes conversations are rare and often seen as unpleasant because they are consequential. The act of design aims to solve this problem through by prototyping or acting indirectly (Doblin, 1987). Most design is predicated upon lowering the stakes of a given venture by creating prototypes, drawings, or maquettes; however, little opportunity exists for people to prototype their difficult or high-stakes conversations. Creating a library of possible conversational prototypes may offer some familiarity with difficult situations. Design can provide structures and suggest processes by which to have prototype conversations. In civic work, irrevocability often comes with major construction projects, necessitating extensive planning and prototype building. Drawings, maquettes, or models all reveal the implications of a project, helping more participants understand how a completed project might affect them. These design tools allow untrained participants to move into the role of designers, playing with different options, which can help to lower the stakes.

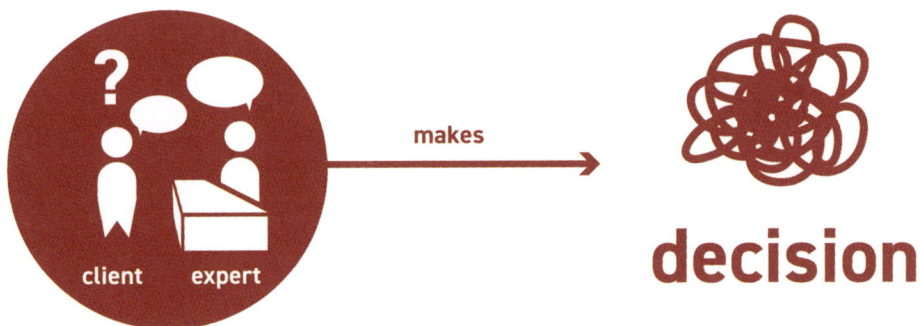

Figure 4: High-stakes conversations

73

WHY ARE YOU HAVING IT?

When you find yourself having a high-stakes conversation, it is likely that you are trying to do something rather unusual. Having a conversation about where we would like to go have lunch together is not a decision that requires the advice of an expert consultant. Even in some more consequential but quotidian decisions, we might disregard or even not consult the advice of an expert consultant. Major life milestones like buying a house, getting married, sending a child to college, and planning retirement investments, may benefit profoundly from the advice of an expert. These may even fall under the rubric that I have defined above of the high-stakes conversation, but nonetheless, some people don't treat these decisions in this way.

High-stakes conversations are rare events for most people, so it is essential that the conversation be designed for optimal sense-making by the participants (with the foremost consideration for the client or principal). A CEO may have a series of conversations with their board about taking a company public. They could lead an initial public offering of stock (IPO) once or twice in their career. By contrast, a lawyer or financial advisor who specializes in the IPO process may shepherd several IPOs per year. The rarity of high-stakes conversations is inversely related to the degree of risk they require. The CEO's risk is bound up to a very high degree with a set of successful conversations and plans associated with the IPO; a consultant's risk is diffuse, spread across their career and client base.

High-stakes conversations are frequently complicated by strong emotions associated with their content (Stone, Patton, & Heen, 2010). We discussed the challenges of difficult conversations in Chapter 3. High-stakes conversations present many of the same challenges. A community group considering a significant zoning change in their neighborhood may have a conversation with city officials about whether to support a proposal with potential drawbacks. These residents may be overwhelmed by the complex emotional aspects of this decision. The future of their homes and community is at stake, making it difficult for them to engage fully in various modes of thinking. In this scenario, the resident is in a heightened emotional state, while the city officials, though sympathetic, may remain more detached and objective. This emotional disparity can create challenges in ensuring that the resident's voice is fully heard and presents challenges to making an informed decision in concert with city-level actors.

When governments convene groups of citizens to have high-stakes conversations, it is usually because a large urban development project or a set of policy decisions are imminent. These government-initiated conversations are a bit different than the expert/client conversations of doctor and patient, lawyer and client. While it may be less consequential than an organ transplant, razing a neighborhood to build a sports stadium complex will profoundly change the lifeworlds of residents.

The City of Pittsburgh Affordable Housing Task Force asked residents to contribute to consequential decisions that affected the future of their community. March 29, 2016, Kingsley Association. Photo by the author, courtesy City of Pittsburgh.

DESIGN-LED APPROACHES TO HIGH-STAKES CONVERSATIONS

An initial assumption of the high-stakes conversation in municipal or governmental practice, is that a group of diverse people will have to come together and agree on an approach. True, in these contexts, a diverse group often comes together. But it is not necessary to have the group agree on a single approach. In fact, driving the conversation towards agreement can be coercive, as it can sublimate important perspectives and values held by less vocal participants in the conversation. When designing for the high-stakes conversation, it is imperative to plan the design in a way that ensures that all voices, not just the loudest, get heard. The following two aspects are essential for the high-stakes conversation, but the rest of Part II covers tactics that may be helpful.

The key question

A key step in the design of a high-stakes conversation is to identify the key question, which captures the essential character of the decision to be made. This question serves as the focal point around which the conversation revolves. To get to this question, designers can employ a process known as *backcasting*, where they think about the completion of the project the conversation is intended to inform and then work backwards to the present state. Backcasting, developed in future studies by Jaco Quist, has been used in various contexts since its proposal in the early 2000s. In backcasting, designers ask: What outcomes does the community need from this conversation? What is the convening organization trying to learn by bringing this group of people together? Beyond the obvious material questions—politics, history, financial investment—what is this conversation truly about? By centering the discussion around the key question, designers can create a more focused and meaningful dialogue that addresses the core issues at hand.

In a meeting during the planning phase of the 2015 capital budget community forums, the controller for the City of Pittsburgh came to a realization. We had a meeting to discuss the different priorities that were at stake in the budget. The mayor had developed a set of goals that he hoped to accomplish. We discussed the forums and how we hoped to find out both what people wanted for themselves and what projects they hoped to have completed in their neighborhoods. We talked about whether the citizens shared and supported the mayor's priorities and city staffers expressed that the mayor hoped that they did. We dug into specifics, talking about whether we needed to explain to forum participants where money for capital projects was coming from. Did residents need to know if funding was coming from community development block grants, pass-through funding from the federal government that the city administrated, or the main pool of tax-derived funding?

When we, as a group, were close to agreeing to dispense with describing the intricacies of municipal funding to citizens, impatient to move the discussion along, I said, "we only have time in this conversation for the essentials. What is that, here?" The city controller, Alex, stopped the conversation. He said, "I think I just realized... a budget is really an ethical document. It is a statement of what we value as a city." The group agreed enthusiastically with his insight, which moved the planning conversation away from minutia and toward questions that all residents can contribute to. We began to structure the meeting format around the set of ethical imperatives that could be contained in the budget. This insight was also an important personal lesson for me. I saw that the dialog that we were engaged in about the specifics of framing this issue for a public to discuss served both the public and the city staff. The generative inquiry of the design process, united with the rhetorical inquiry necessary to structure a deliberation, surfaced this new understanding.

After a course of several meetings, our team of city staff and researchers designed the meeting agenda to help attendees understand and discuss how they agreed or disagreed with the set of priorities that the mayor had developed to guide the budget implementation. Because the capital expenditures varied, a specific dollar figure did not necessarily relate the degree to which the administration *cared* about that budget item. Alex's insight, that the budget is a statement of what we value as a City, led us to the key question for these capital budget forums. We needed to ask the citizens what they value. We gave residents a list of the many priorities that the mayor is considering in the budget and asked which were most important to people and why. Alex's insight into his own work as City Controller came from engaging in a planning conversation that attempted to surface the values of the administration in response to residents' feedback. For Alex, engaging in designing systems where residents give feedback ended up being a value in itself.

For the capital budget conversation, the key question was what the residents valued for their community. Working with PennDOT on a robotic signalization project for an urban corridor, the key question was not where curb cuts were placed, not how to integrate the signalization project with bus stop redevelopment, nor how much authority to regulate traffic should be handled by synchronized timers or by a learning algorithm. These questions were poor choices to put before community members. Specific technical expertise that participants rarely hold is required to answer these kinds of question meaningfully. If an abstract or highly technical question is determined to be a key question that requires resident feedback, effective educational information must support participants' deliberation activities. Developing scaffolding media assets, like a briefing document and pedagogical presentation, becomes more critical to provide participants with essential, contextualizing information.

A different option for developing a key question is reframing a question so it fits squarely within the expertise of the participants. This does *not* mean that the question should be "dumbed down." It does mean asking the participants questions that are appropriate to their deep knowledge and expertise. Community participants are specialists in a particular kind of knowledge: the lived experience of a particular geographic area and a social community. Consulting community participants means that you, or your organization, are convening a group of experts with a particular kind of knowledge. You wouldn't consult a team of expert pediatric neurosurgeons on a hydrology problem for a subterranean construction site. This question would be appropriate for a group of geologists, geological engineers, and civil engineers, but is outside of the expertise of neurosurgeons. Similarly, deep thought must be put into writing key questions that are appropriate to the expertise of the resident group that is likely to attend the meeting.

Conversations exist in a context that Flores and Winograd characterize as effective coordination of action with others, which George Lakoff understood as a "frame." With the use of language, frames can be activated, or frames diffused and different frames activated. Conversational frames determine how the participants will interpret things that are said, influence their responses, and structure how the stories of the conversations are told after the experience has passed. In *Weathercocks and Signposts*, Crompton (2008), citing Lakoff, states that it is imperative to center high-stakes environmental messaging on values of the actors involved in the conversation, rather than attempting to create content and positioning targeted toward a demographic or polled value (Crompton, 2008). When authoring the key question, it is important to understand that it is always local to the group coming together, rather than informed by broad demographic trends that are less relevant to the people in the room. The goal of the key question is providing a concrete framing that participants can think with and react to.

A 2002 article "High Stakes Decision Making: Normative, Descriptive and Prescriptive Considerations" by Kunreuther et al. (2002) presents a list of conclusions from literature regarding low-probability, high-stakes business decisions. Kunreuther et al. propose *prescriptive heuristics* as one approach to making risk analysis more concrete. Prescriptive heuristics involve reframing the probability dimension of risk into a more concrete form. For example, you might say that there is a one in five chance of an earthquake over the 25-year life of a building, rather than a 1 in 100 chance of an earthquake any given year (Kunreuther et al., 2002, quoting Weinstein et al., 1996). Further, multiple studies in medical shared decision-making literature shows that patients have difficulty understanding risk concepts (Sheridan et al., 2004).

In a high-stakes conversation, the key question framing the conversation before the participants is the most salient aspect of design. It guides participants toward the relevant aspects of their expertise and determines whether the convening organization gets actionable data from the conversation. If you can guide participants to the relevant aspects of their expertise through framing, the conversation is more likely to yield insightful, relevant, and actionable outcomes that directly address the core issues and goals. This focused approach ensures that participants understand the relevance of their knowledge and experience, keeping the dialogue productive and aligned with the intended objectives. This alignment ultimately leads to more effective and impactful outcomes.

Convening from the mid-level to the grassroots

An effective design for any conversation begins by considering who will participate, which is doubly important in a high-stakes conversation. The opportunity to host the conversation on a topic that has irrevocable implications for a community entails the ethical obligation to broadly engage the stakeholder community. The question that follows is: How to engage stakeholders by design?

Convening community participants can be productively preceded by working with mid-level stakeholders. At the highest level of city organization are so-called top-down bureaucratic systems of government and the corresponding policy structures that shape intra-organizational behavior. At the lowest level of city organization are the "grassroots"—the formal and informal communities that are the site for much of people's daily experiences. Families, neighbors, our work teams, transactional digital communities, and families of our children's friends (the preschool group) are the networks where "grassroots" movements grow and spread. While significant dialogues are often arranged around the question of top-down versus grassroots innovation, compelling, urgent, and impactful work gets done through the work of many mid-level, non-governmental actors (Lederach, 1997; Maiese, 2003) such as universities, religious organizations, and humanitarian organizations. Rather than explicit policymaking or grassroots organizing, this fertile midlevel is characterized by networks of interpersonal relationships, fundraising, awareness-building, and a constellation of loosely coordinated organizing efforts. Mid-level stakeholders are representatives of these organizations who work in communities affected by the question at stake.

Bringing together the group of mid-level stakeholders serves to lay the groundwork for conversations had by a broader group of community members. Putting these mid-level stakeholders in conversation with one another offers opportunities to discover questions that are latent in the community's thinking. You can also ask, "Who is not in the room but should be?" Then strive to fill that gap. By engaging stakeholders in direct dialog, the conversation can be further informed. For example, these powerful statements emerged from a 2017 mid-level stakeholder convening discussing poverty in Allegheny County:

- The culturally constructed shame of poverty is a key component of the experience of poverty.
- Pittsburgh's system to help people experiencing poverty is fragmented and unable to deal with the holistic concerns of the population.
- Some poverty in the Pittsburgh area may escape easy tabulation. People living in poverty may be invisible, living in middle-class boroughs like Swissvale or Braddock.

Activity is catalyzed by events. Framing civic conversations as events can foment action in the network of stakeholders who surround a given matter of concern. While that action might be framed as contestation, there are many stakeholders and members of the greater community that share values and can realize benefits through models of discourse other than contestation. Designing to foster collaboration and conversations that focus on the surfacing of values can lay the groundwork for collaboration outside of the conversation. Collaboration is just one of many productive ways forward.

CONCLUSION

High-stakes and difficult conversations are often unpleasant and rare. The act of design is bound up with the act of prototyping, or of acting indirectly (Doblin, 1987). Most design in effect is predicated upon lowering the stakes of a given venture by creating a prototype, or drawing or maquette; however, little opportunity exists for people to prototype their difficult or high-stakes conversations. Creating a library of possible conversational prototypes may offer some familiarity with difficult situations, and design can offer structures and processes by which to create these prototype conversations.

Activity is catalyzed by events. Framing civic conversations as events has potential to foment action in the network of stakeholders who surround a given matter of concern. While that action might be framed as contestation, there are many stakeholders and members of the greater community that share values and can realize benefits through models of discourse other than contestation. Designing to foster collaboration and conversations that focus on the surfacing of values can lay the groundwork for greater collaboration outside the system of the conversation. Collaboration is a productive way forward.

In conclusion, designing high-stakes conversations requires a nuanced understanding of their unique challenges. From the inherent uncertainty stemming from the absence of a definitive right answer to the palpable sense of imminence and the weight of consequences, each challenge demands careful consideration. Moreover, the dynamics of power imbalance and the irreversibility of decisions underscore the complexity of these conversations. However, by recognizing these recurring challenges and embracing the importance of framing the key questions and convening from the mid-level, designers can approach the high-stakes conversation with integrity and effectiveness.

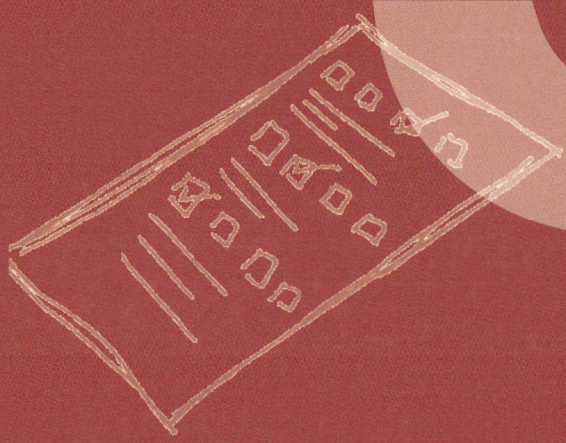

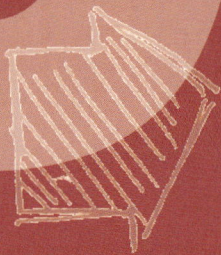

CHAPTER 5

Planning a Conversation

INTRODUCTION

When setting out to plan a conversation, most people start thinking about what they are going to say. When interviewing doctors about how they learned to deliver bad news, they nearly all told stories of senior physicians advising them on how to frame bad news. Like other people, they talked about how they learned what to *say*. When preparing to give a public presentation, many people say, "I've got to write my talk." If an elected official is going to talk with the media, they might prepare their *talking points*. Everyone thinks about what they will say in their talk.

When planning for a civic conversation, most people's first instinct is to plan the words. How should we welcome participants to the meeting? What are the best ways to explain the design project or complicated policy concepts? Most of the planning activity happens before a civic conversation. Of course, no one should short-change the importance of words. In fact, words are terribly important, as they carry meaning and structure. After all, words are the primary medium for this book! But words are only one part of planning.

Decreased perception of the importance of a democratically elected government has created a moment of crisis for proponents of liberal democracy (Foa & Mounk, 2016). The relatively recent rise of factually impoverished and emotionally overabundant political discourse throughout the world has manifested in populist movements in the United Kingdom, the United States, and India. As you read this, it has probably continued to infect the discourse of major governments worldwide. Despite this concerning recent history, when examining discourse at the level of the individual, civic engagement events have shown that citizens can be trusted to discuss issues, share reasons, and come to conclusions (Fishkin & Luskin 2005). Yet, the production of civic engagement events frequently neglects the influence of the system of stakeholders and the power of material interventions to facilitate deliberative conversations.

Civic conversation is vital to civic change's engagement spreading across a complex network of actors. A civic conversation is full of opportunities. It is a place for knowledge transfer, a moment when citizens can understand the needs of the greater community, and where they can articulate what their community needs to surmount challenges. In turn, citizens can hear the needs of their neighbors and perhaps place their own needs in the context of the entire

> *The rise of factually impoverished and emotionally overabundant political discourse has manifested in populist movements worldwide.*

community. The moment of the civic conversation is when government actors can collate critical information to guide policymaking and improve their understanding of the needs of the communities they serve. This understanding serves as a framework or heuristic to guide the creation and application of policy. Civic conversation is a *bricolage* (de Certeau, 1984, citing Levi-Strauss, 1966); in the civic conversation, participants disclose through conversation their relationships with neighbors, membership in community groups, relationship to place, and their historical experience of place. For people participating, they might seize the opportunity to influence their neighbors' views and reconstruct their own views in relation to the question at hand.

The challenge for a contemporary design practitioner designing for civic discourse is to create a conversation that evokes the richness of the participants' lived experiences while maintaining a reflective distance. Such distance helps participants share their present needs, hopes for the future, and the narrative that supports their positions. The civic participation event is the point at which that richness can pass into the polity.

Citizens' involvement in civic life, and their ability to articulate need (Max-Neef et al., 1991) in a way that can inform policy creation, are profoundly influenced by their experiences with organizations that are more part of their everyday lives than the more abstract construction of "government" (Wenger, 1998; Spinosa, Flores, & Dreyfus, 1997). The needs of citizens are aggregated, focused, filtered, and fixed through their involvement in neighborhood associations, community groups, churches, community and economic development corporations, business associations, and community-based and corporate news organizations. Some may say that these mid-level actors represent a toxic influence on the political process, in that they reorient the dialog toward their own ends. This may be true of some political groups, but I have found that most are working with what Spinosa, Flores, and Dreyfus (1997) refer to as a rich awareness of their sustaining practices—how the organization's mission and goals constitute community interest. As I have found in my work, citizens who attend events on behalf of civic organizations find it difficult to simply regurgitate media talking points when events are framed as a conversation with neighbors. The activity of conversation requires a richness that is not easily reducible to talking points. Essentially, when people are invited to a conversation, they must think for themselves.

Through direct experience and conversations with nearby organizations, the individual's understanding of civic life and articulating their needs intersect with the capacities of public authorities, public agencies, and government entities that provide for those needs. At the scope of municipal government, marshaling these mid-level actors—the trusted organizations—facilitates access to citizens and, in turn, helps motivate citizens to participate. These complementary processes that influence the formation of attitudes, values, beliefs, and policies are a dynamic system. Event-based participation is a critical point of feedback within that system.

The set of design choices made by participants that flows from these conversations must encompass the spectrum of needs evoked in the conversation. Voting or negotiation approaches are organized around a zero-sum game that creates winners and losers. However, design—informed by a spectrum of needs and a spectrum of reasons why—can approach true collaboration.

THE CIVIC CONVERSATION AS A SERVICE

Deliberative democracy is an approach to governing that supplements traditional definitions of politics, based on the struggle for power and influence, with debate and deliberation, in which the better argument is decisive (Jenssen, 2008). In the practical sense, as in the convenings of which I was a part, citizens are invited to topical meetings that address an issue that pertains to their neighborhood, municipality, or region. These topical meetings begin with a non-partisan pedagogical presentation with structured agendas encompassing two or three related questions for the participants to discuss. The meeting concludes with each table writing a question they put to a panel of experts.

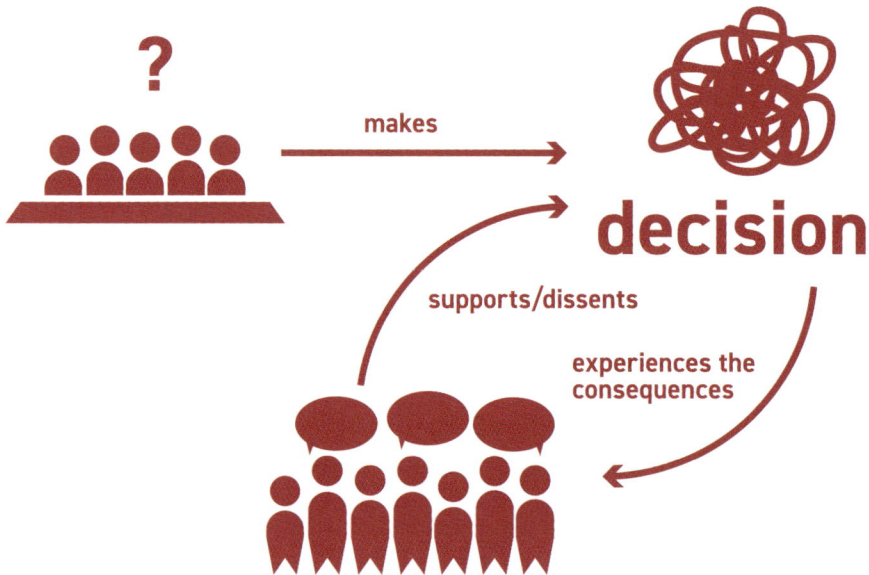

Figure 5: In a civic conversation, a decision-making group within the government has a question and must make a decision. They convene a panel of residents to inform that decision. The residents' relationship with the decision remains indirect.

When? Principally, a Civic Conversation is needed when there are issues before a legislative body that are not well suited to legislation. Issues may be **too complex for legislation,** demanding that a community discuss the complexity surrounding a social or material issue. Rittel and Weber (1973) describe a "wicked problem" as one with a context so challenging that the problem before the community is to decide what the problem actually is. Rather than legislation of a single issue, lawmakers may need to gather broad input to **simultaneously set multiple priorities,** for example, when preparing a capital budget or community master plan. A Civic Conversation may also be needed when an issue needs **richer engagement** by the members of a community than traditional policymaking can give. For instance, a community experiencing a collective trauma or collective grief might have a civic conversation to deliberate upon the experience—an act of healing.

Where? Ideally, the civic conversation occurs at the intersection of an organization's capacity to provide services and the collective needs of its community. These organizations have been principally government organizations, but one could envision other possibilities where civic conversations might support policy-making in hospitals, universities, social service-oriented non-governmental organizations, or even publicly traded for-profit corporations.

How? The civic conversation is developed from the model of the high-stakes conversation detailed earlier (Chapter 4) and is a more complex version of the two-actor expert/client model presented there. The civic conversation convenes multiple actors through a constitutive organization. These convenings evolved into a format that may be usefully thought of as five steps:

1. Convening community stakeholders
2. Designing the process of community conversation
3. Recruiting community members
4. Having a community conversation
5. Communicating results

While convening a community conversation, equity emerges as an important concern. While a full philosophy of equity is outside the scope of this book, in a simple framing, equity means approaching the design of the event, framing the dialog, and designing supporting documentation mindful of being fair or impartial. Equity also has a second meaning, that of a kind of shared ownership. Equity as ownership points to who owns the consequences of policy. In the high-stakes conversation, the matter is owned by the party that bears the consequences at play in the conversation. That is, in the civic conversation, the matter is *owned* by those people within the city who bear the consequences of the policy. Not getting re-elected is a significant consequence for politicians. However, having to live the rest of one's life with an ill-conceived development next door, or having the streets that contain one's vibrant musical scene erased from the city landscape to make way for a hockey arena are far more troubling consequences.

This leads to the question: how should we design for equity? In a complicated community matter with conflicting interests, how might one come to understand who in the community has a stake in the matter at hand? One key step enacted through these processes was first engaging **mid-level actors throughout the community.** These are people who work for organizations or on issue-areas that are near to matters of concern, but perhaps not deeply involved. Mid-level actors could be, for example, church leaders, employees or founders of not-for-profits, and employees at philanthropic organizations.

To develop an understanding of the matter of concern—and what and who is at risk in the situation—these mid-level actors should be convened. Together, they enrich understanding of the issue, inform the agenda for the community conversation, set goals, and anticipate outcomes. Mid-level actors not only have situated expertise that informs the framing of the policy problems for the broader community but also act as conduits to the community.

Once an understanding of the significant aspects of the matter of concern has been surfaced through the advice and participation of the community, a **design for the community conversation** can be developed. While it may seem obvious to state, the event needs to be designed to fit the constraints of the situation. The constraints are familiar to nearly any design project: budget, time, and space. Further constraints include the nature of the topic and the relation of the community to the matter. When working with the City of Pittsburgh under time limitations, key aspects of the design were predetermined. The underlying scheme of the conversation event operationalizes characteristics of deliberative democracy to support inquiry into the matter of concern. Developing an agenda for conversation in collaboration with mid-level actors or community stakeholders is the first significant step. Designing the conversation in collaboration with these mid-level actors helps to frame the conversation for the participants.

How Does it Change Things to View the Conversation as a Service?

Many businesses are arranged around the concept of a "service." A coffee shop is an archetype of a service-oriented business. A coffee shop service can be broken down into a set of definable experiences typical for any counter-service business: people queue, place their order, and wait while staff prepare the order. They then receive their order and either sit and enjoy it or leave. Churches also offer a structured service experience familiar to many. A typical church service includes a welcome and announcements, an opening prayer, hymns and worship music, a scripture reading, a sermon, congregational prayers, an offering, and a closing hymn. Many other experiences are organized as a service, like seeing the doctor, going to the Department of Motor Vehicles, and getting your car repaired. In a similar sense, a civic conversation is a service, and the "order" of the day is encouraging the convening organization to hear what people have to say about a particular topic.

The central thinking of a service design perspective is that design activity creates a *user-centered* service that places the participants at the center of design considerations. This ethical position orients designers toward a different set of needs and goals: those of the participants. Thinking of the civic conversation as a service offers an altered perspective. In a service experience, *things* emerge as useful in different stages of the *experience*. Crucially, things are active in the conversational environment as they shape different arcs of time and parts of the participants' experiences.

Service Design Elements

Before

Recruiting participants is a key first step in planning a civic conversation. Announcements in media such as newspapers, television, and social media—and traditional campaigning methods such as street advocacy or door-knocking by volunteers—can drive attendance. However, in the work I have done, the bulk of engaged attendees come directly from relationships developed by mid-level actors. The participants who will fill the meeting hall where the civic conversation is held will be referred by the mid-level actors who were part of the initial agenda-setting discussions. In conversations where the mid-level actors were uninvolved in helping to recruit participants, few people attended regardless of the density or volume of direct outreach.

A perceived threat to one's neighborhood or business or the potential for a perceived gain typically drive attendance. This is known colloquially as NIMBY (Not In My BackYard) politics. It reflects a narrow focus on personal interests rather than the broader community or societal needs. However, simply opposing developments or changes in one's local area without considering the bigger picture does not effectively address the complexities and interconnected nature of systemic issues. To tackle these challenges, it's important to move beyond self-centered perspectives and engage in discussions that consider the needs and impacts on the entire community. NIMBY politics can be interpreted as a rejection of decision-making by experts (Ravetz, 1999) or as "low-resolution" civic feedback. Boyer & Hill (2013) describe NIMBYs who would like green projects completed but do not want to bear any of the burdens of those projects or experience their consequences. However, in spite of Boyer and Hill's characterization, NIMBY-ism should not be viewed as a problem that must be dealt with. It is important to understand that, especially for people attending a civic conversation for the first time, there exists a strong likelihood they are attending because of a NIMBY-related need. NIMBY-ism, far from being a potential negative, is merely one way to motivate a person to engage in civic conversations.

The other side of NIMBY-ism that drives attendance at civic meetings is what I would call a "pothole mentality." This mentality emerges when participants think about the issue that they are passionate about (e.g., potholes on the roads that they use regularly) without considering the broader context of that project or thinking about their needs alongside those of the entire street or neighborhood. Essentially, though, these needs—whether they are framed positively or negatively—inspire people to be involved in a civic conversation. Perceiving that the civic conversation might be a site to speak about a matter of concern—the pothole—means that participants are properly connecting their perceived needs with the opportunity to speak back to the government. This can be a valuable perspective to cultivate in the community but hopefully leads to a broader, more systemic understanding of needs through the medium of the community conversation.

During the Meeting

This format of the civic conversation is designed to accommodate a larger number of participants than a formal meeting. Over three years of conducting in-person meetings in this format, we have hosted between four and 162 participants at a single meeting. A deliberative community meeting designed in this framework takes about 2½ hours, a length preferred for several reasons. It was generally felt

that the longer form of meeting (one to two days during a weekend) was extremely burdensome for participants and not practical from the perspective of executing events on a limited budget. Perhaps most significantly, the time window was chosen because the City of Pittsburgh hosted similar meetings in the past using that time window. They knew 2½ hours would be appropriate—and most cities have a similar expectation for the length of evening meetings.

To operationalize Fishkin's deliberative characteristics, PDD employs the following structure for each deliberative forum:

1. **Arrival:** Participants receive table assignments and briefing documents from event staff.
2. **Participants Gather:** The table facilitator greets participants and gives them time to meet and read the briefing document. We strongly encourage the convening organization to set aside part of the budget for a light dinner for the participants. If food is provided, the participants eat at this time.
3. **Receive Background Information:** A nonpartisan "teacher" gives participants a short overview of the topic area(s) and collective goals, then explains how data generated by the participants will be used.
4. **Small Group Discussion:** Led by the table facilitator, participants engage each other in freeform discussion of the agenda issue(s). The briefing document is referred to as a source of additional information.
5. **Question Writing:** Led by the table facilitator, participants write questions to pose to the expert panel.
6. **Question Asking:** Participants pose their questions to the expert panel and receive answers.
7. **Post-event Survey:** Participants fill out a survey indicating their opinions on the agenda issues and suggest new agenda issues.
8. **Departure:** Event staff thank participants for their time and thoughts. Participants chat informally with each other and expert panelists.

Figure 6: Elements of a Community Deliberative Forum

All the elements above were iteratively and intentionally designed to facilitate a "smooth" experience. The meetings were staffed by volunteer facilitators and registrar(s), an emcee, a member of the convening organization (who shares key information about the context of the discussion), and a panel of recruited experts.

After the Meeting

The final step of the civic conversation is transferring the results of the conversation into the systems of policymaking. While this is typically achieved by a report and presentation, its format and structure should be carefully designed to achieve optimum clarity and impact within the policymaking body. As with any communication design project, consideration of how information might be most effectively consumed and used by the recipients—in most cases, policymakers—affects the outcomes of the entire process.

In Chapter 2, we discussed the power of reporting the My Brother's Keeper (MBK) conversations. As one model for successful reporting, the ongoing reporting of MBK continued to drive conversation and action long after the original convenings ended. Conversely, poor-quality reporting can effectively erase the work done at the civic conversation, neglecting the work of the staff and participants who brought the event to fruition. Reporting that has no impact on project or policy outcomes but only seeks to match participant feedback with what organizers planned to do before the conversation violates the trust that the participants placed in the process. It disrespects the time and energy devoted to the process by city staff and elected officials.

Evaluating an event's effectiveness is a topic worthy of its own book. In brief, a system of evaluation can determine the effective parts of a civic conversation, and which need further work or deeper consideration. We will address evaluation more thoroughly in Chapter 8 but in short, effective evaluation cannot be done cursorily or retrospectively. Some evaluation is infinitely better than no evaluation! Even one question on an exit survey asking about participants' satisfaction might be all that is possible in the context of a no-budget civic event. However, every effort should be made to conduct a rigorous and multidimensional evaluation of the quality and effectiveness of the civic conversation.

Finally, planning a mechanism to follow up with attendees is a key part of follow-up work. This can be as simple as sharing with them the evaluative report and the data collected at the conversation event. This aspect of the process will be given a fuller treatment in Chapter 8, but follow-up must be considered during event planning, lest planners forget to collect email addresses or another method of contacting attendees during the registration or meeting process.

Service Blueprinting

A service blueprint displays the most salient actors and activities that happen in each stage of service delivery and which actors will complete which activities. A technique developed by Lynn Shostack (1984), blueprinting shows all actors involved listed along the left-hand side on the vertical axis, and service steps shown in chronological order on the horizontal axis. This arrangement creates a matrix that maps out the actions each role will perform. A blueprint distinguishes between actions visible to participants (above the line of visibility) and back-office actions (below the line of visibility). Roles may be filled by individuals, organizations, departments, artificial intelligences (AIs), or other machines. Critical interactions between the participant and the organizers are distinguished by the line of interaction, which separates participant actions from service provider actions, marking the point where they meet.

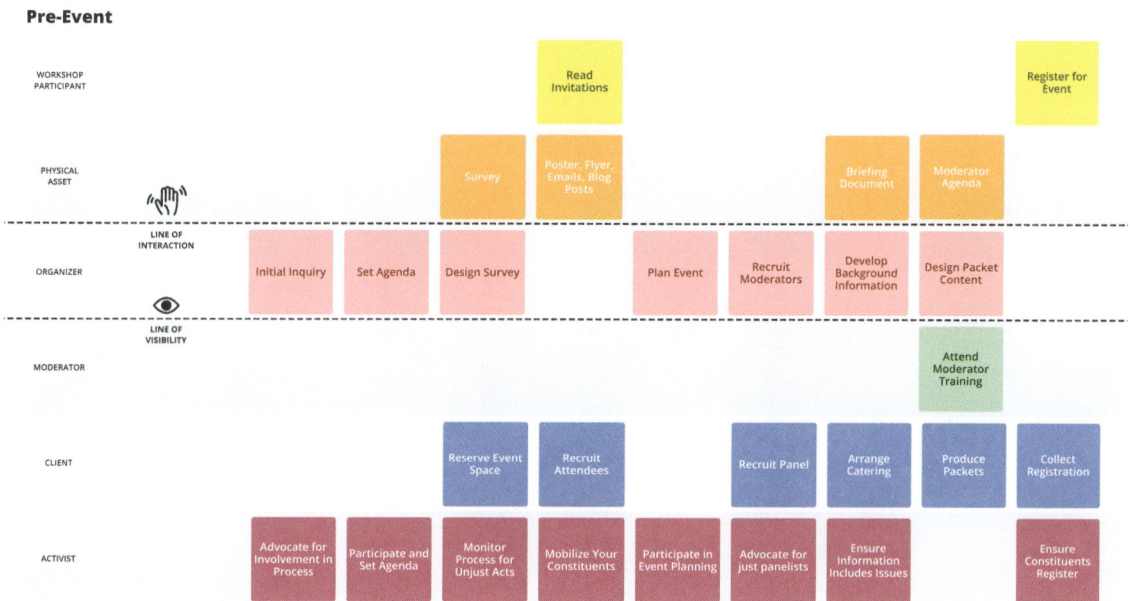

Figure 7: Pre-event service blueprint

Event

WORKSHOP PARTICIPANT	Travel to Event	Check-in	Listen to Presentation	Listen & Deliberate on Agenda Items	Develop Questions	Listen & Ask Questions	Complete Survey	Informal talk with other participants
PHYSICAL ASSET		Registration List	Briefing Document				Survey	
ORGANIZER	Validate Room Setup	Check-in Participants	Give Pedagogical Introduction	Provide Discussion Points	Develop Questions	Run Panel Q&A	Complete Survey	Teardown Event
MODERATOR	Attend Pre-event Meeting	Moderator Welcome		Manage Discussion	Reflect on Deliberation, Recall Open Questions		Moderator Goodbye	
LINE OF INTERACTION								
CLIENT			Give Introduction (Optional)	Observe Event		Participate or Facilitate Q&A		
ACTIVIST			Give Introduction (Optional)	Observe Event		Participate or Facilitate Q&A		
LINE OF VISIBILITY								

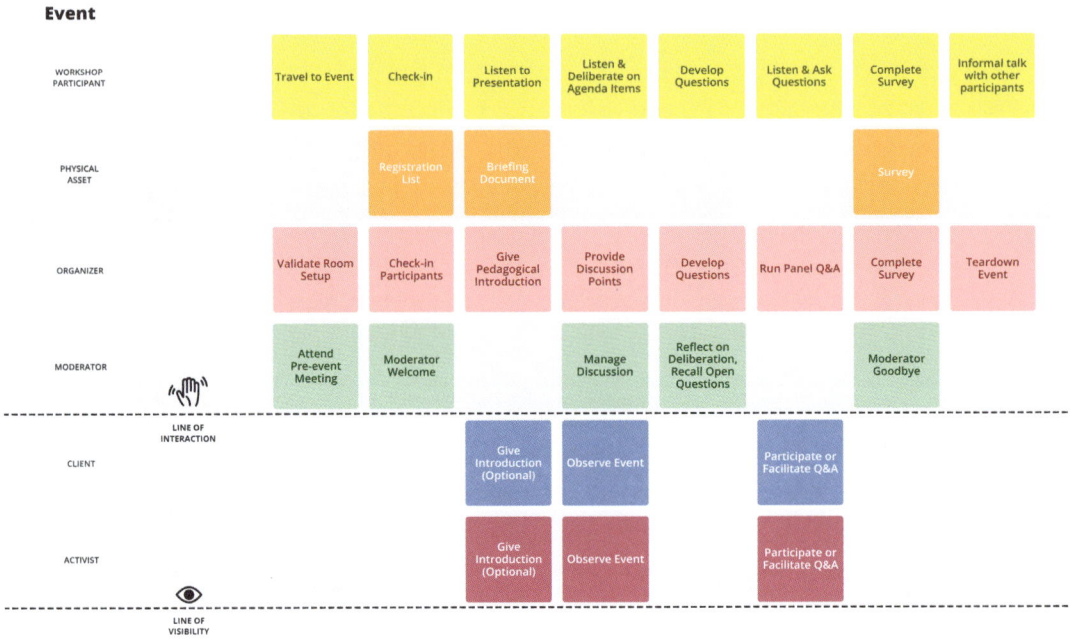

Figure 8: Event service blueprint

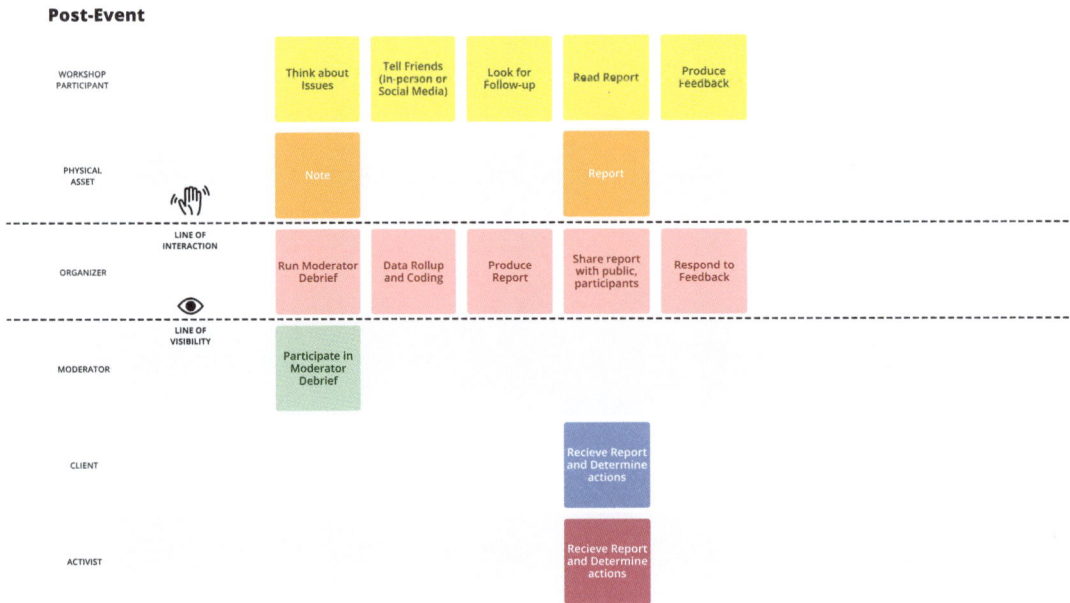

Post-Event

WORKSHOP PARTICIPANT	Think about Issues	Tell Friends (in-person or Social Media)	Look for Follow-up	Read Report	Produce Feedback
PHYSICAL ASSET	Note			Report	
LINE OF INTERACTION					
ORGANIZER	Run Moderator Debrief	Data Rollup and Coding	Produce Report	Share report with public, participants	Respond to Feedback
LINE OF VISIBILITY					
MODERATOR	Participate in Moderator Debrief				
CLIENT				Recieve Report and Determine actions	
ACTIVIST				Recieve Report and Determine actions	

Figure 9: Post-event service blueprint

The example blueprints attached here show an archetypal civic conversation. A blueprint is created for actions before, during, and after the conversation. It includes the community **participants,** important **physical assets** they will use, a group of **organizers** who design the event, and facilitators who attend the conversation and help the meeting run efficiently. The blueprint also includes two actors that are more peripheral but no less important: the **client,** representing the organization that convenes the conversation, and the **activists,** who care about the outcome and perhaps represent groups of people implicated in the conversation.

Diagramming your conversation event may help you to think through these parts of the event planning. Notice how the lines of visibility and interaction shift location before to after the event. This helps emphasize the necessity of ensuring personnel are ready to fulfill critical **front-stage** roles like staffing the event check-in table, moderating conversations as table facilitators, and finding a good emcee to lead the entire meeting. Critical **backstage** functions such as catering, AV services, site accessibility, promotions, and signage must be planned and handled before the event. Post-event **backstage** activities like data collation and reporting happen after the event. A service blueprint that shows the different stages of the event can ensure no critical steps are missed, and participants are well-supported as they consider challenging questions and share their expertise.

Practical Applications

Clarifying the Conversation's Purpose

Achieving clarity about why you are convening a group of participants is an important step that must be accomplished early in the process. If you were to start looking at civic conversations from the perspective of a cost accountant, you might never have one. Civic conversations demand the time of paid staffers (and perhaps consultants) to plan. Someone must collect and process data that results from the civic conversation. There are also costs associated with the implementation, such as room rental, catering, and cleanup. But the most significant costs are hidden costs the community bears—a tremendous donation of person-hours by the people attending. As this is one common mode of thinking about value, let's take a moment to attempt to assign an economic cost to their time donation. For the sake of easy math, let's say that 100 people attend a two-hour event, and we estimate the value of their time at $100 per hour. We'll add another hour of transit time to and from the event, for a total three-hour commitment from each participant: 100 people × 3 hours commitment × $100 per hour valuation, 100 × 3 × 100 = $30,000. Considering each conversation as a large gift of residents' efforts to improve their city is just one argument for a rigorous planning process with a clear purpose.

A civic conversation can serve many purposes, depending upon whose perspective you view it from. Elected officials might see the civic conversation as an opportunity to understand voters' viewpoints on an issue so they can reflect them in their actions. In the case of large construction projects, project managers, architects, and contractors might regard the conversation merely as a statutory requirement that needs to be accomplished. Residents might approach the conversation as a site to share their viewpoints with city staff and elected representatives, or as the only chance to influence a policy or project outcome before it is enacted. Amid all these valid purposes is the purpose of the conversation seeks to fulfill. Whether a statutory requirement, a site for speaking truths to power, or a site for learning what residents care about, conversations are typically constituted around some kind of problem, to which all these constituents will bring their matters of concern.

To avoid misusing everyone's valuable time, it is important to achieve clarity across participants, organizers, and beneficiaries of the data on two key questions: 1) Why are we having this conversation? and 2) What is the scope of the participants' power within this conversation? We might also ask these questions as: 1) What problem are we trying to solve? and 2) What can we accomplish here? One early civic meeting I attended was designed around each participant getting their three minutes at the microphone. The panel, composed of two city council members and staff from the City Controller's Office, Public Works, and Parks and Recreation, was there to hear ideas from residents to determine what kind of capital improvements residents would like to see in the upcoming year. Participants wishing to speak showed up before the meeting and signed up on a sheet of paper for a three-minute opportunity to speak at the microphone. However, there were few cues for the participants to answer either of the key questions above. A public announcement was shared along with a digital document of the proposed capital budget for the coming year, but little direct guidance was given to people who hoped to participate. Some people spoke about issues that were part of the city's operating budget, not the capital budget.

One participant used his three minutes to speak about the unfairness he felt when paying his personal income tax. The City of Pittsburgh does collect an income tax from people who are employed in the city, but tax collection was not a part of the discussion at this hearing. While all the people on the panel may have been sympathetic to the man's feelings, his feedback was misdirected. He needed to know why the conversation was convened and what the scope of his power was in that situation. Instead of interrupting him, the panel listened politely, and the city councilperson thanked the man by telling him that the city income tax was not the subject of tonight's conversation but that the councilpersons would record his comments for reference in a future meeting. Looking frustrated with that ambiguous promise, the man sat back in the audience to hear several other participants speak before leaving. I do not know what his personal goals were for participating in the capital budget feedback session. But I couldn't help but feel he had wasted his time that evening. Such missed connections can be addressed by designing conversations for future participants.

Ranulph Glanville's reading of Gordon Pask's writing indicates a fraught yet powerful aspect of conversations in civic contexts: "It is in this difference that novelty can be seen to arise: indeed, it cannot but arise. Thus... if we construct our meanings differently, we cannot assume our individual understandings will be the same. Therefore, every time my conversational partner expresses back to me his/her understanding, I must assume it will be in some way different from mine" (Glanville, 2007, p. 1190). A challenge in these events is how to help all participants, especially those from the hosting organization, remember that participants may not share goals or values, or even a common language.

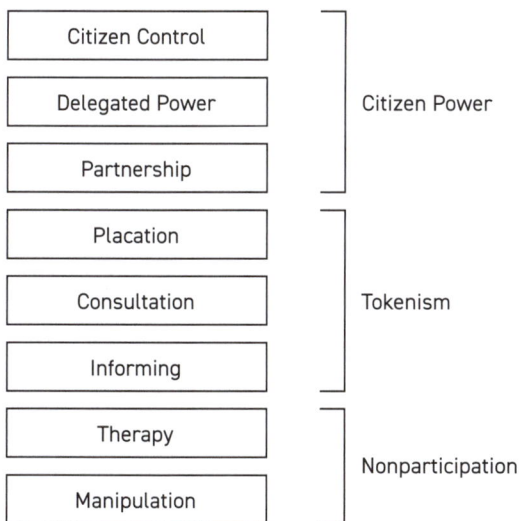

Figure 10: Ladder of citizen participation

Sherry Arnstein (1969) offers the "ladder of citizen participation", Figure 10. Arnstein reminds us that the model juxtaposes powerless citizens with powerful decision-makers. However, she admits, neither of those are distinct populations. Arnstein returns us to the point made in the introduction of this book that mechanisms of citizen participation depend upon a benevolent government. The terms of the conversation are often set by conveners: people in government. Zoning and Planning offices decide what will be built, Public Works professionals plan the next year's capital improvements and offer those plans to the Mayor's Office and City Council. Parks & Recreation staff have wide latitude to determine programs and services that will be available. In many contexts, residents can do little but complain. However, with public innovations such as participatory budgeting, where the structure of part or all of the city's budget is determined through a public process, those upper rungs of participant power can be made available to participants. Part of the design of a civic conversation should use convening to show participants what the scope of their power is.

Tools for clarity

What can a designer do to offer clarity to participants? The answer is tools that most people already know about. We highlight them here to give the designer of civic conversations a richer understanding of how these common tools *work* in the context of the civic conversation.

Processes where artifacts are a key component offering clarity are:

- Invitation (who participates, how people are recruited)
- Deliberation (engaging multiple perspectives, where the goal is to build structures of desirables, not consensus, that are supported by a material environment)
- Action (focused on connecting deliberation to actions, and dependent upon reporting)
- Decision aids (booklets, websites, and software)

I began approaching deliberation from the standpoint of structuring the material environment and designing artifacts that invite, facilitate, and transfer the surfaced knowledge in a deliberative dialog. As I have argued before in this book, these material elements are both a subtle and powerful way to guide people toward productive engagement.

For example, agendas are a crucial tool for guiding action in meetings. The agenda not only sets the framework for discussion but also empowers participants by giving them a sense of the structure of the process. Like traveling a road with a map of the journey, an agenda offers a granular view and an overview of the arc of the meeting. Community conversations' strength is soliciting participant ideas on specific open-ended questions and allowing the spontaneous emergence of innovative ideas and approaches. Similarly, an agenda provides structure to what might otherwise seem to be a meandering discursive process.

Besides a participants' agenda, designers can develop a facilitator's agenda. These can be lengthier documents that include scripted instructions that might need to be delivered precisely, as well as unscripted prompts for participants' common challenges. Ideally, the agenda is supplied well before the event, giving them time to read through and prepare for the event. A facilitator's agenda can also provide context for each step of the event. For example, a column with the goals of each event step can be added. This provides the facilitator additional context, and knowing the goals, an adroit facilitator can steer off-topic conversations back to the topic.

Time	Who	Description	Goal
6:25 5 min	Table Facilitators (breakout groups at tables)	Table Introductions *Facilitate introductions: suggest participants take 20-30 seconds to give their name, where they live, and why they chose to participate in today's forum. Facilitator introduces themself as an example.* *Briefly review "Guidelines for Participation"; explain your role as table facilitator; remind participants that they are free to respond to, ask questions of, and engage directly with other participants*	Build community & trust at the table

Figure 11: Facilitator's agenda

Beyond the steps of what will happen at a meeting, a collective understanding of the topic of conversation helps set common terms for the discussion. A common understanding of the project or challenge facing the conversation conveners gives the people a common frame to work within. To gain that common understanding, several supporting things can be developed. The challenge is how to match supporting things with the needs and preferences of the participants who will attend.

The most straightforward thing that can be developed is a presentation and briefing document. It is a tool to communicate information and build a common understanding of the problem and a common vocabulary related to the problem at hand. Using a briefing document alongside a presentation can be very effective and come at a minimal cost. The briefing document, presentation, and agenda should all be developed with alignment between content. Essentially, for optimal clarity of purpose, participants should receive the same material in the presentation and the briefing document, and then deliberate using that same information. Various pedagogical materials can accomplish this same purpose, but a well-aligned presentation and briefing document is within the reach of nearly any city, regardless of budget or time constraints.

Offered here is a layout example for a sample briefing document. The briefing document should have several parts:

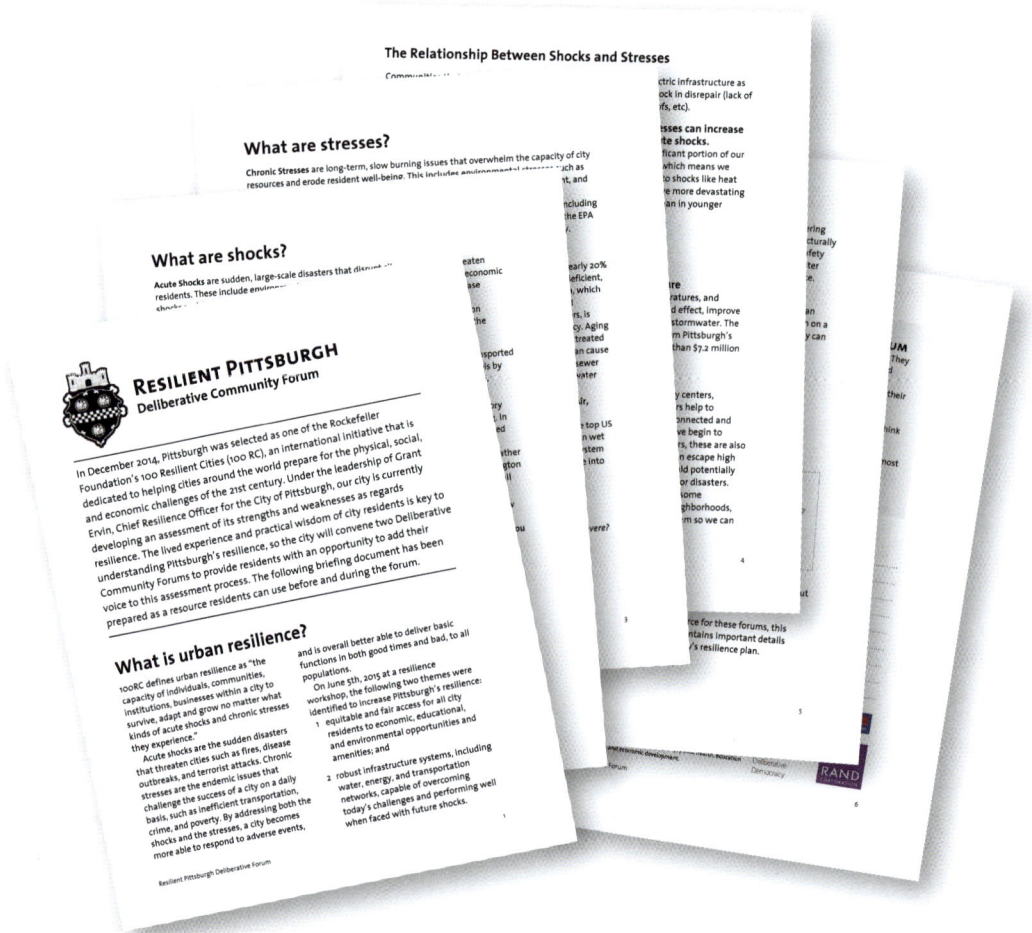

Figure 12: A briefing document is a critical tool for communicating basic knowledge and a shared language to participants.

1. An introduction that explains the **purpose** of the meeting
2. A short description that explains the **format** of the meeting
3. Enough information that people understand the **context** of the meeting among other city processes — for example, what led to this meeting and what will happen afterwards
4. A *minimum effective dose* of **contextualizing information,** which might include examples that are relevant to people's lived experience or statements of values that are up for discussion
5. The key **questions** that participants will engage with at the forum

As before, while it is not crucial that the briefing document be the conveyance for this information, conveying it is necessary. Since I started organizing these community conversations, I have tried various formats. Each has its own benefits and drawbacks. At a forum for students exploring the issue of abortion and women's right to choice at Carnegie Mellon University, we used a theatrical play. It was composed as a series of narrative vignettes, each depicting one aspect of the ethical issues at play in the abortion debate. For this event, a playwright was commissioned several months before the forum to write the play, then worked with a group of student actors to produce the work for the audience. In a half hour, the different viewpoints on the issue were made salient for the audience. Care was taken to show respect for the differing views as regards this delicate issue, and each character was treated with dignity.

Other approaches to conveying information with dignity include using information graphics, documentary videos, and comedic improv. Actors have used performance techniques to depict data using embodied improvisation, and a university professor delivered a brief lesson with contextual information. Any of these can accomplish the goal of clearly communicating the needed information for appropriate deliberation. In times of crisis, national leaders use the data-rich format of *situation rooms* to offer complex and nuanced presentations of contextualizing information. While it may be easy for an eager designer to be carried away with the possibilities of these different formats, the central goal of contextual information must be kept in mind. Participants need to understand the issue to recognize what from their own lived experience is relevant to the questions at hand. After all, as discussed in Chapter 1, participants will bring their expertise to the meeting. The goal of these tools for clarity is to help them understand which of their expertise is relevant.

When The Objectives Are Not Clear

At a community conversation, a table of 6–8 well-oriented people can sufficiently address a well-formed question with about 15 minutes of conversation per question. When people find clarity of purpose together, their conversations are focused and rich. People tell specific stories from their lives and offer lucid insights. Face-to-face and across difference, they show respect even when questioning one another's values and beliefs. Like a train passing at a street crossing, the conversation develops its own powerful rhythms, and the table facilitator becomes almost superfluous, except to guide the participants to the next topic.

When people find clarity of purpose together, their conversations are focused and rich. People tell specific stories from their lives and offer lucid insights.

But sometimes the conversation stalls; people are reluctant to speak. Their body language is telling—they lean back in chairs with tight facial expressions, avoiding eye contact. Their hands go under the table in laps or are tucked beneath the elbows of folded arms.

Sometimes, participants will hold a bag or backpack in their laps like a defensive wall to protect them from the other participants. One reason for these stalls might be that there is a lack of clarity among the participants. Perhaps nobody read the briefing document, or the starting presentation might have been overwhelming with unfamiliar and pedantic detail. After this happens, if you ask people, "Why were you so quiet?" their answer is often, "I didn't know what to say."

The expanded facilitator's agenda can help table facilitators. By offering questions along with several different sub-questions, a table facilitator can use the briefing materials and agenda to improvise a bit to get the conversation going. Here is one example taken from a facilitator's agenda prepared for MyVA Communities, a US Department of Veterans initiative funded by the Heinz Endowments:

> Military life and civilian life have differences that can be challenging to navigate. **Have you or someone you know experienced a 'military/civilian gap' in Southwestern PA?** What types of challenges or concerns resulting from a military/civilian gap in the region have you, your family, or someone you know faced? Were you able to access support during that time? How could it have been more effective?

The central question, shown above in bold, may be insufficient to start the conversation. The follow-up questions, as well as an acknowledgment of a common experience at the beginning of the question, give permission for participants to disclose problems that might otherwise be embarrassing. The main objective—gathering information about the difficulty of transitioning between military and civilian life—is supported by related questions that offer different vectors toward the same objective.

ADOPTING A LEARNING MINDSET

Working with the government, it often seems like we are surrounded by experts. People within government have dedicated their careers, sometimes their entire lives, to the good of a community, a set of issues, or a type of work. Even some of the least experienced people in government get tested by attempting to execute projects with low budgets and intractable constituents. They are sometimes subjected to profoundly negative interactions with "the public." Policies are questioned, approaches are protested, and the satisfaction of government service can often feel like a burden. But following the complicated path that is "doing the people's work" brings the immense satisfaction of helping people accomplish their goals and making their neighborhood a better place. It can often feel like city staffers have a deep and unassailable expertise regarding "what is best" for the community. But the habit of thinking of "us expert insiders" and "those resident outsiders" only fosters a brittle administration that fears failure.

Over the years, the best people I have worked with have cultivated a learning mindset. Researcher and Professor Carol Dweck spent her career studying mindset, and had this to say about the students that inspired her research:

> Research shows that people with a malleable theory are more open to learning, willing to confront challenges, able to stick to difficult tasks, and capable of bouncing back from failures. These qualities lead to better performance in the face of challenges such as difficult school transitions, demanding business tasks (e.g., negotiations), and difficulties in relationships (e.g., dealing with conflict). (Dweck, 2008, p 392)

Better at difficult transitions, demanding negotiations, and dealing with conflict... does this set of tasks sound familiar to you? Dweck says that students with this attitude view mistakes as feedback that they might need to do something differently. Students with this attitude view effort as enjoyable rather than being overly focused upon the outcomes. What Dweck refers to as a "malleable theory" is what I call here a "learning mindset." It is a crucial attitude for the organization to maintain for the successful planning and execution of civic conversation events. Even more to the point, business scholar Chris Argyris writes about the consequences of avoiding public testing of underlying assumptions that structure organizational behavior:

> People get trapped by using patterns of behavior to protect themselves against threats to their self-esteem and confidence and to protect [...] organizations to which they belong against fundamental, disruptive change."
> — Chris Argyris, *Organizational Traps: Leadership, Culture, Organizational Design*

Rather than fundamental, disruptive change, organizations can invite feedback and the opportunity to question underlying assumptions by planning a pattern of feedback opportunities through the medium of the civic conversation. Viewing these events as sites for learning creates opportunities for continual growth.

Strategies for Adoption

A learning mindset can be difficult to cultivate in any organization. Public organizations face an underlying tension in their work—elected officials who constitute administrations are elected through a combination of the strength of their personalities and their values communicated through policy positions. It seems intuitive that the public organization, personified by the elected official, should avoid change and seek to embody the personality and values that got them elected in the first place. However, this instinct is a recipe for stagnation and failure, as the engagement with "the public" is a dynamic engagement characterized by change. Administrations that resist evolving fail to stay engaged. In a concise and lucid booklet prepared for Sun Microsystems by Hugh Dubberly, Peter Esmonde, Michael Geoghegan, and Paul Pangaro, they discuss the challenge of this dynamic:

- When an organization changes from within, it does not redefine itself, or its mission. It simply seeks to gain greater equilibrium, to become more efficient at what it already does. [...]
- The source of new language is questions— questions that spark new conversations, questions that create controversy.

- Ask yourself: What questions should we ask? And more important, ask yourself: What questions are we not supposed to ask? (Ask those.)
- Ask yourself: Who aren't we conversing with? And then ask them: What are your questions?
- Ask questions that don't come easily— questions that are tough, awkward, even taboo.
- Ask unnatural questions.

Dubberly, H., Esmonde, P., Geoghegan, M., & Pangaro, P. (2002). Notes on the Role of Leadership & Language in Regenerating Organizations. In *Driving Desired Futures: Turning Design Thinking into Real Innovation.*

To adopt the learning mindset in a public organization, staffers must balance the equilibrium and resultant efficiencies with a continual source of new questions from outside the organization. While these questions seem disruptive, they strengthen the organization as it receives and processes new inputs and fields new questions.

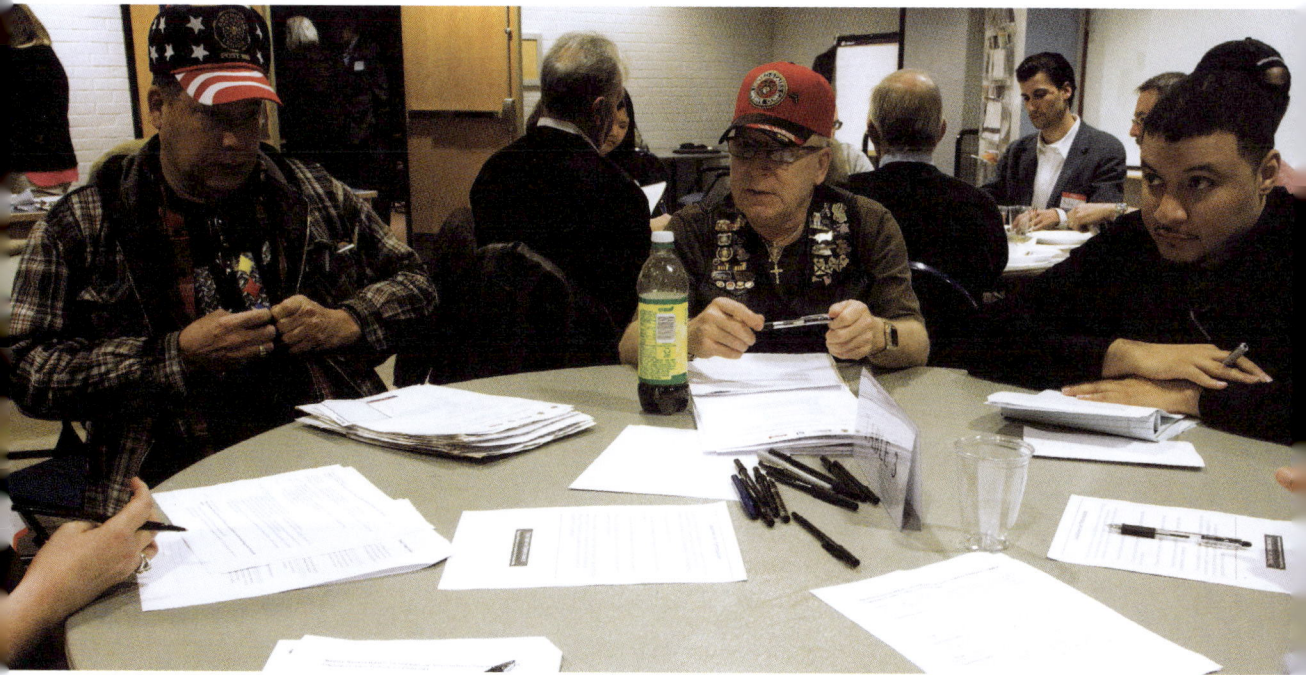

The US Department of Veterans Affairs sought to engage in new conversations with the community of veterans they serve through the locally led, community-driven initiative, MyVA Communities. Conversations with veterans were a vital part of this initiative. Feb 8, 2016, Community College of Allegheny County, Boyce Campus. Photo by the author, courtesy US VA and the Heinz Endowments.

DOUBLE-LOOP LEARNING WITH STAKEHOLDERS

In single-loop learning, organizations seek to correct errors by modifying their actions based on existing policies, goals, and frameworks without questioning their underlying assumptions. Single-loop learning is the reaction of a system to a particular stimulus. The archetypal example of this system is the thermostat that turns on the heater when the temperature in a room gets too low. The thermostat reliably serves its function in a single loop, monitoring conditions and responding to changes in conditions with a predetermined response. But the thermostat doesn't know if its response is "correct." It only has one response to a change in conditions: to turn the heater on or off. If I accidentally leave the house with the window open and the temperature drops suddenly, the thermostat has no way of knowing the window is open! It will faithfully respond with its single-loop approach, turning on the heater and attempting to heat the room with the window open. Double-loop learning is when a human being (perhaps my spouse!) comes by and notices that the window has been left open, the heat is blasting, and we are warming the New England outdoors. The underlying assumption of the thermostat's response—heat the room when it gets too cold—is questioned, and a new response is formed outside of the single-loop program: close the window. Hopefully, this example isn't too pedantic, and your mind is already brimming with applications of this paradigm to your work! Let's discuss an example of how double-loop learning might be relevant in a civic context.

A city government sets up a public communication and feedback system to monitor the success of a program to encourage the community to recycle more household waste. A coordinated messaging program of articles in local news sources, a promotional video produced by the city's media team and distributed on digital social platforms, and postcards added to residents' water bills talk about the impact of reducing trash and the need to recycle more. Success metrics are tracked by a data-sharing relationship with the highly responsive and collaborative trash vendor that monitors the weight of trucks headed for the landfill. The underlying assumption is that less trash equals more recycling—a successful program. After a three-month period to set a baseline and retrieving data from the previous year to correct for seasonal changes in trash volume, the program is implemented. Trash weight and volume decrease immediately and stay low during the monitoring period. The program is declared a success! A press release is prepared, and the local newspaper runs an article about how the city is a new recycling hub. Double-loop learning rears its head when the recycling vendor calls and says that they have had a surge of nonrecyclable materials being added to the communities' recycling stream. Their quarterly reports show that labor costs have more than doubled, and they have identified your city as the source of an excess of non-recyclable materials that have to be manually removed, and they will have to reassess billed costs under the agreement. This new information from another source results in a second loop of feedback. The second loop caused the city to question the underlying assumptions that drove its perceptions of success in the first loop.

The Importance of Stakeholder Engagement

Stakeholder engagement is often the key second loop. As staff strive for efficiency and optimize processes, stakeholders add a valuable second loop of correcting data to the system. Soliciting feedback from diverse stakeholders adds valuable richness to the data, which in turn creates more resilient programs and services and, by extension, a more resilient organization.

Difference can often be seen as a "problem" to be overcome. One way to think about difference in public life is that the solution to a roomful of diverse viewpoints is to build consensus among stakeholders. If we have a consensus, then we can move forward. The normative force that coalesces behind a consensus is one way to drive policy forward. However, when consensus becomes the end, the system can easily slip into the efficiencies of a single-loop model, never questioning the underlying assumptions that drive organizational behavior. For this reason, we invite our stakeholders into the room, trusting them to tell us that the window has been left open and the city's thermostat system has run amok.

Strategies for Effective Engagement

Throughout this book, I have expounded on the value of interacting with the mid-level actors in a community. As previously mentioned, these groups serve to coalesce communities of interest and can be relied upon to be where community values and beliefs are distilled and made legible. Mapping those organizations and the arguments that they bring to the issue can serve to uncover additional areas of inquiry that may be helpful for designers planning the conversation.

Mapping is one way to create a shared visualization of the problem space. One approach to mapping complex issue spaces is Jeff Conklin's IBIS-based software

Compendium, an argumentation mapping software. It provides a restructuring of conversation as a rational argument, an understanding of the diffusion of the political power of the various actors in the conversation, and a refocusing of the conversation upon the act of the shared creation of a visual artifact.

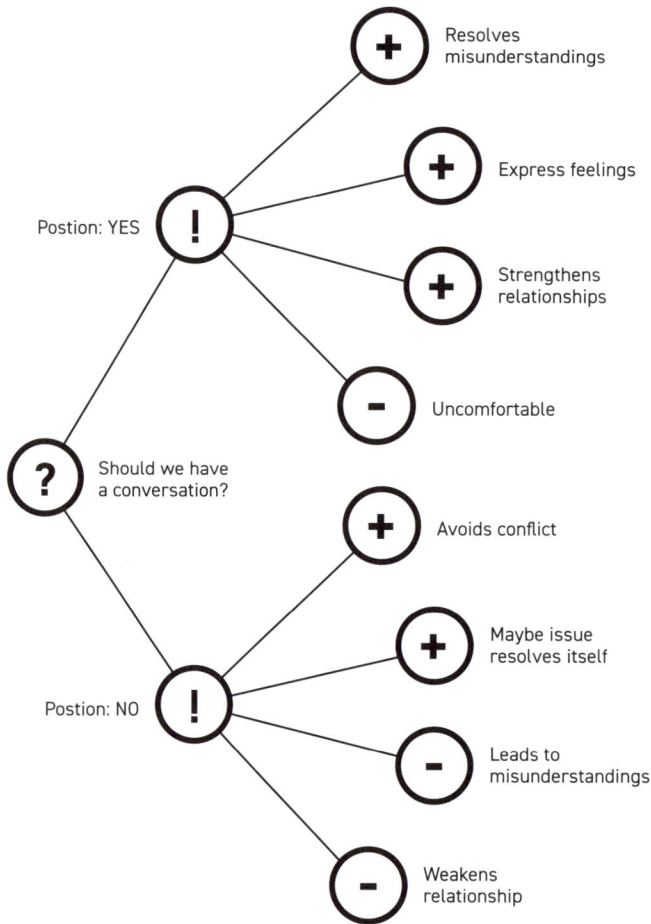

Figure 13: IBIS argumentation mapping, developed by Horst Rittel can be used to organize an argument into supporting or detracting points.

Conklin, a student of Horst Rittel, created *Compendium* to structure the social complexity of arguments about problem spaces, or to "defragment" problem dynamics (Conklin, 2006). Fragmentation occurs when the stakeholders see themselves as more divided than united. Defragmenting is not consensus, as warned above, but offers opportunities for stakeholders to see the relevance of each other's viewpoints. Stakeholders might not agree on the problem definition or a specific approach, but they can all agree that each other's perspectives and approaches hold value.

Compendium, a descendant of Rittel's IBIS system (Kunz & Rittel, 1970), can be used to map the hierarchy of ideas that contribute to an argument. *Compendium* mapping has a few "nodes" that can be described in everyday language: questions, ideas, supporting points, detracting points, and proposals. When it is crucial that policymakers "get it right," taking the time to map out all the arguments in a space, as well as the stakeholders that support or dissent from those arguments, shows the issues at play in a community. Further, mapping the issues in order to understand the conversations that may result offers an understanding of the terms of resistance to particular approaches. Resistance manifests because people feel that their voices have been marginalized inside of the official channels of structure (Young, 2000). While voices of resistance are an important component of democratic dialog, and designing conversation systems must leave room to accommodate them, designing an intentional set of structures to accommodate resistance is antithetical to the idea of resistance. From the perspective of the design of conversation, resistance must always be negotiated.

CONCLUSION

Planning a civic conversation is a rich and complicated process that extends beyond merely thinking about what words will be spoken. It involves rethinking the civic conversation as a service and working within the user-centered paradigm by guiding people toward the inquiry. Reaching out and meaningfully involving diverse stakeholders and residents to clarify the conversation's purpose and set objectives offers access to the particular wisdom of the community in the processes that shape discussions and outcomes. Through a combination of structured and improvisatory experiences, participants can be guided toward a deeper understanding of their own knowledge and expertise as it pertains to the problem at hand and surfacing that knowledge for the benefit of policymakers. Engaging new voices to question underlying assumptions leads to new understandings of context and helps civic organizations to become more responsive and resilient. This approach not only builds knowledge to address immediate issues but also builds a foundation for ongoing, productive civic engagement, ultimately fostering a more inclusive and participatory community.

6

How Things Support a Conversation

INTRODUCTION

Objects and spaces play crucial roles in our everyday lives, shaping our interactions, behaviors, and perceptions. These things are not merely passive backdrops to human action; they actively participate in and influence social practices. The design and arrangement of objects can reveal or obscure power dynamics, facilitate or hinder communication, and support or disrupt community cohesion. Recognizing the agency of things in our social worlds opens up new possibilities for design that is attuned to the complexities of human and non-human relationships.

When we have a conversation, *things* facilitate or detract from the understandings we develop. The things in a conversational space are like a team of agents working for or against you and the participants. Understanding the environment for conversation as a participatory and procedural space creates the opportunity to design events for richer engagement. Conversations create structures for participants engaging with matters of concern and each other.

Noortje Marres (2012) has explored how material objects can mediate public engagement and participation. Marres argues that things can shape the way issues are framed and discussed, influencing the dynamics of deliberation and the formation of public opinion. Further, Elizabeth Shove (2012) explored the cyclic interplay between material objects, competencies and meanings. Extending the arguments of Madeline Akrich, Shove discusses how competencies emerge from the dialog between objects, competencies and meanings. This is firmly the designers' territory, and these perspectives offer valuable insight into the set of relationships designers engage in as they design for conversation. By paying attention to the role of objects in these processes, designers can create spaces that enhance the quality of interactions and foster a deeper understanding among participants.

HOW OBJECTS CREATE DEMOCRATIC SPACES

In the realm of deliberative community meetings, the role of material environments and objects cannot be understated. The setup of the space, the availability of information and resources, and the design of the tools of engagement all serve to support the overall effectiveness of the civic dialogue. Creating an environment conducive to open, respectful and productive discussions involves more than just bringing people together. It requires a thoughtful consideration of the material environment, of how things influence the flow and quality of the civic conversation.

Rather than waiting for a turn to speak, a deliberative community forum participant converses with neighbors about the difficult issues that affect their neighborhood.

Generally, people don't respond to the prospect of a civic meeting with bubbling enthusiasm. In fact, the prospect of attending a civic meeting to speak on a topic we care about may cause the more fainthearted among us to experience anxiety and worry about conflict.

However, attending a deliberative community meeting is a bit different. Rather than finding a line for a sign-up sheet where nervous, perturbed residents queue together to acquire one of the limited number of 3-minute speaking slots, a participant who attends a deliberative community forum is greeted at a registration table. They are offered a briefing document that outlines the main questions and proposed topics, and are then directed toward a buffet with sandwiches or pizza. They don't spend time sitting, waiting, or listening to other residents take their turn at the microphone, mentally practicing what they will say when their turn to speak comes. Instead, a deliberative community forum participant converses with neighbors about the difficult issues that affect their neighborhood.

Effectively, the objects surrounding "traditional" 3-minutes-at-a-microphone public comment sessions induce undesirable behavior. The lectern, the microphone, and the arrangement of the audiences (both other residents and the government staff) signal that public comment is a space for performance. The person at the lectern is elevated over all others as they typically stand at the architectural focal point of the room. Other people either remain silent and attentive or shout cheers, encouragement, boos, or heckles. Outside of an actual performance situation, can you imagine an experience that convenes more performance metaphors? People who attend a traditional public comment session are given all the framing cues (Lakoff, 2010) that they are in a performance situation, and they respond by performing.

Fortunately, the distracting architectures of power are often absent in community meetings. Deliberative forums are usually held in transient spaces that lack ceremonial character. I have hosted deliberative community forums in settings that are spartan at best. Over the past year, I have organized deliberative forums in church meeting rooms, civic building meeting rooms, recreation center auxiliary spaces, library basements, and the meeting room at a county-supported residence for low-income retirees. Churches minimally adorn meeting spaces by decorating meeting rooms with evangelical posters and other devotional messages on the walls; otherwise, the rooms where these forums are held offer little more than empty space. The rooms are designed to economize cost and have a temporary character. They have very few (if any) aspects of place and contain little evidence of the hosting organization. The furnishings of these spaces are similarly spartan, disposable, and movable/foldable; walls and flooring are beige or gray and do not lend any sense of place. Generally, participants at these events sit in folding chairs, at round or square folding tables. In general, the meeting rooms had none of the ceremonial character we typically associate with city council chambers, school board meeting rooms, or other stereotypical places for governmental deliberation.

Spaces of statecraft have their own scripts. When advocating for the reconstruction of the destroyed British House of Commons in a 1943 session of Parliament, Winston Churchill famously said, "we shape our buildings, and thereafter, they shape us" (HC Deb, 1943). Churchill followed this statement with a structured argument detailing how the design of the chamber both reflected and curtailed British party politics. He argued that the small size of the chamber improved the character of presentations and made debates take on a more conversational tone. The smaller space didn't seem echoingly empty when less than the full Parliament was in attendance.

In deliberative democracy, setting is one aspect that organizers of deliberative fora have only lightly considered. Church basements, dusty union halls, and Veterans of Foreign Wars meeting halls with leaky ceilings contribute a sense of place. However, the places that contain these generic meeting rooms are each invested with unique cultural meanings other than democratic engagement. In these meetings, the lack of civic ceremonial character subtly influences the people who attend. Regardless, the influence of the setting should be considered, including the history of the organization's actions within the community. While some may find comfort in attending a meeting in their own church basement, others may feel unwelcome in that same institution. Similarly, the use of a semi-public space may be perceived as either an endorsement of the city by the institution or an endorsement of the institution by the city.

The tension and kind of silence that exists in a courtroom, hall of state, or council chambers is a function of the formal character and the social conventions and learned behaviors of those spaces. The ceremony of these places can be overbearing. By contrast, the people who attended sessions I was a part of remained conscious that they were engaged in an important activity. Instead, the casual-yet-structured atmosphere encouraged direct, focused participation, while also providing space for off-topic social interactions.

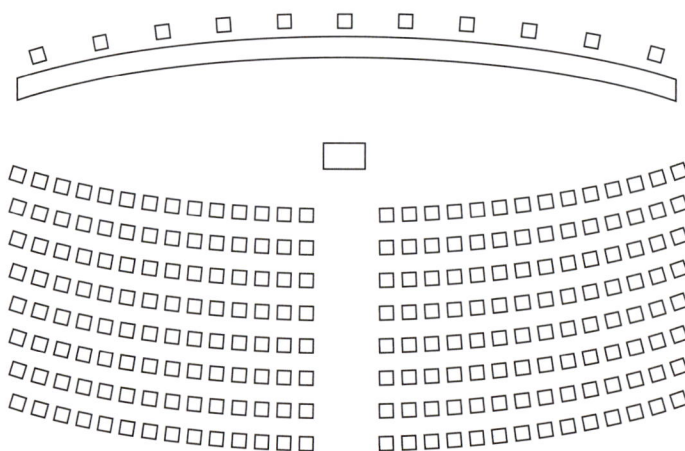

Figure 14: Room layout for city council chambers. Note how closely the space planning mirrors a performance space, like a movie theater or music hall.

In contrast, the deliberative community meeting is constructed around a different set of framing metaphors. There is no audience; the only "authority" is a reasonable, friendly host (moderator) who cleverly directs the conversation so everyone who wants to can speak. The goal of the evening is not to communicate what "I want to say" but to discover what the group does not know and where their knowledge gaps exist. This set of cues activates a different framing: a dinner with neighbors to discuss a difficult problem.

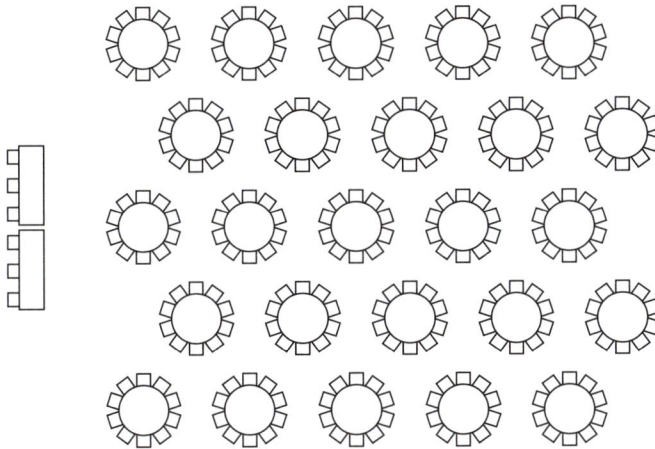

Figure 15: Room layout for a deliberative community meeting. Note that the room layout is more similar to what might be used for a reception or party.

After conducting more than 30 large, formal, deliberative community forums and countless other smaller community gatherings, a neighborly dinner-table format is mostly successful because of the compelling change of metaphor used to organize people's framing. By reframing public participation in this way, and the participatory design work that is being done in other areas, these metaphors might be carried through (Schön, 1984) into other areas of civic life. Participants' experiences can also be enhanced by thoughtful intervention in the physical environment of the deliberation event. Ertel and Solomon (2014) offer a checklist in their book *Moments of Impact* for designing the material environment. Their checklist suggests ensuring:

1. The room works for the number of people and activities planned.
2. The room can be adapted to different activities if needs change.
3. The room is comfortable. They mention seating, temperature, acoustics, and minimal distractions as essential elements.

We will cover spaces again in Chapter 8 when we discuss evaluating the civic conversation, but the main aspect I would add to Ertel and Solomon's list is ensuring the space is compliant with Americans with Disabilities Act (ADA) requirements. Accessible entrances, sufficient space between tables for people with mobility impairments, and accessible bathrooms all contribute to the basic needs and dignity of all participants. High-quality building ventilation can reduce participants' exposure to infectious diseases, which is particularly important for older or otherwise health-vulnerable participants.

Coming together and eating communally creates successful deliberative events. Beyond mere symbolism, the experience of a shared meal is an intimate one. Framed thusly using objects—tables, chairs, lecterns, and microphones—meetings offer a moment of coming together and discussing community challenges. Civic conversations create a special moment for the participants. These events are distinct from everyday life and offer an opportunity for focal practice: a moment of mastery when we can become skillful and open with one another (Spinosa, Flores, & Dreyfus, 1997). However, other political needs might demand a different type of spatial configuration.

Situation Rooms

The White House Situation Room, as a work of the U.S. federal government, this image is in the public domain.

de Soto's situation rooms are a critical subversion of the government situation room (Delinikolas, DeSoto, & Dragona, 2013). Occupied by citizens and powered by free and open-source software, de Soto uses the situation room to create alternative cartographies to society's dominant paradigms. In other words, de Soto's work uses the tools of empire to reinscribe the geography with citizen, ethnic, and post-colonial viewpoints. His situation rooms become environments for a kind of conversation with the geography and lines of language that overlay, structure, and provide a technological interface to the natural world. de Soto facilitates the creation of non-cartesian, non-dualist geographies through these rooms by opening opportunities for post-colonial understandings of space and place.

Situation rooms involve key activities such as assembling, monitoring, exploring, converging, and consolidating information (Landgren & Bergstrand, 2016). Designers might be interested in creating these kinds of "situation room" environments to support public deliberation. Little research exists to describe how situation rooms might function when supporting residents rather than topical experts in emergent conditions. A public situation room could support new forms of citizen engagement that will help bridge the gap between urban publics and the various agencies charged with policymaking, and building and sustaining urban environments. By partnering with both municipal governments and local community stakeholders designers could foster the difficult conversations that are necessary for ensuring equity and access within and between communities.

Designing a Conversational Environment

Another useful break from designing for information clarity is to think of the design-facilitated conversation as a holding environment for deliberation (Culmsee & Awati, 2012). The concept of the "holding environment" was first articulated by psychologist Donald W. Winnicott as the environment where an infant is raised by its mother. Later, it was defined by Robert Kegan as a set of *cultures of embeddedness*, is that environment and mindset where an expert helper or facilitator will provide an environment of understanding, and through the expert's experience of the client's problems will aid in the sense-making process for the client (Kegan, 2001).

Each of these environments functions in a way that shapes the conversations that are had within.

To return to earlier works, Pablo de Soto's "Situation Room" installation designs a cartographic conversation with an environment, as surely as the concert hall is designed to prevent and limit conversation between audience members, assuring that they remain mute and respectful (Small, 1998). Each of these environments functions in a way that shapes the conversations that are had within. To return to Jeslma's point regarding behavior shaping, poetry may be read or songs sung in any situation room, but the design of that socio-technical environment provides specific paths that are easier to follow. These special rooms are more like the interface designs of Winograd and Flores (and many others since) which have produced theoretically grounded sets of garden pathways that privilege certain acts and facilitate certain outcomes. But as Winograd admits of his own work, within and without those interfaces there remains space for resistance.

The Role of Objects

One level of design to consider when designing a civic conversation is material artifacts. Here, design operates at the most foundational, constitutive level: the look and feel (Houde & Hill, 1997), choice of material, and the arrangement of objects. Designers might put objects on the tables to stimulate participants' thinking, such as models, game boards, tokens that represent concepts, and facilitator's game cards. There are also the supporting things that tend to recede in our perception, such as tables, chairs, desks, podiums, and microphones.

Round tables are generally better for deliberative conversation events than long, rectangular banquet tables. If the only available tables are banquet tables, organizers can push two together to make a square, though the combined table is just slightly better for the conversation dynamic than seating eight people at a long rectangular table. Because of the side-by-side seating that the banquet tables afford, banquet tables inevitably divide the table into small subgroups. Lines of sight are difficult to maintain. When a person turns to talk to their neighbor, both seated at a rectangular banquet table, much of the rest of the group is hidden from their sight (Figure 17). Often, participants end up having two discussions, one at each end of the table. Participants who are committed to engaging and seated at banquet tables will scoot their chairs out in the middle of the long edge of the table, simulating a more circular table. But it is difficult for participants to escape the discipline of a rectangular table.

The most effective meetings had a distinct parallel construction between the agenda questions, briefing document, pedagogical presentation, and survey. Essentially, people can participate more effectively when the forum documents share an overarching structure. Participants must know the framework for discussion and understand that the framework is supported by factual information. At the end of the event, participants are surveyed on the same information that they have deliberated upon. Functional parallelism throughout the event serves as a recurrent structure that eases and stabilizes interactions.

Paper materials used during deliberative sessions offer a familiarity to participants. While paper materials are perhaps not the most sustainable, participants who have sufficient visual acuity can interpret materials and respond to surveys created with ink on paper. In current times, there is a strong temptation to digitize these kinds of supportive materials. However, the openness of simple materials provides a site for both discourse and dissent. Simple paper materials offer an opportunity for participants to operate outside of the systems of access and control (logins, registrations) that are deployed along with a digital solution.

OBJECTS STRUCTURING CONVERSATIONAL SPACES AND PLACES

Steve Harrison and Paul Dourish explain the social context of conversation through concepts of space versus place. Place is constituted through a set of associations and ideas of behavioral appropriateness in spaces:

> Physically, a place is a space which is invested with understandings of behavioural appropriateness, cultural expectations, and expected activities. We are located in "space", but we act in "place". Furthermore, "places" are spaces that are valued. The distinction is rather like that between a "house" and a "home"; a house might keep out the wind and the rain, but a home is where we live. (Harrison & Dourish, 1996, p. 69)

In successive scholarship, attention to place has emerged as an important element when context is considered. Moving the site of civic discourse out of ceremonial places, like council chambers or the city hall building, and into local places, like church basements, recreation centers, or senior centers, quite literally moves the civic conversations out of the halls of power and into the territory of the familiar.

Winston Churchill, Prime Minister of the United Kingdom during World War II, had a lucid understanding of the intersection of conversation and place. Following the destruction of the House of Commons meeting room in World War II, in an address to Parliament, Winston Churchill stated that, "We shape our buildings and afterwards our buildings shape us" (HC Deb, 1943).

Churchill and the members of the House of Commons spent time discussing possible design approaches, though, and whether reproducing the old chambers would be the most effective for planning for a new type of dialog. (HC Deb, 1943). Their underlying argument was that place shapes the behavior of those present. It prefigures Akrich, Latour, and Jelsma's arguments that we should consider objects determining the social world (Akrich, 1992; Latour, 1996; Jelsma, 2003). Continuing this line of thought, Emilie Gomart and Maarten Hajer (2003) examine the relation between behavior and place with the question "Who acts?" or "What acts?" Their psychological experiments, begun in the 1950s, examined the sexual performance of rats during mating. In the first set of experiments, the rats were in small cages, and the female in estrus (or "in heat") was dropped into the male rats' cage. In these experiments, the female rat exhibited submissive behavior, while the highly active male rat exhibited dominant behavior. Gomart and Hajer then turn to later experiments, where the two rats were placed in larger cages with semi-natural environments. In these cages, the female rat showed a highly active role in the encounter. Gomart and Hajer write, "as the experimental setting (the cage) is transformed, so is the phenomenon of female rat sexuality" (Gomart & Hajer, 2003). I would take this a step further and say that the experimental setting *designed* the rats' behavior.

The concept of place I use in this book is oriented toward supporting design for conversation. The context that place provides—salacious bedrooms, adolescent hangouts, or halls where revolution is planned and enacted—influences the nature and types of conversations that take place there. I hypothesize that placeiality shapes high-stakes conversations. The images, spaces, and objects near to the high-stakes conversation also, to reference Akrich again, "define a framework of action" for the participants and observers (1992).

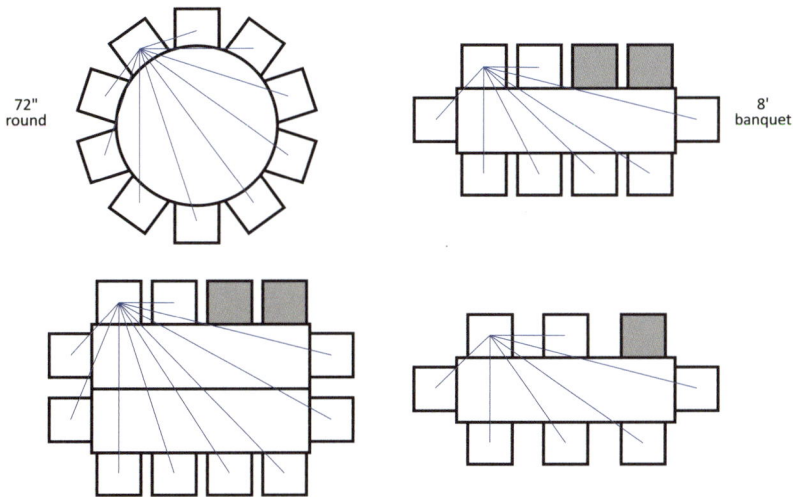

Figure 16: Lines of sight on various types of seating arrangements.

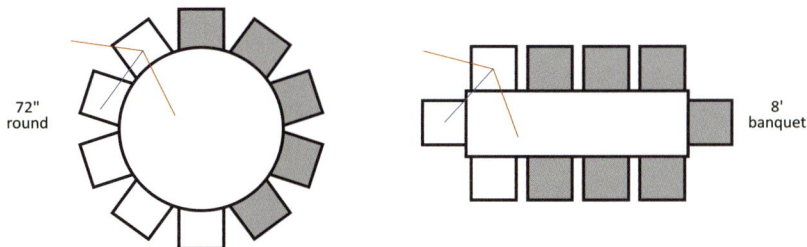

Figure 17: Fields of vision when turned towards another participant on round and rectangular tables.

OBJECTS AND CIVIC METAPHORS

Microphones also have a strong disciplinary effect. Having only one microphone in the audience and controlling that microphone subdues participation in a plenary session. To keep the question-and-answer portion of the meeting from running over time, the emcee can hold the microphone while a participant speaks without turning over control of the device. The microphone can also place the participants at risk. For example, the participants might feel unjustly controlled if the moderator uses the microphone to rephrase their question. In this case, if questions are rephrased for concision and clarity, turning to the participant and asking, "Did I get that right?" after the rephrasing helps participants feel that their concerns are heard. A participant or an expert going over time can be asked to pass the microphone to another individual.

Deliberative community forums ensure that all voices, not just the loudest, get heard.

On August 15, 2016, then-presidential candidate Bernie Sanders yielded his microphone to two protesters from Black Lives Matter (Merica, 2015), a group that campaigns against systemic racism directed toward Black people. At the time, Sanders' action was covered extensively in the news media, and then-candidate Donald Trump called it "weak" (Murphy, 2015). The functionality of a microphone that elevates one's voice is both a functional necessity to help people with low hearing and a powerful proxy of one's own voice. When I speak with members of city governments, I use a common trope: "deliberative community forums ensure that all voices, not just the loudest, get heard." The power that a microphone has to amplify voices is quite seductive.

Other elements of the material environment have a civic character. Meetings are often held in expedient places such as churches, union halls, Veterans of Foreign Wars or American Legion halls, and senior centers. Metaphors can work in these settings in several ways. Familiarity with the meeting site lends a sense of comfort to those who come there to have a conversation and perhaps lends a sense of urgency. The meeting is so timely and crucial to understanding the public's view that city staff must use any site available.

The objects used in a deliberative community forum can confirm or upset expectations for a city meeting. As discussed in chapter 4, the metaphors that frame the conversational event must be carefully considered to reorient the participants toward fuller participation in the event. While encouraging participation is a goal, opportunities for protesting and voicing the concerns of marginalized groups must be held open. Here, the design, unlike our 311 reporting app from chapter 2, must be held open a degree to permit sites for alternative viewpoints and for unsanctioned ways of speaking into the system. Openings in the design of structure of the conversations for Lucy Suchman's heterogeneity offer a wider potential bandwidth of inputs to the overall system.

I can state conclusively that deliberation works, but not always for the reasons the democratic theorists think. The principal component that drives deliberative democracy practice is the use of the things of meeting design to evoke participants' rich understanding of how to be convivial (Illich, 1990) with other people and harness their cultural knowledge. Essentially, we must say through our designs, "this is how we have a civil discussion; this is where we come together to talk through our problems." Let's discuss further how a designer might activate some of those powerful objects to support community conversations.

OBJECTS IN GAMES

Several Carnegie Mellon University design students play a vintage version of Trivial Pursuit (approx. 1990).

Trivial Pursuit has had very little traction as a competitive game. While *Monopoly* players hold annual tournaments and chess players have elaborate tournament and ranking systems, *Trivial Pursuit* is more... "trivial" in a sense! The enjoyment of the gameplay derives more from sharing random facts and engaging in the conversations than whether a player successfully answers the most trivia questions correctly. The game questions are designed to be mildly provocative—to evoke nostalgic recollections of the time period referenced, perhaps even to provoke collegial arguments, or at least discussion over the veracity of the *Trivial Pursuit* cards. The game contains all the highly structured elements of a competitive game. The players roll dice, move their pawns, draw cards, and add pie slices, but the game experience centers around discussing the facts brought to light by the gameplay. Though highly structured, the game is a thin gloss for provisioning topics of conversation. The turn-taking nature of the gameplay ensures that the conversations do not go on too long. If a player is less interested in a top-40 pop song, the conversation is over before the urge to tune out becomes overwhelming.

Trivial Pursuit, as an object, is an excellent place to start talking about orienting with things. Specifically, the objects of the game act in a facilitative role. Strangely enough, as I was thinking about the problem of objects facilitating conversation, someone left a bag of cast-off board games in the hallway outside my office. *Trivial Pursuit* was one of those games, which set in motion this line of thought. I started considering how sometimes the object of a game is not to win but to foster enjoyable conversations about some minutiae with a shared cultural currency. Here, Parlett considers the ongoing development of games in which the objects move away from the center of gameplay and take on a more facilitative role:

> Wandering further away from the board, we reach a game like *Trivial Pursuit* and its derivatives, in which all the real play takes place off the board. The board is almost an irrelevance: it does little more than keep a score, like a Cribbage board. Finally, we reach fantasy games, some of which involve a board as a convenience for keeping track of inter-player relationship, but most of which are boardless role-playing games, overlapping with 'play' in its theatrical rather than any other sense of the word. (Parlett, 1999, p. 347)

Like Parlett says, games create theater, a shared *place* where objects facilitate conversation. Games like *Trivial Pursuit* are perhaps the most common, well-known, frequently played, and least abstract. One way to consider structuring the understanding of objects facilitating the conversation is to consider the degree to which the objects are present in the role of facilitation.

Objects might take a dominating role in structuring interaction. These objects impose their content, their haptics, and perhaps even their worldview upon the user. These objects permit and structure a directed play scoped within the playing field. Conversely, other objects recede in an interaction and enable or encourage behavior, acting in a way that highlights the behavior or the interaction as the central aspect of the experience. In the context of a game, some of these objects assume both an important component of the *mise en scène* of the playing field, and also take on symbolic meaning. Cards can become the player's voice and pawn the player's body. Consider the language that occurs around gameplay in *Sorry!*: "You sent *me* back to home!" You would not say, "You sent *my pawn* back to home!" For some, playing a game may become visceral, eliciting a feeling of "stuck-ness." The arcade video game *Golden Axe* (Uchida, 1989) has player-characters options that include only a hyper-masculine barbarian, a bikini-clad Amazonian woman, and a dwarf. If players want to use the game, they must don one of those identities. Less dramatic, perhaps, are the boards, the dice, and the pawns of a game board, yet players inhabit those game objects to a degree.

When considering everyday conversations or civic conversations, objects remain an aspect of the setting and act similarly. The symbolism of the objects remains, yet their role is backgrounded in gameplay. Games contain experience thresholds where these objects become animated. The pawn in the box is rather less animated than the pawn on the gameboard. The facilitation of these objects—how they become a part of the player, and the player becomes a part of the object—is a profoundly significant aspect of games. Through roleplay, the actions are delegated to the game objects and become less consequential to the player's life.

Encouraging Turn-taking

Rarified objects that act in supportive ways are common in gameplay. They can be a game board, slips of paper, tokens, or nearly any other item. Although everyday conversation rarely uses these types of items, exceptions exist. The Mi'kmaq—an Indigenous group native to the American Northeast—materialize the right to speak using a "talking stick" during discussions of problems. It is an ordinary or specially carved stick used during community discussions to authorize speech. In practice, during the discussion, the individual who wishes to talk about a problem holds the stick and speaks. All other participants must listen. The stick is then passed to the next person, who then speaks about the problem without repeating what the previous speakers have said. This continues until all who want to speak have spoken and the stick is returned to the originating person (Donaldson, 1998, quoting Knockwood, 1992).

Other examples of objects that structure conversation can be found in politics and specialized occupations. At the beginning of sessions at the United Nations, speeches are structured by a voluntary 15-minute time limit. The speaker's time at the podium is shown through green, yellow, and red lights on the speaker's podium that indicate when the speaker's time is nearing its end (Ruder et al., 2017). While they do not sanction speech, medical practitioners use decision aids—pamphlets that explain risk factors or aid in planning treatment for complex, costly, and/or life-threatening medical situations (Collaboration IPDAS, 2005). However, artifacts do not come into play in everyday conversation. If objects facilitate a conversation, it is almost invariably a very unusual speaking situation or a game.

Designers of civic conversations can similarly use game objects to help structure portions of the event. Hypothetical discussions of budgets in municipal budget meetings might be made material by giving each participant fake money. Participants can then distribute the funds into buckets based on how much they want to support each budget priority. Using the metaphor of money this way becomes a common-sense version of weighted voting. Asking each participant to distribute an allowance of game money also incorporates turn-taking into the meeting experience. The other aspects of games—such as spinners, dice, a game board, and cards—can be used this way. Because these game elements have common metaphors of use that bridge many cultures, they exert a subtle structuring force on the meeting format. The sequential playing or choosing of cards—or really any game-like experience where people normally take turns—can be modified by designers to encourage turn-taking in a civic conversation.

Creating Boundaries

Games create a special kind of social space—a construction in which the formalism and structure of the game take precedence over other rules and conventions of the outside world. Katie Salen and Eric Zimmerman (2003), quoting Johan Huizinga (1950), wrote about the "magic circle" of gameplay—a space where the game rules preempt norms of behavior. Similarly, John Dewey (1958) defines an "experience" as bounded in time and space. For Huizinga, games are so bounded by time and space, and their boundaries are established by the act of play. Within the context of the act of play, there is a shifted hierarchy of rule-following. In the adult card-matching game *Cards Against Humanity* social conventions may be flaunted and even broken within the magic circle of the game. Within this protective magic circle, players may, as a part of the gameplay, adopt the personalities of fictional characters. They may commit fictional crimes and unfairly leverage other players in ways that would be unseemly if done outside the magic circle.

Games permit behaviors that are otherwise impermissible. For instance, *Twister* allows a set of behaviors that would not be considered appropriate for friendly company outside of the game space. Similarly, *Cards Against Humanity* makes racism, sexism, and ableism permissible in the context of the game space. While *Cards Against Humanity* uses the magic circle of the game space to permit prurient giggling, it points to a special agency that games are imbued with. Games allow us to *play* with aspects of our culture and allow people to engage with topics or perform behaviors that are otherwise taboo, or perhaps just difficult to discuss.

Within the context of the game space, participants are permitted to talk about difficult or taboo subjects as a matter of ordinary conversation. The space of the game and its lack of consequences lighten the stakes of the experience and help people talk through challenging issues. Gamifying an experience can be one approach that can enable participants to deal with difficult topics. This approach is evident in such games as *Never Have I Ever...* a speech-only game principally played by teenagers. In the context of its gameplay, teens can choose to touch on taboo subjects. Also, the game *My Gift of Grace*—described as "a conversation game for living and dying well" (Common Practice, 2016)—uses a thin gloss of game experience to encourage participants to discuss preferences and fill out what is essentially a questionnaire about the person's preferences for end-of-life care.

Establishing Rules

The game *1000 Blank White Cards* has rules that are manipulable by players. Played with a large stack of index cards and pens, players write anything they want on the cards (Morehead et al., 2001). The game develops based on the cards that people draw and write. The game has no predetermined end, no predetermined rules, and no predetermined way of winning. In a word, the game is nomic—its rules and structure are generated as people create and add cards to the deck. According to the website BoardGameGeek, "it is in the spirit of the game to spite and denounce these conventions, as well as to adhere to them religiously" (BoardGameGeek, 2018). The objective of the game is to instigate conversation about the game's rules, structure, and drawn images.

Although this is not prescriptive, *1000 Blank White Cards* games can be thought of as having a three-part structure:

1. Card creation
2. Gameplay
3. Card evaluation

During card creation, players write rules and draw pictures to create a starter deck of cards. When players decide that enough cards have been created, they are dealt to the players and gameplay begins. Customarily, the player to the dealer's left goes first, followed by structured turn-taking by other players. However, this custom may be altered by the community or the cards that players create. After an amount of play, the game may end and one player declared "the winner"... or not. After play, the cards are evaluated, and some saved for future gameplay. In a long-running game, introducing a new card that is well-regarded is a coup of sorts.

1000 Blank White Cards, *created by Carnegie Mellon design students and the author.*

Some commonly popular cards award (or decrement) a player's points, modify the system of turn-taking for gameplay (skipping turns, losing turns, or reversing the order of play), and require players to discard or draw cards.

An interesting aspect of *1000 Blank White Cards* is that the materialization of the game assets, rather than being created by a designer, is turned over to the players. Design itself becomes the locus of play. Players might ask themselves: "How can I materialize this rule in a funny way? In a way that might delight the other players?" Because the ruleset is totally fungible, questions of winning or losing are set aside, and the gameplay becomes about enjoying clever manipulations of the game space. The game becomes not an exploration of the play space defined by the ruleset but a discourse about the ruleset itself.

While teaching a design course that explored the design of procedural environments, I played this game with my design students. The cards they made were a mixture of inside jokes, pop culture references, absurd references, and commands to perform physical activities. These were paired with commands that added or decremented points or dollars, or ended the game. Most groups chose to play in a style vaguely like the game UNO, where there was a discard pile and a draw pile, and each player held a small hand of cards.

Dice, paper, and pencil are all the materials needed to play Peter Suber's game Nomic.

Another interesting aspect of playing nomic games is that giving players control over the game's structure doesn't mean the structure is left entirely open. Players' approaches to *1000 Blank White Cards* are structured through the materiality of the cards themselves. Cards and card games evoke links to participants' past understanding of what a card game is. References to other card games like *UNO*, *Crazy Eights*, *Slapjack*, *Go Fish*, and *Spoons*—as well as references to childlike pastimes and references to social settings where card games are played—become part of constructing the ruleset for *1000 Blank White Cards*.

1000 Blank White Cards is the same type as the eponymous game *Nomic*—a game where all gameplay is players changing the ruleset. Introduced by philosopher Peter Suber, the game *Nomic* is a game of making, changing, debating, and voting on rules. *Nomic* has two types of rules: immutable (numbered in the 100s) and mutable (numbered in the 200s). While points are accumulated by each player throwing one die and adding it to their score, Suber says that that mechanism of points accumulation is included only so that it may be amended or changed by the players (Suber, 1990).

The material elements of the game are quite simple: a pencil, paper, and one six-sided die (though not specified in the ruleset, a standard die is assumed). The game begins with 29 rules, 16 immutable rules, and 13 mutable rules. Mutable rules may be changed, amended, or repealed. Immutable rules must be changed to mutable rules first before they are changed. At the start of the game, each player's move consists of a dice throw and a rule change proposition, which all the players will vote on. It is not possible to comment definitively on this game beyond the starting conditions, as each gameplay situation is unique.

Suber created the game with the intent of making it a model for examining rule-making activities in legal systems, specifically the activity of amending a ruleset. Suber admits that amendment-making is an esoteric feature of a legal system, and while this may be true in the context of examining legal systems, an aggregating process is a key feature of designing systems for public comment— where citizens' views are collected, counted, and coded, with the goal that those views will guide future change in legislation or policy.

Writing on *Nomic*, Douglas Hofstadter (1985) extends the concept of hierarchical rule systems to biological systems, customs, and etiquette. He discusses contingency, or what players must do when another player disobeys the rules. For Hofstadter, understanding contingency helps maintain the integrity of the game space, which some might think is counterintuitive (p. 76). Considering the game in light of other rule-bound systems (like democracy!), though, a systems design is only as robust as its structures to recover from errors. A customer can only understand the depth of an organization's commitment to service when the service fails.

Hofstadter points out that *Nomic* blurs the distinction between constitutive rules and rules of skill. In *Nomic*, play may be arbitrarily extended outside the game field. While Nomic remains a game and the key aspect of the gameplay is changing the ruleset, Nomic play is structured by implicit rules within the gameplay experience. Unlike most games, Suber goes to great lengths to make the implicit rules explicit, offering them up for modification. For example, Rule 101 (an immutable, or less mutable rule) states that: "All players must always abide by all the rules then in effect, in the form in which they are then in effect." A tacit understanding of what a game is, however, and Suber's original goals—that people will play this game to explore the nature of amendment—are beyond the reach of the rules, be they mutable or immutable. For example, a rule could be created and made immutable such that the game's goal is solely for personal enjoyment; however, that activity falls under the original set of goals that Suber created *Nomic* to fulfill. In short, some higher-level social structures may be out of the reach of the rules of a game with even so broad a reach as Nomic. Despite the game's evolution, the players continue playing with the same goals. Once playing, players cannot opt out of Suber's goals for the game.

Remaining Flexible and Thinking Systemically

The examination of rulesets that are adjusted through games and game-like practices might also be a useful approach to understanding the behavior of systems. Donella Meadows cites the manipulation of rules and the power to change the rules as higher-level ways to induce change in a system (Meadows, 1999). Systems of governance or evaluation—and other systems that include hierarchical rulesets—could be modeled with a *1000 Blank White Cards* experience or type of nomic game. In short, conversations about game objects, rather than being a structural curiosity, model the interactions that occur when rule changes are made in the system. Far from indicating breakage or failure, conversation about the game objects represents an interesting point for investigation.

When designers work with these public conversations, they are working at the intersection of several interlocking systems: the system of the neighborhoods, networks of social good organizations, the local business economy, as well as government. When Donella Meadows was writing about systems, she introduced the concept of "leverage points" strategic places within a system where a small shift can lead to a significant change in system behavior or outcomes. These points are not regularly distributed throughout the system, but represent key nodal points that might vary in effectiveness or impact. Meadows categorized these leverage points into twelve levels of impact ranging from locally impactful within a particular subsystem to paradigmatic. Considering Donella Meadows' concept of "leverage points" in light of Peter Suber's *Nomic*, it becomes clear that she is articulating the degree to which the system's rules are either mutable or material. As leverage points move toward level 1—the "power to transcend paradigms" (p. 132; see the complete table of leverage points below), the leverage point that Meadows considers the most powerful—the manifestation of the leverage point becomes more materially, even linguistically diffuse.

Most "regular" games operate at Meadows' level 12, meaning a game is played by manipulating a set of game constants into a more desirable configuration. However, games like *Nomic* or *1000 Blank White Cards* operate at Meadows' level 4 or 5. These levels contain rules that materialized through rule sheets in games and as statutes, laws, or constitutional provisions in society. Games that center around game conversations are conceptually slippery. Suber notes nomic games are fraught with the potential for paradox—especially when rules countermand other rules.

	Meadows' Leverage Points	How do they exist in the world?	Material/ Immaterial
1	The power to transcend paradigms.	Tacit understandings.	Immaterial
2	The mindset or paradigm out of which the system—its goals, structure, rules, delays, parameters—arises.		
3	The goals of the system.	Usually unspoken, but articulate-able.	
4	The power to add, change, evolve, or self-organize system structure.	Contained in a ruleset, materialized as a hierarchical set of laws.	
5	The rules of the system (such as incentives, punishments, constraints).		
6	The structure of information flows (who does and does not have access to information).	Materialized as a network.	(Mostly) Material
7	The gain around driving positive feedback loops.	Materialized within the system itself (as control system or reward system such as money, resources, popularity, and thermostats).	
8	The strength of negative feedback loops, relative to the impacts they are trying to correct against.		
9	The lengths of delays, relative to the rate of system change.		
10	The structure of material stocks and flows (such as transport networks, population age structures).	Materialized as infrastructure.	
11	The sizes of buffers and other stabilizing stocks, relative to their flows.	Materialized as warehouses, reservoirs, streams, forests, oceans, and ecosystems.	
12	Constants, parameters, numbers (such as subsidies, taxes, standards).	Standards applied to the material that the system is processing.	

Figure 18: Collated from Meadows (1999) with the two rightmost columns by the author.

Game conversations are key to developing a prototypical situation where participants can explore, modify, and amend rulesets to understand the consequences of their modifications. Conversation is necessary to constitute a system in which participants can rectify imbalances in the system. While all games have a degree of conversation baked into the game experience, *nomic* games foreground conversation.

CONCLUSION

Playing with ideas within a ludic space enables creativity and experimentation in civic conversations. The careful planning and use of things—objects, spaces, and systems—cultivate meaningful and impactful civic conversations. These elements act as scaffolds by providing tangible and visual aids that help participants engage more deeply with civic topics. Establishing clear boundaries and rules provides a framework for productive discourse while encouraging turn-taking and active participation. By creating an environment where participants feel free to explore and innovate, conversations can lead to more innovative solutions and stronger community bonds. By grounding abstract concepts in the physical, conversations become more inclusive and dynamic, enabling diverse voices to contribute meaningfully.

CHAPTER 7

Fostering Authentic Participation

INTRODUCTION

We were short by a few table facilitators. The My Brother's Keeper community conversation at the Allegheny County Housing Authority Homestead Apartments Community Room was about to start, and we still had two tables that needed coverage. I had sent messages to anyone I thought might be available, but there was no response. The Homestead Apartments have a robust service plan for elderly persons, and with the meeting in the building, we were getting even more attendees than we were expecting. Slipping into one of the empty chairs with the facilitator's agenda and briefing document in hand, I waited while my colleague opened the conversation and welcomed the introductory speaker to the microphone. The meeting room set aside for senior citizens' activities was exceptional. The chairs were comfortable, and the overhead lighting was bright without being harsh. The room's floors were covered by a thick, plush industrial carpet that muted excessive noise but was still a stable and firm walking surface. I remember thinking that, of all the meetings I had hosted in Pittsburgh, this was the space that was clearly the nicest, the most well-appointed, and well-maintained. I made a mental note to check on scheduling future events in this space.

As the introductory speaker outlined the importance of the evening's conversation, describing the challenges faced by young men and boys of color in Pittsburgh and the systemic barriers they face, I quickly reviewed the facilitator's agenda. I had written much of it and designed it, but using it to facilitate (when I had planned to collect observational data for our post-meeting evaluation) made me review my own design work. After the introductory speaker finished, the first question for me to field was a "softball"—an easy warm-up question designed to break down social barriers between strangers at the table: "Let's take just a moment to go around the table, share your name, what part of town you live in, and what brought you to this meeting tonight."

Following my script and modeling the introduction for the other participants, I introduced myself by name. I mentioned that I was here as part of the organizing team, and I hadn't planned to facilitate a table tonight. But we were glad that many people came and I had just switched roles to help with this important conversation. Perhaps I overemphasized the word "important," but the young woman in her early 20s sitting across from me didn't wait to speak up next. She introduced herself by name and then shared that she was one of her parents' four children. The rest of her siblings were brothers, and she was the only one of her parents' children still alive. She said that this conversation was necessary because the work we hoped to do was important. She was here tonight because no one should ever have to lose a brother.

The table sat silent.

Several breaths were taken before anyone spoke. An older woman broke the silence, saying, "Let's see what we can do, then." The young woman's story produced a moment that could not have been designed but could be designed *for*. Sharing her raw and personal story shifted the mood of the table and underpinned that night's work with a different sense of urgency. The confluence of circumstances and design work that had led us all to the Homestead Apartments Community Room on a Wednesday night in September provided an opportunity for the group of us at the table to participate authentically. Each night, when hosting a meeting, I aim to create a space where people can engage with honesty, openness, and sincerity. For participants, this means sharing genuine thoughts and feelings while truly hearing the thoughts and feelings of others. Authentic participation requires vulnerability, willingness to be honest about experiences and viewpoints, and a commitment to co-producing the environment where the conversation takes place. This kind of participation helps build trust, mutual understanding, and meaningful connections among participants.

EMBODIED PARTICIPATION

Embodiment is an odd thing to talk about. To some, to state that an experience is "embodied" might not seem that useful. However, if you think about it, it's not possible to disentangle bodies from thinking, knowing, and acting. Following the writings of Hubert Dreyfus, we understand that it is only through our bodies that humans relate to one another and the world. The most disembodied experiences I can think of—reading, using the computer, and listening to music—might be cognitively rich. However, they are all still experiences tied to a body with a heart that beats and lungs that breathe. To think about embodied participation is not to argue that some participation is embodied and some is disembodied. Rather, embodiment highlights the richness of potential engagement of bodies when we think about participation.

For the sake of this discussion, we will not discuss neuroscience, brain chemistry, or the network of biological systems, but we will rely on this example from sociologist Harry Collins (2000). Say that we were to imagine that knowledge could be transferred between two people using a sort of "mad scientist" type knowledge-transfer device. Hooking my brain up to the brain of a basketball player to transfer their knowledge of basketball playing to me would be a useless exercise. The basketball star is likely much taller, has a physique developed over years of dedication to the sport, and might even have superior fast-twitch muscle fibers due to their particular genetic advantage. If I tried to use this newly transferred basketball knowledge, it would likely result in me throwing out my back. I'd probably seriously injure myself if I attempted to utilize the player's running, jumping, blocking, or shooting skills in an entirely different body. Our brain-to-brain knowledge transfer device might be able to transfer the memories of basketball playing, but much of the knowledge of playing is not in the brain but distributed throughout the arms, legs, and core musculature.

Thomas Nagel also writes about this challenge of the non-transferability of knowledge and perception in his famous essay "What is it like to be a bat?" The bat flying around "seeing" the world by emitting hypersonic yips and gauging its sonic echoes off different objects and insects is knowledge partially embedded in the bat's physicality. It is simply incommensurate with human knowledge and experience—even if we could transfer knowledge by hooking up my brain to the bat's.

Therefore, when we talk about embodiment with participation and community engagement, we highlight there is some non-transferable, non-articulable knowledge that each participant brings to the community conversation through the sum of their lived experience. People know "what it is like" to live in a neighborhood or ride a particular train over 200 times a year. Inviting people to "participate" in an embodied way asks them to bring their complete perspectives on their lives to share with their neighbors.

Looking back to Chapter 5, we discussed the importance of planning not just the words of the civic conversation, but also planning for things. Beyond the words and the things, one important aspect was only touched on in our earlier chapter. When a participant is invited to engage with their body, more of the person's intelligence is brought to bear. If you ask someone to build a model, draw a diagram, or even arrange post-it notes on the wall, you are asking them to use the knowledge of their bodies in concert with their cognitive abilities.

Importance of Physical Engagement

Participatory environments are an open and responsive architecture in which people can engage. Here, I use the word architecture in its broadest sense—meaning not only the space defined by the building itself but the set of cultural constructs that are organized around the building and the way that particular building is placed or invested with cultural and behavioral understandings of appropriate interactions (Harrison & Dourish, 1996). Returning to the civic conversation, a building might be considered a participatory environment in a similar sense as the types of games elaborated upon earlier. A building has designed inputs, rule structures, system controls, and known outputs. Yet the power of the material structure of participatory environments is sometimes obscured from the users—and even creators—of those architectures.

I participated in Priscilla Cheung-Nainby's 2016 workshop at the Design Research Society conference. Cheung-Nainby has developed a freeform method of using bamboo sticks, strings, binding materials, and paper tags to allow people to construct brainstorming artifacts that are also three-dimensional concept maps or system maps. The experience is compelling, but Cheung-Nainby's descriptions of the experience of participation in this format—that participants are "designing by envisioning and enacting participants' collective imagery in physical forms in an iterative cycle of deconstruction, construction, and reconstruction" (Cheung-Nainby et al., 2016) or that "[t]he structural connectedness of ideas and data give rise to the creative emergence of a design concept" (Mulder-Nijkamp &

Chueng-Nainby, 2015)—downplays perhaps the most fundamental point of the experience: the process-light co-construction of a three-dimensional representation of a problem space puts the bodies of the participants into a different relationship with the artifacts of the conversation. Participants are not facing the ideation space (whiteboard) or surrounding the ideation space (co-design activities) but are in and around an immersive ideation space.

In Cheung-Nainby's workshops, connecting tags and sticks of bamboo while having a conversation about their meaning is an inherently embodied activity. Reshaping the form of the conversation by asking participants to engage by making creates new and different opportunities for people to relate to one another. People can step up, move back, walk around, even go inside the central sculpture, and view it from different perspectives.

Constellating with Communities

The technique of constellating was developed by psychotherapist Anton "Bert" Hellinger, originally as a method for exploring the nuances of interpersonal family dynamics and the impacts of generational trauma. Over time, this method from family systems therapy has evolved to applications in organizational and systems theory work and has been applied in business, academic, and civic contexts. Drawing from existential phenomenology, this unique method aims to help participants reveal a pattern of relationships (Wade, 2004). This is done through a deceptively simple-seeming approach of asking people to embody different aspects of a system and having another person (the "constellator") position them in relation to one another. Once the people are positioned, the constellator can ask them questions.

In constellating, people role-play beyond simply assuming another person's characteristics. A person might be asked to role-play elements of built or natural systems (like a river, bike path, or coal barge), abstract concepts (such as economic development forces, social or political movements), or even systemic controls (e.g., laws, policies, or bureaucratic institutions). Essentially, participants are asked to volunteer to embody any aspect relevant to the system of relationships under consideration (Arnold, 2016; Arnold & Fischer, 2018). There is no requirement that the role-play characters are of the same level of abstraction or the same "type." A conversation might be elicited between a person embodying a network of bike paths and another embodying restrictive zoning laws as a third person role-plays a local business owner. For the sake of memory, participants might hold signs or wear nametags that help other participants remember the network of relationships.

The constellator then asks what people see from their different vantage points. Drawing from the efficient and engaged work of Helen Wade (2004), these questions should center around five different concept areas:

1. **Time** might be the history of an organization or the evolution of particular competencies.
2. **Give-and-take** involves exchanges with other parts of the system, like systems of remuneration or other value exchange.
3. **Roles and functions** of the different parts of the system, suppliers, competition, upstream allies.
4. The **hierarchy** of relationships between the different elements being embodied, networks of priority.
5. Feelings of **belonging**, or examining where loyalties, partnerships or conflict emerge.

Wade's method aims to construct and illuminate the relationships between different elements of a system. Conducting a workshop with a facilitator trained in constellation techniques can reveal patterns of relationships that might become salient when they are embodied by participants. They can literally speak back to you.

Coming Together as an Embodied Practice

Physical relationships also, like city systems, are dynamic and evolve over time. My work with Dalcroze Eurhythmics practitioner Stephen Neely reveals the value of examining temporal aspects of human experience (Neely & Arnold Mages, 2024). Eurhythmics is a practice of synchronized movement that principally informs the performance of Western Classical-style music. This kind of engagement has broader implications for understanding human experience. For example, when people come together to perform a collective action, the act of coming together may occur in several

> *Entrainments can happen between people and other people or creatures, people and things, people and natural systems, and things and natural systems.*

different and definable ways, depending upon what kind of coming together is happening. We call this act of coming together an *entrainment*, meaning essentially a synchronization of one person or group with another. Entrainments can happen between people and other people or creatures, people and things, people and natural systems, and things and natural systems. These different entrainments can each have a different character that an interested designer might well be interested in.

For our civic conversations, consider the "syncing up" that occurs, the confluence of time arcs that each participant moves on as they journey to and away from the collaborative event that is our meeting. Traveling across town on buses, trains, ride-share services, or private vehicles, they all arrive at the arbitrarily chosen mechanical time of 6:30 pm for check-in. As participants struggle with whatever mode of transit they need to attend the meeting, they remain fixed upon a *mechanical* entrainment of being at a specific place for the start time at 6:30. Here, broader action is organized by the mechanical and unrepentant start time of 6:30.

A different kind of embodied entrainment might happen during the conversation. As participants queue and file in the door or out at the end of the event, they exhibit *subconscious* entrainment. All of them move together as a group, coordinating with one another without seeming to coordinate. With subconscious entrainments, offering familiar cues that don't require much thought to follow provides a smooth and familiar path for participants. Subconscious entrainments are evident when participants feel "swept up" with emotion or become "carried along" in the conversation and could lead to participants adopting the prevailing attitudes held by strong-willed or vocal participants.

A designer might help people come together in a more *choreographed* way. Perhaps participants all give similar introductions or play a game that incorporates highly scripted turn-taking. Having a group entrain together in a choreographed way will often take a bit of instruction or training as the group members learn a more structured script for behavior.

Designing to get people to come together or *entrain* mechanically, subconsciously, or choreographically are common design tasks. Think of the set of signals that an industrial designer places at the edge of a moving walkway to show people that they must "match up" with the speed of the walkway. Walking on a crowded city sidewalk or being swept up in a protest march is a potent subconscious activity as deeply seated as animals moving in a herd or birds in a flock. The final two modes of entrainment are the most complex and challenging to design for but can be held as aspirations that may not always be attainable.

An example of *algorithmic* entrainment might be seen in a sports team, where everyone shares goals, directions, and knowledge of a set of patterns of movement and response that might advance the entrained group toward a goal. Think of the dynamic "plays" of a skilled soccer or basketball team. A goal and a means are agreed upon, and a set of general motions are prescribed, but entrained members make responsive choices to move the group toward a goal. To apply this coming together in the design of a civic conversation, you might think of your own events team, working together with a prepared set of "plays" to ensure a successful event for the participants. Algorithmic entrainment might even be a set of responses to emerging circumstances. For example, a "play" I had discussed with my team before it was necessary was "helping people in distress." We hypothesized that, at some point, we might have an angry participant who wanted to disrupt the meeting. We discussed nonviolent ways to engage with the person and some approaches for safely de-escalating difficult situations. We didn't realize that it would be many months before we needed that "play." When the time came, it wasn't a belligerent person but someone who was under the influence of alcohol. Despite the incongruity, the team kindly helped this individual to a place where they could relax, and engaged with them in a respectful, caring way.

Improvised entrainments are perhaps the most sophisticated and flexible network of embodied relationships. They cannot be designed but may be fostered through design. A group of participants who are aware and responsive, who are collaboratively co-authoring a discussion or deeply engaging in a community-focused co-design session are the context where improvised entrainments may emerge. Improvised entrainments are different than a skillful facilitator artfully guiding the conversation. Rather, they involve participants exchanging leadership with one another, perhaps contributing their expertise as appropriate and receding when different expertise is needed. The phenomenological characteristics of a group coming together in improvised entrainments are like the togetherness found in improvisatory jazz ensembles (Barrett, 2017; Hagberg, 2014)—the group is of "one mind" or "one heart" as they play together.

In an example more legible to civic practitioners, Jilly Traganou (2019) described the case of an improvised coming together at the Standing Rock protest against the proposed construction of an oil pipeline under the Missouri River. To support the protest, the group engaged in an embodied improvisation of labor division. With no designated leader and no imposed hierarchy, camp residents took on roles such as cooking, sourcing food supplies, and installing solar energy. Others focused on protest activities like sign-making, occupying spaces, and enacting resistance. This dynamic organization of tasks reflected the complexity of society itself. At Standing Rock, the camp's resistance came to life through this embodied network of coordinated actions and material flows, culminating in a powerful act of improvisatory coming together.

Techniques for Fostering Embodied Participation

Not all approaches need to be as radical or dramatic as the ones listed above. Embodied participation can be fostered by acts as simple as collaboratively building a model of ways that we hope to redesign our city or even a simple act of putting stickers on a shared map.

Although many might consider a map a simple and inert object, the participants' interactions revealed its dynamic role in shaping their dialogue. This map was initially provided to the participants in the Route 51 redesign project so they could mark important locations like homes, places of work, and "third places" like favorite shopping, exercise, or social spots. Yet the map dominated the participants' discussion past its intended use in the first exercise. Its central position on the table and the initial directive to mark places with colored dots transformed the map into a focal point, influencing throughout the session. The map remained active, as participants gestured to it and waved hands over areas as they talked. Even though the meeting agenda moved on to other activities, the participants were reluctant to end their embodied relationship with the map.

Courtesy of PennDOT and the Remaking Cities Institute.

143

The image on page 143 provides a clear example of embodied participation. Even though one participant is speaking, all participants are oriented around the map. The dominance of this forceful object remained evident throughout the session. In the context of map's mediation, the different models of corridor development were taken hyper-literally. Participants discussed each model and pointed to locations where two large destination developments might be located, then discussed specific locations for each neighborhood center. Although they were not asked to do so, they discussed the possible consequences of uncontrolled development and specific neighborhoods that might be vulnerable.

Toward the end of the meeting, I walked up to take a few final photos, and the participants turned to me as one. "Well, we've decided," one of the participants said with a clear sense of accomplishment. Gesturing at the map, he stated, "We want a transit-oriented development here, this part to be a green boulevard. This section should have neighborhood destinations." The relationships enabled by the map facilitated a collective decision-making process, underscoring the surprising power of physical objects to mediate complex discussions and foster unity. The event emphasized how much more powerful these discussions can be when participants have something to *do* as well as something to *say*.

Ambiguous Objects

Design researcher Estefania Ciliotta Chehade developed the practice of making conversational facilitative objects. These abstract shapes are used as material prompts to inspire participants to think about their culture and share stories and cultural associations. About the size of a paperback book, each facilitative object is an abstract outline that can relate to any number of concepts or material artifacts. The toy-like quality of Ciliotta Chehade's objects invites people to play with them, hold them up, compare them to one another, and even to mime behaviors with them.

This playful engagement creates a shared physical and emotional experience, fostering deeper connections and opening doors to mutual understanding.

While it is tempting to think of these things as foremost being material, they also demonstrate and shape embodied relationships. Physical interaction with these objects encourages participants to express themselves not just verbally but through gestures and movements. This playful engagement creates a shared physical and emotional experience, fostering deeper connections and opening doors to mutual understanding. The facilitative objects become extensions of the participants' thoughts and feelings, representing aspects of their personal history as connected to their cultures.

They illustrate how design can transform abstract concepts into tangible, interactive experiences that enrich the dialogue and promote genuine, embodied participation.

Objects don't need to be entirely abstract to foster an embodied relationship. Delanie Ricketts and Dan Lockton (2019) developed a toolkit of paper representations of natural phenomena. These models of mountains, trees, and weather events invited participants to build landscapes that reflected their experience of working together on a project. By arranging these facilitative objects, the conversations about the work project teams engaged in were further empowered by the structured yet improvisatory format. The act of constructing these landscapes and attributing names to elements (e.g. "plateau of exhaustion," "hell," and "marsh of uncertainty") illustrates how physical and metaphorical language can merge, helping participants articulate their experiences in a shared, embodied way.

These models also have a utility that is active across levels. The methods Ricketts and Lockton discussed have applications that range from individual reflection to small-group, community-based participatory design workshops. The creation of fantasy landscapes as metaphors could be constituted in a larger, more durable way to create public environments where residents could engage with and play with their ideas and landscapes of thought. Embodied participation can help communities reflect on and learn about their collective thinking, enhancing shared understanding and collaborative problem-solving.

Overall, manipulatable play-able things like Ciliotta Chehade's "evocative objects" and Ricketts and Lockton's "mental landscapes" invite participants to engage more fully with their whole bodies. Beyond sitting and talking, creatively engaging in this way offers an opportunity for people to embody their experiences in physical forms. Through these activities, participants can better express and understand their emotions and thoughts related to the more abstract work of government and policymaking.

DESIGNING FOR LISTENING

When we discussed conversation in the introductory chapter, one of my first steps was introducing conversation as interlocking loops of thinking, saying, and listening. Since that introductory chapter, we have talked about conversation in a more holistic sense, thinking about how to set up conversational systems that help people have the conversations that they want to have. We have discussed how the conversational environment is surrounded by spaces, engaged with and supported by material and processual things. Let's devote a section of this chapter to thinking about designing for listening.

Designers might be tempted to think about designing for listening in the same way they think about using negative space in physical designs. But designing for listening is more than shaping an absence. Listening is an active and aware mode of noticing, relating, and reflecting. Listening well means connecting what is being said to a wealth of knowledge and experiences oriented toward constructing new meanings. Throughout this section, we

> *Listening well means connecting what is being said to a wealth of knowledge and experiences oriented toward constructing new meanings.*

will discuss some approaches that can enhance participants' listening activities. As discussed in previous chapters, material forms can play an influential role in shaping behavior and creating space for listening. Cards, map-making, and model-play will be discussed with an emphasis on how these things shape opportunities for listening and provide gateways for deeper engagement. These approaches transform listening from passive reception into an engaged, co-creative process that enriches both the listener and the speaker, ultimately leading to more meaningful and impactful outcomes.

Techniques for Enhancing Listening

Prompt Cards That Ask Participants to Respond to Each Other

Apples to Apples, a game by Mattel, asks participants to create nonsensical and humorous matches between "red apple" and "green apple" cards.

One technique that can be applied in civic events is to design and use cards to create structured cycles of prompting and responses. They ask participants to engage with and respond to one another. To illustrate this approach, we will discuss the popular card games *Apples to Apples* and *Cards Against Humanity*. Both use the same mechanic of play, asking each participant to match one central prompt card with one of the response cards they hold. Through these examples, we will see how each creates space for listening by focusing participant attention on engagement with others' responses.

Apples to Apples is a card-matching game played in a small group. Players attempt to win the subjective judgment of the player acting as the judge for a given round of play. The game is played using two types of cards: red cards and green cards.

All players are dealt a few red cards containing descriptions of persons, places, things, or events. Each player plays the role of judge for a round. When the judge's role passes to a player, they draw a card from the second pile of green cards, each of which contains a description of a characteristic. All other players, choosing from their hands of red cards, offer a potentially matching person, place, thing, or event for the drawn characteristic.

All players submit their cards face down, and the judge mixes them and reads each match aloud. As an informal part of the gameplay, players may make suggestions or advocate that the judge choose or disregard a particular match. *Apples to Apples* cards contain people from US and European pop culture, such as "David Beckham (1975-, soccer player whose ball-bending kicks inspired a movie title and landed him a posh Spice Girl.)"; places like "Dog Parks (Where dogs go to scratch and sniff.)"; and things, such as "Twilight (The diffused quality of light that occurs when the sun dips below the horizon. Very flattering for vampires.)" (Kirby, et al., 2010). These can be matched with descriptors like: "Delicious," "Xenophobic," and "Old-fashioned." The player acting as the judge awards the best match to a given player.

Because of the limited number of cards a player might have in their hand and the random choice of cards selected from the pile, most matches are imprecise. At the mercy of the judge's subjectivity, the award of a win for a particular round may be the most humorous or the most bizarrely creative rather than the most accurate match. This imprecision requires players to listen carefully and understand the judge's perspective, perhaps sparking nonsensical conversations about whether Beyoncé is more depressing than Area 51. Players use their listening and personal knowledge about the judge's likes, dislikes, personal history, and inside jokes to offer matches that appeal to their sensibilities.

While the game fosters conversations, the gameplay itself offers structure and limits, providing topical information and a forum for discourse centered around the topics the cards present. Listening plays a crucial role as players gauge the judge's reactions and preferences. Still, the conversations typically do not venture into participants' personal lives, expose personal attitudes or beliefs, or open discussions on more significant issues. *Apples to Apples* guides the interaction primarily through the content, colors, and typefaces on the cards. The game's content and activities, rather than content generated by the players, steer interaction, making listening an essential skill for winning.

The gameplay of *Cards Against Humanity* (*CAH*) closely mirrors that of *Apples to Apples*; however, the cards' content is much more provocative. The tagline on the game's box, "A party game for horrible people," reflects the edgy attitude of its creators. In *CAH*, players are dealt ten white cards containing references to people, events, activities, or concepts. Unlike *Apples to Apples*, *CAH*'s references are often risqué or obscure and include sexual content, visceral imagery, and charged racial content. Prompt cards such as "Donald Trump's first act as president was to outlaw _____." or "Batman's guilty pleasure is _____." elicit responses that can range from humorous to offensive (Dillon, et al., 2017). Controversially, a significant number of cards contain charged racial content directed toward Black people (Strmic-Pawl, 2016).

Reviewers note that the game allows players to bypass social norms of politeness (Dean et al., 2015; Brooks, 2016). I would go further. Using the cards as a medium, players can express racist, sexist, or otherwise inappropriate behavior without taking personal responsibility. The game's thrill comes from this delegation of bad behavior to the cards, providing a sense of "safe" transgression. Players can make controversial statements through the game artifacts and absolve themselves of responsibility by saying, "It's not me, it's the cards." Working at the limits of what is acceptable and sometimes transgressing those limits requires players to listen carefully to gauge the reactions of others and to understand the boundaries of the group's collective sense of humor.

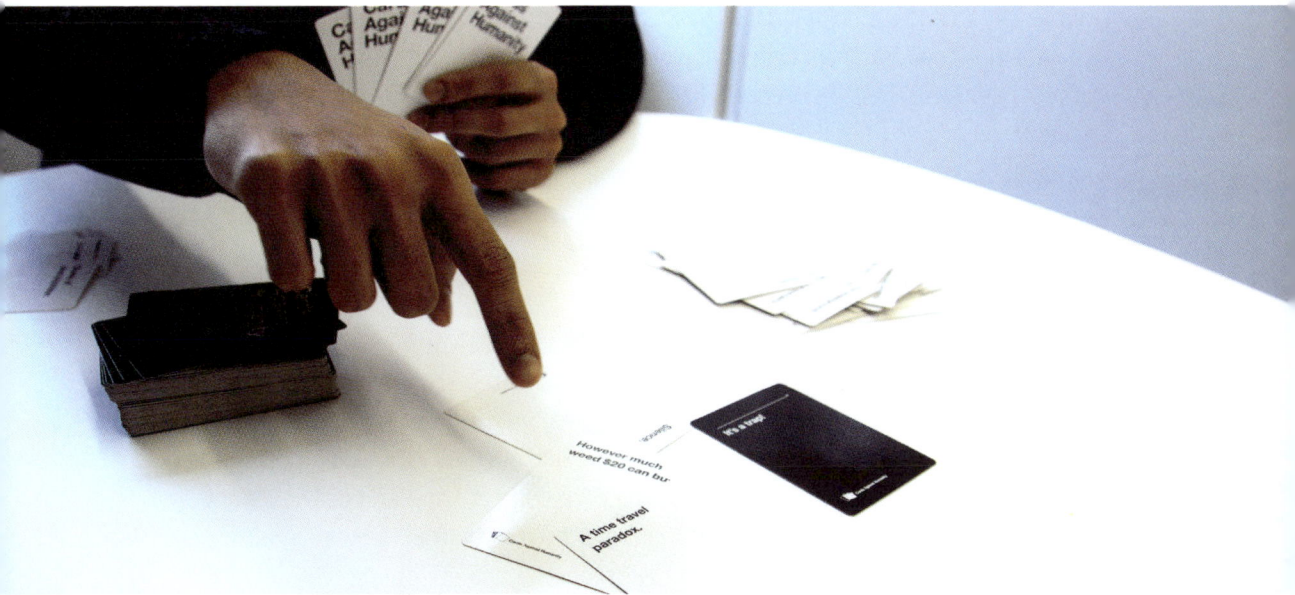

Cards Against Humanity has identical game mechanic as Apples to Apples, but the content is very racy, resulting in very different gameplay.

Similar to *Apples to Apples*, *CAH*'s gameplay offers the opportunity to argue the superiority of a player's match over another. While it might be delightfully absurd to advance a rationalization on the point of whether "Skunks" or "Running out of Toilet Paper" is more "Explosive" (*Apples to Apples*), the experience of *CAH* is derived primarily from vicariously feeling transgression through the medium of the objects. To keep their distance from this transgression, in the gameplay I experienced, players are sometimes hesitant to advocate for a particular match. Therefore, they are not enticed to add to the game from their own life experiences or perspectives. The game becomes about recombining and regurgitating the content provided by the game designers rather than exposing the personalities or humor of the people who play the game.

To state this more directly, the materialization of the statements as cards allows players to delegate racist, sexist, or otherwise socially inappropriate behavior to the game objects. In *CAH*, the thrill of the gameplay comes from the titillating experience of delegating bad behavior to the objects of the game. Players are allowed to say taboo things or make controversial statements through the game artifacts and are absolved of responsibility for the inappropriate remarks: "No friends, it is not I who say these things, it is these damned cards. I am merely an innocent bystander."

What can we learn from these approaches? If you are working with difficult material that people may be reluctant to speak about, the power of delegation can offer a way to engage with it. However, you should allow participants to maintain a critical emotional distance. One danger is that difficult content may result in a gameplay experience that revolves around manipulating the pre-existing content of the cards rather than the unique knowledge or wisdom of the participants. Listening becomes crucial as players navigate these boundaries, deciding how far they can push the envelope while remaining within the group's comfort zone.

Prompts as Creative Catalysts

One early example of a game-like experience serving as a creative catalyst is the *Oblique Strategies* cards created by Brian Eno and Peter Schmidt. *Oblique Strategies* is a deck of cards that function as creative prompts when a person is stuck, trying to generate new ideas, or change approaches. When using these cards, the user thinks of the problem or the challenge at hand and draws a card randomly from the deck. Some cards contain statements like "Remove specifics and convert to ambiguities" or "Honor thy error as a hidden intention". Part of the experience of using *Oblique Strategies* is the moment of surprise and confrontation between the card and the user. Turning over the card and being confronted by disruption is the essential element. To quote Eno on the materiality as a function of use:

> I would go into the studio with a list of ideas I wanted to remember. [...] They were difficult to use in a list because you tended not to be so surprised by them. You would just go to the one that was least disruptive. Whereas I found I put them on cards, and I found if you pulled a card out, and you said to yourself 'I'm going to do whatever this card tells me', then you would get somewhere interesting, because it would break you out of your rut. It would push you into a kind of behavior you wouldn't normally make, and sometimes that was very productive. (Cocker, 2010)

In considering the aspects of play (solitaire and catalyzing creativity) within the context of conversation, a person approaches a deck of *Oblique Strategies* cards with an unspoken question in mind. The deck serves as an oracle, offering godly wisdom to the supplicant. These cards are crafted to fulfill a distinct purpose: inspiring creative action. The challenges inherent in creative endeavors often involve move-making in a field of incomplete information, further complicated by the uncertainty of the final form the creative work will take. The process of engaging in creative acts is consistent across diverse fields, such as painting, filmmaking, design, and music composition. Thus, the open-ended poetic nature of the *Oblique Strategies* statements enables them to function effectively regarding a wide range of creative problems. Unlike *CAH*, which is anchored to its specific topical associations, *Oblique Strategies* rely on eliciting a response from the user's existing knowledge and associations. The surprise and cognitive dissonance triggered by the card's statement drive the creative process forward, prompting the user to find innovative solutions.

Oblique Strategies supports active listening by encouraging users to listen to their own internal responses. While *Oblique Strategies* does not attempt to carry on a lengthy, complex conversation, it was created to give effective responses in a specific context. Unlike *CAH*, which offers prurient or provocative content, *Oblique Strategies* cards rely on evoking a response from the user's own internal content. This dynamic interaction between the card and the user leverages the user's intelligence and creative thinking. In a sense, it prompts you to do the creative work yourself.

Oblique Strategies was composed by Eno and Schmidt to solve the creative block; users might be thought of as engaging in a time-shifted conversation about creative direction with Eno and Schmidt. With the framing given by the instructions card, the replies received are situated in response to a creative block and are engaged by applying the response in creative activity. One might think of *Oblique Strategies* as a conversation with an Eno/Schmidt-powered creative block chatbot. Although chatbots algorithmically reflect statements back to the user, *Oblique Strategies* is more of a conversation with human intelligence, albeit deferred.

Considering the *Oblique Strategies* messages, some cards read with the air of the last line of a Zen kōan: "Gardening, not architecture," "Be less critical more often," and "Remove specifics and convert to ambiguities" (Eno & Schmidt, 2001). All these phrases can be seen as advice on nearly any topic. This universality speaks directly to the functionality of *Oblique Strategies* as part of a conversational process. Eno and Schmidt's design helps users think processually and relationally rather than remaining stuck on the material work of creativity.

Some cards give a particular direction like, "Take away the elements in order of apparent non-importance" (Eno & Schmidt, 2001); however, this requires the reader's intervention to localize the application of the directions to their work. If one is working on music, "elements" could be interpreted as instruments, melodic ideas, harmonizing orchestration, or rhythmic embellishments. If a user is working on a software application design, "elements" might refer to interface elements, available affordances, or visual stylings like gradients, colors, outlines, and application screen states. Never mind what "apparent non-importance" might be defined as or what the processes for "taking away" might imply for the so-called different elements. The point is to reassess the creative process by reflecting on making, grounded in active listening and interpretation of the card's directive within the context of the user's current project.

> *Tools like Oblique Strategies and Change Cards create space for listening in creative and problem-solving processes.*

The technique of *Oblique Strategies* has inspired other similar tools. In the realm of public policy, the United Kingdom's government Policy Lab created a set of cards called *Change Cards* (Policy Lab, 2015) that function similarly. *Change Cards* is a deck of 45 provocations divided into six categories for different types of challenges. Not all categories have the same number of cards, and the text of some cards is specific to the British government. The *Change Cards* focus on broadening the user's perspective by reframing problems, considering different perspectives, and exploring new approaches and resources.

By engaging with these cards, users are invited to listen actively to their own responses and those of their peers, deepening their understanding and reflection. This listening-centric approach encourages creativity and facilitates a collaborative environment where ideas can be shared and developed more effectively. Interested designers might create their own set of ambiguous prompts to use in civic projects. They could use them in a testing environment and notice how the structured nature of turn-taking and listening moments scripted by gameplay affects participants.

Tools like *Oblique Strategies* and *Change Cards* create space for listening in creative and problem-solving processes. They create opportunities for users to engage more deeply with their thoughts and those of others, promoting a dynamic interplay between external prompts and internal reflections. By doing so, they support the generation of innovative solutions and foster a more nuanced understanding of complex issues.

Listening in the Civic Conversation

Utilizing a deliberative format for our civic conversation informs the kind of listening that is supposed to happen at these events. For most people, the idea of deliberating might bring up thoughts of furrowed brows and faces in intense concentration. Indeed, defining deliberate as a verb ("to deliberate") means thinking carefully about something. Yet, there is another meaning to deliberate as an adjective; to describe something as "deliberate" means that it was done with purpose or intention.

A common facilitation technique for deliberative conversations is to ask for purposes and reasons why. A well-trained table facilitator will only let unqualified statements or assertions pass if the participant explains the reasons for their statement or belief. This attention to the deliberate aspects of speaking reorients the other participants toward careful listening.

Specific activities of the civic conversation can be set up to promote listening. In Chapter 5, we learned about how to design deliberative community conversations. One of the steps of that process is worth extra attention and consideration from the perspective of designing for listening. At the end, when participants deliberated upon the agenda items of the evening, they had an opportunity to ask questions of a resource panel. Each table works together to write a question that a table representative will pose. The collaborative process of question writing begins with the table facilitator recounting questions that were open, things that participants at the table didn't know, and identifying the gaps in the table's collective knowledge.

Collaboratively writing a question that the table *doesn't* know the answer to requires listening, considering, and reflecting on what was said that evening. The table facilitator can help by recounting earlier stopping points from their notes. The room facilitator can help by re-sharing the contextual information shared at the beginning of the meeting, but the most important work of writing these questions lies with the participants. While question writing, participants must listen to one another to attain the goal set for them. The group asks each other where the knowledge gaps lie, suggesting possibilities, going through their conversation notes, and proposing alternatives.

Collaboratively writing the group's unanswered questions is more than an exercise to fill up time at the end of the meeting. The culminating question-and-answer portion of the meeting reframes the civic conversation for participants. Rather than "sharing my idea," participants are "searching for the gaps in our knowledge together." The goal facing the table is to sort through the issue and figure out what we, as a microcosm of the larger community, *don't* know about the issue.

DISCLOSIVE DESIGNING

Disclosive designing is an approach that seeks to uncover hidden or latent issues within systems or communities. Like the surfacing conversation described in Chapter 1, disclosive designing emphasizes the importance of designing to reveal values, issues, and perspectives that may be obvious to some participants but not to others.

Other design approaches might focus on communicating information—telling you something—while disclosive designing creates contexts for interactions. Disclosive designing aims to create experiences that acknowledge and embody a set of learned associations that people may have with images, objects, and spaces. It reveals these to other participants so that associations become visible and legible so they can be a platform for action. Disclosive designing means that through our work, we create the opportunity for participants from one world to see another world meaningfully.

Techniques for Disclosive Designing

There are many possible techniques for disclosive designing, each aimed at challenging perspectives and uncovering latent assumptions. One effective method is using theater to illustrate scenarios from other worlds.

Decision Point is a play that was developed in cooperation with the Carnegie Mellon Program for Deliberative Democracy to explore the issue of abortion with college students. Led by Tim Dawson and featuring a group of professional and pre-professional actors, *Decision Point* used the technique of presenting issues through a series of narrative vignettes. Characters enacted different challenges faced by young women or couples considering abortion. With the aspiration to open a view into another world, presenting these issues though a theater experience, coupled with the knowledge that they would shortly be invited to deliberate upon these issues, implicitly charged viewers to consider the questions that the characters were faced with. Using theater as a disclosive design approach allowed participants to reconsider, clarify, and reshape their own understandings. Theater helped viewers understand how the issue of abortion might be embodied and enacted through private struggles with individual decisions. Disclosive designing through the medium of theater offers a window into those private moments, revealing latent realities rather than the surface political rhetoric.

Beyond depicting specific scenarios, theater can also offer a window into the world of data-based representations that often inform public life. To that end, with a large and multidisciplinary group of colleagues and in collaboration with a local community partner interested in supporting more green spaces in Boston neighborhoods, we developed a practice that we call *community-engaged data theater* (Snyder-Young et al., 2024). This practice involves collecting quantitative data and presenting it through a theater experience. In our explorations, collaborator Jonathan Carr was a skilled practitioner of the improvisatory theater method called *Viewpoints* (Bogart & Landau, 2012), which invites theater participants to improvise non-narrative or movement-based responses to prompts. Here, we substituted prompts that may be more familiar to theater aficionados with quantitative and policy data.

We experimented with representing data using theatrical variables such as time (e.g., tempo, duration, and repetition) and space (e.g., shape, gesture, architecture, and topography). Theater practitioners then developed a set of compositions—brief non-narrative scenes—that depicted different relationships in the data. Re-embodying data collected from participants in the community offered a surprising perspective on the practices of working with data in civic contexts. As the actors worked to show abstract concepts like increasing rent prices or the consequences of the rising displacement of residents that occurred over the years, it became clear that the counts of those occurrences represented the experiences of real families. Even though the medium drew from abstract representations, theater practices offered participants and audience members a window into the experiences of the community. Theater highlighted these experiences by directing all participants to regard the representations with sensitivity and attentiveness to what was unusual about the data. By working through the data and the antecedent human experiences that it represented, participants and audience members were able to rethink the data and their relationships with people's lived experiences.

Whether through theater, mapping, or other semi-structured forms of inquiry, disclosive designing aims to uncover latencies in situations. While it seems simple and straightforward to say, *noticing* is a principal act. In the data theater exercises above, the student actors noticed that the data they were representing ultimately tied back to representations of people's lives, which they wished to represent with dignity and respect. This kind of aware noticing, a prerequisite for all researchers, points to the core act of disclosive designing, which Charles Spinosa (1997) calls "uncovering disharmony."

Uncovering disharmony, as described by Spinosa, involves identifying and addressing underlying conflicts and inconsistencies. In disclosive designing, this concept is crucial for engaging in an activity that amounts to more than just "finding a problem." While it may be a common reaction for skilled designers to start reframing a situation as a set of problems and solutions, uncovering disharmony asks the designer to take a different perspective. If you were to imagine a designer or urban planner viewing a neighborhood like that along Pittsburgh's Route 51, they would have a rich perspective on each of the problems that face that neighborhood. When there is heavy rain, the storm sewers pour collected runoff into the neighborhood's sanitary sewers, causing the combination to flow into the rivers and streams near Route 51. This can be framed as a problem, and it is imminently solvable by renovating these miles of pipe. A problem/solution framing would identify this challenge and seek to apply a solution in response to the known quantity.

However, a designer aiming to uncover disharmony might take a different view. They might regard the combined sewer overflow as manifesting in an area that requires deeper investigation. Projects to reconfigure the network of systems that result in combined sewer overflow might take a variety of approaches that don't submit to being neatly understood as direct action under the problem/solution dichotomy. For instance, rather than proposing and specifying solutions, a designer might engage in the practice of noticing the challenges of this area from a more holistic perspective. They could engage in the everyday activities that a resident or business owner does but with an awareness of what is unusual. The designer might go through the typical activities of conducting civic meetings, interviewing key community stakeholders, and utilizing data analysis of sewer activity—but also others in the corridor. Through intense and ongoing probing of the site, disclosive designing offers a more deeply engaged perspective toward the world in which the designer aims to intervene. It may be that the problem does not need to be "solved" in the traditional sense. Rather, through surfacing the disharmonies of the corridor, we come to a new understanding of the systems and practices of its communities and environments.

Benefits of Disclosive Designing

All the practices discussed above, especially the engaged activity of disclosive designing, aim to improve human society's replete and complex relations with natural systems. At the close of this chapter, I would like to enumerate some of the benefits of designers using these practices. The benefits may be distributed unevenly across a community, some may be realized, and some may be nascent.

Your community may see additional or different benefits than those I describe here. However, I can say that when advocating for this work, these benefits have been quite real, although you might initially miss them.

Solidarity is a feeling that can be ambiguous. It's the feeling that you are "part of something," which may come from direct engagement with a larger group of people or a more symbolic association. For instance, a group of people who engage in the same practices and share the same concerns, like a group of bicycle enthusiasts advocating for more bike lanes, might feel a very active solidarity as they engage in civic conversation with other residents. Many groups could emerge and recognize solidarity with each other. One of the more well-documented groups in my sphere was "hilltop communities" (Crowley, 2011). They emerged after common needs and identities were found through bridging work via partnerships and engagement with the Coro Foundation. These communities found solidarity by recognizing a common set of needs, similar population demographics, and a common relationship between their municipalities and the City of Pittsburgh.

Much has been written about **infrastructure**, the supportive structures that help maintain communities. Here, a significant benefit comes not in what might be typically thought of as infrastructure (e.g., roads and bridges) but social infrastructure. Social infrastructure includes the relationships between neighbors on a street and community knowledge of knowing who to call in the community to address specific challenges or needs. It's the kind of infrastructure that is supported through disclosive designing and civic conversations. You can see it in action when participants stay after a meeting to talk about issues, exchange phone numbers to meet up later to talk, or go immediately for a coffee or beer at a nearby pub. These subtle connections improve community resilience in many different scopes and scales. They are just as much of the connective community tissue as the more material systems that are present in the city.

Social harmony and friendliness might not be the first thing that city staffers consider when thinking of community members. Still, a repeated and committed program of engaged conversation with the community can result in more **conviviality** in our cities. By providing open access to the hidden tools of the city through the medium of civic conversations, residents gain the freedom to engage in new ways with their city government. Our schools, libraries, and community centers are where convivial community emerges, and the impact of engaging with and through these systems lends a tone to our design work and our community convenings that are not accessible if held in, for instance, the offices of the city council.

When community members were asked to redesign a major transportation corridor that spanned multiple municipalities, facilitative things helped them to respond to the challenge. July 14, 2015, Brentwood Public Library. Photo by the author, courtesy PennDOT, Metro 21, and the Remaking Cities Institute.

CONCLUSION

In conclusion, fostering authentic participation is a deeply engaged process that requires more from designers than the typical set of approaches they have used and likely found productive throughout their careers. Rather than a positivist framing of "problems to be solved," fostering authentic participation opens an opportunity for emotionally aware designing. Considering the needs and knowledge of the body, thinking about structuring active opportunities for listening, and engaging with the latencies and hidden layers that exist across communities and environments offer the designer transformative approaches to uncovering and addressing hidden issues within systems and communities. By fostering solidarity, enhancing infrastructure, and engaging with communities in a mutually meaningful and convivial way, designers can support a robust network of engaged community participants. Ultimately, this is how designers contribute to more healthy, beautiful, and vibrant cities.

CHAPTER 8

After the conversation, what to do with the data?

INTRODUCTION

Organizers often see the end of the community conversation as when the participants leave the room. In a successful event, participants recorded contextualizing information regarding the problem at hand and shared and discussed their matters of concern. They felt that they were informed by the views of their neighbors and recorded their perspectives in a structured way that could be shared with policymakers. But ideally, for the organizers, the event continues as they collate the narrative from the community members and frame it for policymakers. A key final step to plan for throughout the process is the collection of evaluative information. Evaluation, in the context of civic conversations, is the use of structured methods and measures to collect information about the validity of the process. For example, if one of the goals of a community conversation is to reach members of an underserved community, only evaluation activities will tell us if that goal was met.

THE CHALLENGES OF EVALUATING CONVERSATION EVENTS

Evaluating conversation events offers various ways to understand the experience. John Gastil (2012) enumerates some of the challenges particular to evaluating deliberative events—a specific subset of conversational events:

> ...a narrow focus on a particular aspect of the event, such as its deliberative quality; the exclusion of attention to important elements of deliberation, such as participant selection and speaking opportunities; an over-reliance on first-person interviews and self-report data; selective vignettes that usually showcase specific participants' positive experiences; particularly compelling moments in an uneven process; the favorable summary judgments of officials or witnesses with no training in ethnography or evaluation; and the optimistic and unsubstantiated attributions of policy or cultural impacts, as proclaimed by public agency staff, columnists, or event organizers. (p. 206)

An additional challenge surfaces when taking a positivist, experimental approach toward understanding conversation events. Validating a method or approach through experimental practices that include an experimental group and a control can prove difficult, even problematic. First, these events are constantly unfolding, producing innumerable variables that are aspects of the experience of the civic conversation. Variables of interest may include the degree to which the issue at hand impacted the lives of the participants, or what the stakes of the discussion were for various participants. Second, many situations can be

> *High-stakes conversations, by definition, have serious consequences for the client participant.*

understood through the lens of the high-stakes or difficult conversation models, which have to do with the history and contingencies of the participants. For example, the participants' own social identity could impede their full participation in a conversation. Past experiences of being made to feel vulnerable or disrespected because of aspects of participants' social identity creates a barrier, preventing them from fully engaging in the conversation. Third, high-stakes conversations, by definition, have serious consequences for the client participant. Those consequences are driven by the specificity of the moment of the conversation. For a researcher to artificially create high-stakes situations to test theories or practices would be challenging and perhaps unethical. Stakes cannot be replicated in an experimental situation.

Experimental situations, by definition, are largely stakes-free zones. For many of the events I conducted, a single representative might attend to share the opinions of a church, neighborhood, or community group. Degrading that person's experience to generate experimental data can degrade, by proxy, the voice of an entire community. Additionally, many of the events conducted served communities that are distressed in some way. People from these distressed communities may also have a history that has been negatively informed by interaction with research experiences. As a researcher observing these events and constructing approaches based on these observations, I closely observed the naturally occurring differences between various events.

Data that Cities Care About

Over a period of three years, I worked iteratively with the City of Pittsburgh, deeply involved in planning and conducting various events in different venues on topics that attracted a variety of participants. After deliberative events, the City of Pittsburgh, guided by our design team, surveyed participants and made that data publicly available via the city's website and through other reporting formats. Invariably, participants were asked to self-report their satisfaction with aspects of the deliberative process. During those three years, the following elements were cited in reports prepared by City of Pittsburgh personnel as evidence of a successful deliberation:

- The number of people engaged through outreach efforts prior to the meeting
- The raw number of people that attended
- The perceived amount of diversity of people that attended
- The participants' self-reported satisfaction levels
- If the city received actionable information from the participants at the event
- If the meeting was conducted in an orderly, efficient fashion
- The general feeling of success of the city staff that attended the meeting

Some of these metrics are quite reasonable for the city to monitor. Several of them require a great deal of subjective interpretation to create an account. Many cannot be recorded in a systematic fashion. Depending upon the city staffer that attends the event, the reports of events may be rather or wildly different. For actionable data across diverse events with different attendees, it is critical to create evaluation processes that can be applied evenly. This does not mean that subjectivity or people's opinions on "How it went" are unimportant. But it is important that subjective metrics be recorded with rigor and presented with sufficient framing.

In community engagement events, institutional evaluation documents nearly always collect the number of people who attended the event. The appeal of collecting attendee numbers is easy to understand; total attendance is easy to collect, and the data is very easy to understand. When considering planning for future meetings, it might be useful to know how much food and how many chairs, tables, moderators, and other elements might be appropriate to provision. Raw numbers of attendees can speak to the success of outreach events that precede the engagement events, but they only sometimes bear upon the quality of the event itself. Regardless of the metrics selected, this kind of digitization of experience is insufficient to tell the full story of a civic conversation.

Another element of data frequently collected by cities is the number of touchpoints. In the context of public outreach, a touchpoint might be any connection between the government and residents: a postcard, an email message, 'impressions' of postings on social media, door-to-door solicitation, or announcements on public access television or through the newspaper. Again, this kind of monitoring may have value for entities within the city that ensure compliance, but this kind of data is ultimately less useful for designers who want to improve their practice.

WHO EVALUATES CONVERSATIONS?

The question of "who evaluates" these events is worth considering. Typically, it is the convening organization or agents of the convening organization who evaluate the deliberative event. More rarely, a participant or witness will write an evaluation of an event. In the course of my work, I have only encountered these accounts when a participant has a negative experience. Caitlyn Luce Christiansen (2017) authored an evaluative account of the public organizational meeting of Indivisible Pittsburgh. She focused on a conversation that happened after the meeting ended, in which two women of color (an attorney and a community activist) confronted a meeting organizer (a Carnegie Mellon faculty member) about the lack of inclusion of people of color in the meeting and the organizational structure of the new organization. The particulars of this account are compellingly written and detail the significant challenges that people experienced, which resulted from a crucial lapse by the organizers of the event. As a tool to improve participant experience from a design perspective, however, this account principally underscores well-understood foundational principles of constructing an inclusive dialog in a public space. An aggregate of personal accounts constructs one aspect or understanding of events.

This is different from saying that informal or de-institutionalized evaluative accounts have lower value to the design process. When designing to engage with communities that have experienced trauma at the hands of other groups, we should center accounts (like Christiansen's above) that question the trustworthiness of the conveners or the convening organization. For many participants, civic conversations are not one-off events but are perceived in the continuum of a history of acts by a political administration or other organization. The above account details a broken trust and the trustworthiness of an organization is itself valuable. Considering the organization by extending the idea of interpersonal trust, people come to a civic conversation with the history of their relationships with organizations and with the hope that positive outcomes will result from the engagement. People from groups that have experienced trauma at the hands of another group may have a deep-seated mistrust of such events. It may take years of successful testing for people to begin to believe that an individual or organization might be trustworthy (Stalvey, 1989).

Evaluation cannot be dissociated from perspective. Evaluation, like any kind of authorship, influences the construction of how the evaluation is framed, how the data that shapes the evaluation is collected, and how it is analyzed. Whether a conversation goes well or poorly offers a perspective on the conversation, which civic conversations contain in multitudes. Even within a city, demographics and interest groups belie a complexity and diversity of perspective that is a rich and fertile ground within which new understandings of the city can grow. One might even hope that, through understanding that ground, there is access to a perspective-less *truth*. However, explicating that richness, attempting to examine every facet of citizen viewpoint and understand the rich histories and perspectives embedded in the participants, is ultimately a futile act.

Touching the depth of experience bound up within each participant that informs the construction of their perspectives can, in the best of circumstances, be an asymptotic exercise. We can approach truth but never arrive at it. However, knowledge creation in civic conversations should not be thought of in such a paralyzing way. Rather, a design researcher may try to understand the convened group as a singular system at the level of the convening. The effect here is not to blunt the richness of the individuals that make up the group but to understand the organism of the group at the moment that the group is brought together. We want to see the group within the context of the event as a particular historical moment and attempt to understand the conversation event and group as a holistic entity.

A rich constructivist approach to evaluation can be found in Egon Guba and Yvonne Lincoln's book *Fourth Generation Evaluation* (1989). According to Guba, four conditions are necessary to start a constructivist evaluation:

1. The study must be pursued in a natural setting (understanding a reality is dependent upon the time and context of the constructors that hold that reality).
2. We cannot frame an evaluative context a priori. We cannot assume what we must ask.
3. Qualitative information must be collected.
4. Tacit knowledge must be incorporated.

My methods of evaluating civic conversations were inspired by Lincoln and Guba's approach. Entering a design situation from the perspective of an engaged learner is a powerful approach to conducting inquiry. If a designer openly acknowledges their inexperience in certain domains of knowledge, it allows that designer to ask questions that, from an embedded practitioner, might seem challenging, rude, or otherwise inappropriate. Apart from the influence that comes from assuming pre-existing knowledge, constructivist evaluation provides designers with a high level of flexibility when entering a new area. This approach acknowledges that knowledge is not fixed and can change based on context and experience. Instead of relying on rigid guidelines or established rules, constructivist evaluation encourages designers to adapt and respond to the specific needs and dynamics of the situation they are working in. This adaptability allows for a more nuanced and responsive design process, where solutions can evolve and improve as new insights are gained and conditions change. Because the designer assumes no prior paradigms of knowledge to work against, they are freed up to subordinate themselves to the needs of the project.

Cities and not-for-profit organizations desire particular forms of evidence. However, this type of evaluation is an emergent process that presupposes nothing; thus, no form of evaluation may be completely constituted in advance. Further, constructivist paradigms of evaluation privilege thick descriptions and qualitative analysis. Constructivist paradigms are ways of knowing that are not easily reducible to scalar values, which is what governments hunger for in their data. Perhaps most problematic, Guba and Lincoln's recursive paradigm has no predictable stopping point. Done properly, constructivist evaluation is completed when consensus is reached. For political processes, this can present particularly knotty problems.

In essence, from a constructivist perspective, it is important to plan evaluation activities with your community stakeholders, with participants, with the people who will be subjects of as well as those receiving and interpreting the evaluation. Having an off-the-shelf checklist for all events will obscure important data that might be localized to a particular conversation, issue area, or group of community stakeholders.

WHAT SHOULD WE EVALUATE?

Starting down the road of evaluation, designers might ask: What kinds of things should we put on our evaluation checklist? If you've just skipped to this section, you might go back and read the earlier part of this chapter, where I've argued that this isn't the best way to construct an evaluation. Ideally, the evaluation procedure flows from the general ethic of the meeting design in a common-sense way. For instance, if we hope that our meeting design will help us reach a particular community, we should plan to collect data in our evaluation that demonstrates whether we were successful or not. If we hope that our meeting design will help people generate creative ideas for neighborhood problems, in our evaluation, we should collect data that shows whether we succeeded in helping people generate creative ideas. Evaluation data can be broken down across some key metrics:

- **Effectiveness**: how well the conversation met its goals
- **Inclusivity**: the extent to which participants' voices were heard and respected
- **Outcomes**: the tangible and intangible results of the conversation
- **Participant satisfaction**: the participants' feelings about the quality of the meeting design

A multimodal approach to evaluation is often the most effective. Each of these metrics can be addressed through a different mode of evaluation. For instance, participant satisfaction and inclusivity might be collected in the exit survey, participant interviews, and observation. If the basis of the evaluation is well-constructed and examines the challenges that the conveners and community hoped to address, then having redundancy in the form and structure of the evaluation will offer a clearer view of what happened in the events.

As discussed earlier in this chapter, it is ideal if the evaluation of the community conversations is co-constructed, that is, if community stakeholders help shape the form and measurements of the evaluation. Too frequently, evaluation is added to an event as an afterthought. Bringing stakeholders to the table to define metrics helps inform the discussion of the workshop design, as well as collaboratively defining what success means for each of the community stakeholders. The following are a types of evaluations that you may want to consider for your civic conversation.

How People Feel

Liz Sanders discusses the problems that non-designers have in attempting to engage in design dialogs during co-design activities:

> One is that too much time is spent on one early idea instead of exploring many possibilities. Another is that it can be difficult to get people to create ideas when they feel that they have insufficient knowledge. A third problem is that people who are brought into co-designing experiences may feel that they are not creative. (Sanders & Westerlund, 2011, p. 1)

While the first and second problems are logistical issues that have been discussed in this book, and can be overcome with proper planning and effective facilitation, the third challenge—whether participants feel creative—is more difficult to surmount. Unfortunately, Sanders does not provide a clear way to understand or recognize success in co-design practice; rather, the topic of the article is how to create co-design spaces that scaffold creative thought by the participants.

The second problem is one with which I have had significant experience. Low domain knowledge might be effectively handled by scoping what is asked of the participants. In a situation where participant domain knowledge is perceived to be low, improved engagement can be found by reframing the question to an area where a broad range of participants can comment (Secko et al., 2009; Burgess, 2014). In the capital budget community forums mentioned in Chapter 4, rather than giving participants play money and asking them to construct a budget themselves, we asked them to comment on their personal and neighborhood dis/agreement with the Mayor's priorities. Participants can be better engaged by moving the problem discussion towards the participants' expertise.

Participants' expertise can be further acknowledged, and designers can address the difficult challenge that Sanders' describes by re-presenting participants' contributions with authority. This may mean designing on-the-fly representations of participants' contributions. Sometimes called *graphic recording* or *graphic facilitation*, trained artists can be hired to make real-time illustrations of participants' contributions that can then be digitally projected back to the meeting. Designers might also prepare digital slideshow templates for participants' quotes, typing them live and projecting the quotes back into the meeting space during the ending phase of the meeting. This type of reflection not only shows participants the respect meeting organizers pay to their contributions, but it these same materials can be shared in reporting as part of the evaluative materials from the meeting.

Outreach Methods

Are our methods of connecting with important community stakeholders and community members successful? Often, we can distribute flyers to neighbors, knock on doors in the days before an event, post on social media, and send emails to community discussion lists. Only a few of these methods will be successful in a particular neighborhood. Different communities often need different tactics for outreach. One community may attend if the meeting is publicized in a popular church newsletter. In some Pittsburgh communities, a church minister mentioning the importance of a particular community conversation from the pulpit was enough to ensure that hundreds of community members turned out. Other communities responded more readily to social media messaging or flyers posted in the windows of local businesses. If designers track what methods help participants feel motivated to attend a community conversation, they can begin to map how to be more efficient in publicizing future events.

Workshop Evaluation

Did we do what we planned to do? How well did our event go? What aspects of the plan were successful, and which need to be reconsidered? Were there any "fatal errors" in planning or execution that created a gap in the participant experience? These questions can be answered in a variety of ways. As mentioned, most evaluations stick to "the counts" or easily recorded data about participants that can be collected passively in exit surveys. The number of participants, participants' demographic information, as well as information about where participants live, are cheap to collect and easy to understand.

From the organization's perspective, the appeal of data like this is hard to ignore. Yet, I would argue that we only should collect data that we can actually *do something* with. Why are we collecting the participant's demographics? Did we make a special effort to reach specific demographic groups? Do we want to know if that effort was successful? Then, great! We have a task to accomplish by collecting that data. If we are merely collecting the data because it might be interesting to someone eventually, the greater likelihood is that we are burdening all people in our system with the extra labor of maintaining that data without a view toward a significant outcome.

Exit surveys can often serve as an effective tool to gauge the impact on participants. The time-honored net promoter score, traditionally a measure of customer satisfaction with businesses, takes the form of a single question: "How likely is it that you would recommend this to a friend or colleague?" This is followed by an eleven-point scale with numbers from 0–10, where 10 means "extremely likely," 5 is neutral, and zero is coded "not at all likely." Responses of mostly 9s or 10s mean that the group was satisfied with the experience to the degree that they would be willing to recommend attendance to neighbors and friends. Scores averaging 6 or lower indicate that participants are more likely to have negative feelings towards the experience and are more likely to speak negatively about it.

Questions on exit surveys can also serve as a collection point for distilled data from the meeting. At the end, when the conversation has been had, and participants have had an opportunity to think deeply about the information, exit surveys can ask participants to record their condensed thoughts and opinions. Asking participants what they think is the single most important issue under discussion can offer a view on the communicative effectiveness of the meeting design. Questions that ask: "Did the meeting cause you to consider points of view that you had not previously considered?" or "Did the meeting make you feel as though your voice has been heard by the city?" or perhaps "...allow you to share stories and experiences with residents from other parts of the City? ...make you more likely to become engaged in making your neighborhood stronger?" specifically address how meetings can be designed to help residents share viewpoints with other residents, and think about how they might translate those viewpoints into actions.

Exit interviews can also measure impact. Be mindful of participants' time when asking for an exit interview. Some participants may be challenged to participate if they are using public transit, in which case, a phone interview is better for follow-up. A brief exit interview of questions like "Were you able to have the conversation you wanted to have tonight?" or "Were your expectations met?" can speak to the match between the participants' preconceptions and the conversation they had at the meeting. Exit interviews are often when residents have combined the information provided with their own opinions and the views of other residents. They will have pithy and valuable feedback to offer. Booking the meeting space for an additional half-hour beyond the meeting time can facilitate a social exit from the meeting and provide a leisurely atmosphere where organizers can talk with a few participants.

Meeting observations, when recorded in a structured way, provide another way to evaluate the quality of work. When meeting observation can be done unobtrusively, it is ideal. Simply taking notes on whether people get to speak without interruption by other participants can provide some perspective on whether the meeting was facilitated effectively. The best practice for meeting observation would be to create a checklist that includes the most salient items that the designers are interested in tracking. An example of room setup is shared below:

- Room setup:
    - ADA Accessible entrance & restrooms
    - Type of tables/chairs
    - Wheelchair adequate space between tables
    - Unobstructed view of projection/lead facilitator
    - Audio amplification used that is compatible with hearing aids
    - Adequate lighting
    - Food/water available
    - Childcare or care assistance available
- Are materials and facilitation available in the preferred language(s) of participants?
- Did staff share supporting materials with participants? (slideshow and briefing doc)
- Did staff/facilitators model respectful behavior to participants?

Straightforward yes/no observational checklists can be implemented by nearly anyone and can support broad data collection across many meetings. By preparing a checklist or heuristic, designers can obtain data that speaks to the quality and effectiveness of their work and can guide the design of future conversations and workshops.

A final note about the evaluation work follows. Evaluation activities can make people nervous. Even when done well and sensitively, evaluating people can remind them of negative experiences from their past or make them feel put "under a microscope" in an uncomfortable way. Further, all civic conversations are done in partnership with community stakeholders, people who manage the building where the event is held, and participants who turn up to share their lived experiences and wisdom with the conveners. Evaluation should begin with the assumption of positive intent from all those involved. Assume that everyone is trying their best for the event. The purpose of these evaluation processes is not to criticize or belittle our partners; it is not an exercise of "grading" our partners. Evaluation works to identify performance gaps—the places in the design where opportunities for improvement exist.

HOW DO WE EVALUATE CONVERSATIONS?

Evaluation activities (as described above) produce two different kinds of data: qualitative (quotes from pullout or exit interviews, focus groups, or the after-meeting discussion with table moderators) and quantitative (participation metrics including demographics, participants feedback on surveys via scores or Likert scale formatted questions). The key to effective evaluation involves combining these two approaches in ways that offer insight into how well the meeting design served the needs of the participants.

One of the primary qualitative approaches involves **pullout or exit interviews**. These interviews are conducted immediately after the conversation to gather in-depth insights into participants' experiences, thoughts, and feelings. These personal interactions allow evaluators to hear individual perspectives, capturing the emotional and cognitive impact of the conversation.

Another effective qualitative method is organizing **focus groups**. These small group discussions facilitate a collective exploration of participants' perspectives, providing a rich tapestry of feedback on the conversation's process and outcomes. Focus groups encourage participant interaction, often revealing collective insights and common themes.

Post-event sessions with table moderators also play a crucial role in qualitative evaluation. Moderators who have guided the discussions are well-positioned to identify key themes, challenges, and successes. Their observations, combined with participants' feedback, offer a comprehensive view of the conversation's dynamics. Ideally, a comprehensive approach is best, but if you can do no other evaluation, this post-event debrief session is perhaps the most valuable and informationally dense.

Finally, all qualitative data collected through interviews and focus groups can be analyzed using **thematic analysis**, particularly grounded theory-based approaches (Charmaz, 2014). This method involves coding and categorizing data to identify recurring themes and patterns, which can provide a deeper understanding of the conversation's impact and effectiveness. This method can be particularly useful for evaluating civic conversations, as it allows designers to uncover underlying themes that might not be immediately apparent. By systematically organizing and interpreting themes, identifying and counting the occurrence of themes can help designers draw meaningful conclusions about the effectiveness and impact of the conversation.

In addition to these qualitative methods, quantitative methods can translate participant data into scores that, properly contextualized for others, offer a view of participants' experiences, satisfaction levels, and agreement or disagreement with policy proposals in a structured format that can be analyzed statistically.

One common tool is the **exit survey**, which is distributed to participants as they leave the event. If organizers wish to measure a change in perspective as a result of the event, a **combined entry/exit survey** can be utilized. Participants complete a survey before and after the conversation, allowing evaluators to assess shifts in attitudes, knowledge, or understanding. While this method is more academic, it provides valuable insights into the conversation's impact on participants' viewpoints.

Another important quantitative measure involves **participation metrics**, particularly demographic data. Tracking who participates in these conversations helps ensure that diverse voices are heard and can highlight any disparities in engagement. Statistical analysis of this data can reveal patterns and trends, informing future efforts to improve inclusivity and representation.

Combining qualitative and quantitative approaches is key to effective and comprehensive evaluation. **Mixed methods** provide a more holistic understanding of civic conversations, merging the richness of personal experiences and the compact nature of numerical data. By integrating insights from interviews, focus groups, surveys, and demographic analysis, evaluators can paint a complete picture of the conversation's effectiveness, inclusivity, and impact.

Evoking the Gradient of Opinion and Knowledge in The Room

Approaching designing for a civic conversation is different from other design activities. When evaluating whether the event was successful or not, quantitative metrics can often tell a story that doesn't align with participants' own experiences. In a subtle and complicated situation like a civic conversation, understanding participants' feelings is worth the effort.

Perhaps the most well-known work on this kind of knowing is Michael Polanyi's writings on tacit knowledge. His ideas highlight how some knowledge is difficult to express in words or measure with numbers. When evaluating both the methods used to tackle a problem and the effectiveness of a conversation, it is important to recognize that these elements often resist straightforward explanation or quantification. This kind of knowledge is often understood through experience and intuition rather than through clear-cut definitions or statistics. As Polanyi tells us, knowing what to look for, having a sense of the qualities of an investigation, and understanding how to extend the inquiry are all based upon a tacit understanding of phenomena (2009). This description is particularly suited to responding to the question of whether a civic conversation is "good or not."

As described by Pelle Ehn (2008), the two central values of participatory design are legitimating democratic participation and informing the design process through participants' tacit knowledge. Though the civic conversation is not participatory design, it is a closely related activity. The central goal of an event is to evoke the gradient of opinion and understanding within the room. Because participants construct their perspective of the issues based on relation to others' perspectives (Spinosa et al., 1997), conversational activity is highly relational.

Outcomes and feedback

> First, from a political standpoint, the senior citizens seemed to be saying, "There is a relationship between mobility and dignity for older people, and when we are isolated to one side of the street we lose self-respect. Further, the government should help older citizens maintain their independence and dignity." Second, the astute politician is not indifferent to the idea that if the governing body authorizes a traffic signal against the engineer's advice, it invites every neighborhood group to demand traffic control at their intersection regardless of engineering advice. Third, the people demanding the signal probably have never been involved in politics before and a refusal to respond to their request may alienate them from future involvement. From the engineer's perspective, I suspect that there was a "right answer" to the problem, and the engineer might have asked, "Will the council have the political courage to accept it?" But, as an elected official, I did not see the right answer. I saw a very complicated set of forces and a problem infused with choices about values symbolized by a decision about a traffic light. (Nalbandian, 1994, p. 534)

Another way to think of evaluating civic conversations is to consider the outcomes of the conversation. If people deliberate and produce clear outcomes, the needs and priorities found through those deliberations are effectively transferred to the government staffers. If the participants' recommendations are never followed because of compromises made for the sake of political expediency, then participants might legitimately wonder: "What is the point?" Deliberations are generally non-binding and may not generate directly actionable outcomes.

Yet, outcomes might legitimately be outcomes besides directly influencing policy. One outcome that has emerged several times from different instances of deliberative community forums is a continued conversation informed by the participants' perceptions that initiated dialog in a designed engagement.

In the quote from Nalbandian above, the decision may be to deny the request for the traffic light. Or the decision may be, despite the city engineer's recommendation, to install the light. In either case, *feedback* (Ashby, 1957) is a key component to an ongoing successful relationship with the community in which the government is embedded. While the design of effective feedback in resident/government communication is another complete research project, it will suffice to say that feedback needs to be considered, directed, and designed effectively to (in this example) let the senior citizens know: that, based upon the engineer's advice, that particular intersection is not in need of a traffic signal, or that a traffic signal will be installed, but that this is a special case with extenuating factors beyond the engineer's advice. Outcomes may be preferred by some community groups and reviled by others. Regardless, for the governing entity to maintain effective relations with the community, feedback is critical.

WHAT'S THE VALUE OF EVALUATION DATA?

The data generated by these conversations has been used in various ways. The trajectory of that data is typically established by the convening organization before the event. When working with the City of Pittsburgh, participants filled out surveys at the end of the event that were a combination of open-ended and closed-ended questions.

Completing surveys at the end of the event is not the ideal time for this activity. Participants are tired from the event and the emotional labor of making a personal exegesis of need for themselves and their neighborhoods. Keeping participants in the space by surveying them at the end of the event, however, greatly increases the likelihood that they will complete the evaluation.

> *Completing surveys at the end of the event is not the ideal time for this activity. Participants are tired from the event and the emotional labor of making a personal exegesis of need for themselves and their neighborhoods.*

To avoid survey fatigue at this critical point, the closed-ended questions were predominantly Likert-type survey responses, which, when tabulated, produce scalar values that depict agreement or disagreement with a statement. The open-ended questions were typically transcribed, and a count was made of related responses.

To serve the greatest potential number of participants, surveys were supplied on paper for all City of Pittsburgh events. While paper surveys required additional effort to encode digitally, the effort of that labor was borne by the convening organization. City employees encoded survey data from the meetings. Additionally, using a technology that was as widely understood as pen-and-paper surveys allows participants to "color outside the lines" in a manner of speaking. Participants can speak back into the process by crossing out and rewriting parts of the survey questions, offering commentary on the process itself, or offering corrections of wording or rankings to be more specific to their experience. Digital surveys lock participants out from that kind of creative reworking of the survey itself.

I suggest that an amount of the scheduled meeting time be saved for the end of the meeting so that participants can fill out the surveys. During two agenda-setting deliberations for WQED, the organizers and I jointly decided to provide participants with a digital survey that would allow them to sort priorities for possible content elements for upcoming shows. In this scenario, participants were asked to provide feedback via email after they had left the meeting site. Many participants did not complete the post-event online survey and we had a response rate of less than 50%. Responses took a lot of work to get after releasing participants. In city meetings where the participants fill out the survey at the end of the meeting, a greater percentage of participants respond—typically between 80–95%. Participants who elected not to complete the survey typically left the meeting early. Having the survey completed during the meeting—positioning survey completion as a communal activity—greatly increased response rates and the validity of the evaluation effort.

The formal data generated by these meetings—meaning, the data that are the principal output of these meetings—represents the public discourse in its most concrete form. This information is recognized and represented in other conversations by city government officials as a snapshot, or "frozen" image of the conversations that took place. Great care should be taken to frame the data outputs of these meetings, as they effectively become the meeting from the perspective of the convening entity.

WHAT HAPPENS AFTER EVALUATION?

Some designers think of the end of the meeting as the conclusion of a cycle of performance. The city had a question. We convened a group of people to refine and deliberate on that question. Then, they shared their feedback, and we wrote the report. Done! It is tempting to think that the loop of participant feedback has been closed at that point. We needed to hear from the community, and we did that. I'd encourage you, however, to think of the community conversation not as a single loop that completes but as more of a cascade that fosters new conversations in other parts of the city. The report that contains the results of a civic conversation is like an electricity converter that we might use when traveling in a foreign country. The report takes the power of the resident wisdom and channels it into other parts of the city, allowing it to generate new activities and conversations. The report is more than just a straightforward reporting of what happened; it is a tool for translating the complex data of the civic conversation to a group of elected officials and staff who want to learn what the community has to tell them.

The exit survey is a key tool to receive feedback. Participants filling out exit surveys in-meeting average between 80–95% completion rates. Photo by the author.

The additional loops of subsequent conversations sparked by civic engagement can lead to change across the organization. By viewing the process of the civic conversation as an ongoing cascade rather than a single closed loop, we acknowledge that the insights collected have an ongoing influence. This dynamic creates a more vibrant organization, informed by the wisdom and energy of the people that surround it. It not only enriches decision-making and policymaking processes but also regards the community with dignity and respect for the wisdom shared, fostering a sense of ownership and continued engagement in civic matters.

Furthermore, distributing the report should be seen not only as the conclusion of the public comment cycle but as the beginning of a new cycle of dialog and action. Officials and staff can use findings to reveal new areas of action, create policies that address multiple objectives simultaneously, and identify new areas of collaboration with residents. Fostering an iterative process ensures that the feedback loops of conversation remain open and active and support an organization that evolves to serve community needs, leveraging the collective wisdom of the community to drive meaningful change.

CONCLUSION

Throughout this chapter we have explored how to understand what happened in a civic conversation. We have considered how, with the help of stakeholders, community members, and our own organizations, a constructivist paradigm for evaluation might be implemented. This paradigm emphasizes the co-construction of knowledge, recognizing that the perspectives and experiences of all participants are valuable in assessing the effectiveness of civic conversations. We also evaluate our work by starting from the standpoint that our residents' needs should guide our actions.

Planning for evaluative work to be done throughout the development of our civic conversation is important to create an ongoing process that tells us whether our goals and objectives were met. By integrating evaluation from the outset, we ensure that our methods and approaches are not only reflective of the process but also adaptable to the evolving conversation. Such a proactive evaluative approach allows us to identify key metrics, gather data, and adjust as the conversation unfolds. This kind of iterative "tuning" focuses attention on the community's needs, as well as being supportive and respectful to our participants.

Moreover, embedding evaluation into the structure of our civic conversations fosters a culture of continuous learning and improvement. It enables us designers to engage in a cyclic critique of our own work and fosters an attitude of engagement with the participants and the broader community. Evaluation and reporting are other conversation loops that begin from a desire to engage with our community. By committing to a robust and dynamic evaluation framework, we not only validate the voices of our community but also engage them in improving our civic landscape.

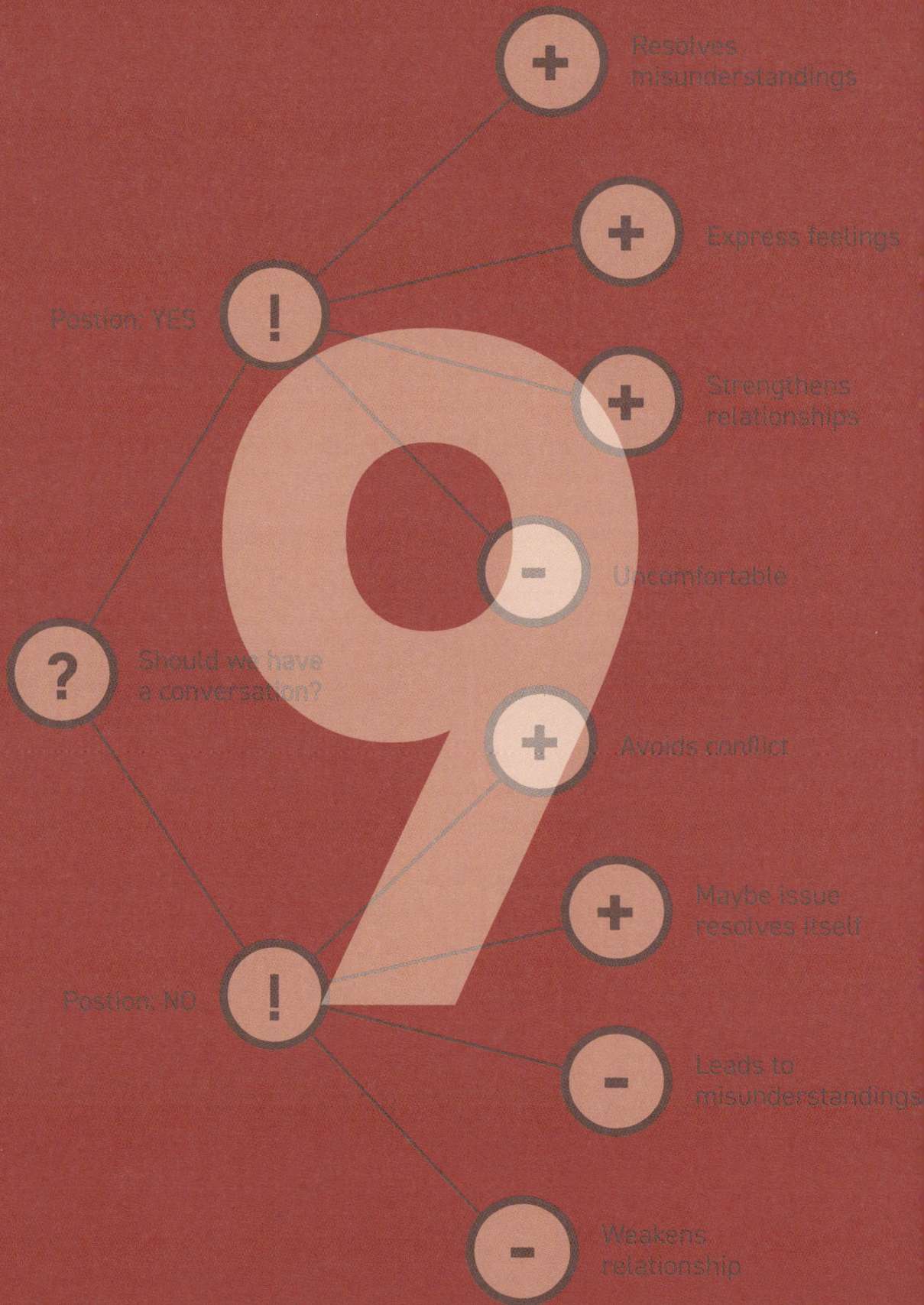

+ Resolves misunderstandings

+ Express feelings

+ Strengthens relationships

− Uncomfortable

+ Avoids conflict

+ Maybe issue resolves itself

− Leads to misunderstandings

− Weakens relationship

Postion: YES !

? Should we have a conversation?

Postion: NO !

CHAPTER 9

Conclusion

INTRODUCTION

In this concluding chapter, we explore the transformative potential of conversational design, synthesizing the insights and strategies discussed throughout the book. The aim is not only to reflect on past research but to chart a path forward, integrating diverse disciplinary perspectives and emerging practices.

When people come together to learn, to make decisions, and to navigate uncertainty, conversations are the medium through which they work. Design, when oriented towards analysis, sense-making, and action, can significantly enhance these conversations, unlocking latent expertise and fostering authentic participation.

Spinosa, Flores, and Dreyfus (1997) argue that humans are at their best when engaged in actively trying to change their world. Active engagement means that humans operate in the disclosive space that opens world to world. Through this work I endeavored to create change through disclosive, conversational spaces for the residents of Pittsburgh, residents of Boston, veterans who receive services through the US Veteran's Administration, students who want to look more deeply into legislative issues, teachers working with their school system to redesign their system for retention, tenure, and promotion, organizations and residents working for social good who wish to create more green spaces in their low-income neighborhoods. Considering civic and public conversations as sites for design and approaching designing from the point of facilitation reveals that the material environment that surrounds the event is a richer and broader system than we, at first, might think. Through embedded research designing facilitative objects for these conversations, I have come to understand the varied ways the material environment facilitates at the meeting, and how the intervention of the meeting itself causes an alignment of resources and activities in stakeholders and communities.

Designers hoping to engage in this work must immerse themselves in the discipline of noticing (Mason, 2002). Because so many things in meetings are assumed, it becomes very easy to miss crucial details or patterns that are nascent in the information field. Questioning the underlying assumptions of how things work leads to richer engagement with the experience and to the opportunity to reframe things and events to produce deeper engagement and fuller disclosure from participants. Further, I do not propose that these levels and modes of conversation described in this book are exhaustive, or complete, but that they represent a useful model for structuring understanding of conversation events.

Diagrams and models are used throughout this work. In fact, one of the contributions of this book is an understanding of this set of precedents as cases and models for further work. However, despite the best efforts of design, the best intentions of convening organizations, the greatest degree of earnestness by the participants, conversations are never as clean or elegant as the models might suggest. Conversations are rife with missed connections, implicature that goes awry, lost threads, misunderstandings, double meanings, unintended offense, irrelevant information. In civic contexts, with the radical differences in the histories that participants bring, it is astonishing that conversation works at all. In 1933, mathematician Alfred Korzybski wrote "the map *is not* the territory, but if correct, has a *similar structure* to the territory" (Korzybski 2005, p 58). The models presented here aim to offer a similar structure, providing a framework for understanding the dynamics of this work. They also offer designers working with government and communities a way to help people affected by policy to surface important stories, learn from their neighbors, and communicate meaningful insights to policymakers.

Findings from this work can be thought of as existing across three levels: material, metaphorical, and systemic. This kind of categorization is porous. Assigning a particular design approach to the levels that are being proposed here does not mean that it has no implications outside of those levels. For instance, stating that a chair has force at the material and functional level does not mean that it has no force or low force at a metaphorical level. It depends on the relationship between the chair and the user.

There are four types of conversations that are particularly important to practitioners in public organizations: surfacing, planning, difficult, and high-stakes conversations. Surfacing aims to evoke latent knowledge, planning aims to help people make commitments to one another, difficult acknowledges that emotions represent critically important data, and high-stakes attempts to balance agency across power. All these conversations have one aspect in common — that through the conversation, people aim to do something, aim to take some action. I have mentioned before the statement that sometimes arises forcefully in public conversations, "Why don't we stop talking and *do* something?!?" The response to this question is to ask, quite sincerely, "What do you think we should do?" Because the answer to that question, nearly always, is something that we as a community need to talk about.

These modes of conversation relate back to the critical question of goals—both the goals of the civic organization convening the meetings and the goals of the people we hope to engage through our work. Cities cannot solve all problems, but as embodiments of our communities' collective will, they serve as guiding lights for our hopes and dreams of better futures. The intersection of residents' needs and goals with the government's capacity to address those needs and goals is where residents meet public organizations. When residents attend public meetings to express complaints, those of us who design and facilitate these meetings must remember a simple reframing: the act of showing up to complain is fundamentally an act of optimism and hope. People voice their complaints because they believe the city might act, indicating a degree of trust in the system of public engagement. Residents' participation reflects their hope that their concerns will be heard by those in power and lead to change. As designers and conveners, we have a responsibility to honor that hope by ensuring their voices are effectively communicated and addressed.

THE AGENCY OF DESIGN

Design has the power to shape conversations and influence systemic change. By engaging with communities at a deep level, designers can access the latent expertise that often remains untapped. Ethical design at the systemic level involves considering the broader impact of our work, ensuring that it is inclusive and fosters genuine participation.

Designing for inclusivity in a broad urban area faces many challenges. In the United States, the equal protection clause in the Fourteenth Amendment to the Constitution guarantees the government may not deny people equal protection of its laws and policies. Many other democratic countries have similar protections. By extension, design for civic engagement should not work to unduly benefit one group over another. However, hundreds of years of design has shaped (and still all too often continues to shape) a civic environment that has many inequalities. Participation is a luxury affordable only by those who can donate their time and costs of transportation. Considering deeply how to design to support participants in an inclusive way is not enough. Thinking from the standpoint of "How do we include more people?" means that we have already begun with an attitude of defeat. Inclusivity more than inviting the groups that can afford to participate, and then offering subsidies to support those who might not.

Instead, begin designing by considering the most challenging cases of participation. Do people need transit passes to attend? Childcare? Dinner? Dinner for their children? Compensation for missed work? If we, as designers in the public sector, are committed to inclusivity in public conversations, these costs of participation must be considered as part of the design process. Ignoring these needs designs a format accessible to some but not all. On a per-person basis, it is possible for an administration or organization to bear the costs of resident participation. If convening residents is not worth a meeting design that values them equitably, maybe we shouldn't have the meeting in the first place. The agency of designers is that we are often in the room when this conversation might be had. A designer can, for example, emphasize the importance of including young parents in the conversation. If a community meeting is scheduled around dinnertime, providing childcare and food is essential to encourage the participation of these key groups. And this is only one example of an inclusive design. Different conversations might have different needs based on the population.

Inclusion goes beyond simply inviting different groups of people to attend; it involves actively removing the barriers that prevent them from participating. By considering these practical needs in the planning stage, designers can help create environments where everyone can participate in the conversation. This approach not only broadens the scope of participation but also enriches conversations with the diverse perspectives that might otherwise be missing. Fuller treatments of designing with equity can be found in the writings of Sasha Costanza-Chock (2020) and Lesley-Ann Noel (2023). When we begin from the standpoint of addressing the challenges people face in attending, we demonstrate the commitment of our organization to genuine community engagement. This proactive approach can foster trust between residents and public organizations, signaling that their voices matter and that their contributions are vital to shaping policy decisions that impact their lives.

COMMITTING TO COMMIT

Achieving meaningful change requires a sustained commitment to the design process and the process of engagement with residents. This involves not only carrying through the meeting design to a successful completion and reporting out, but a long-term dedication to nurturing and supporting community involvement. The impact of such commitment is profound, leading to lasting improvements in neighborhoods, cities, and cultures.

Developing a vibrant scene for public conversation involves building trust with residents in a process that may extend over years. Often, an administration might make a few half-hearted stabs at engagement events, doing more damage than good. But building cycles of invitation, conversation, analysis, and reporting to the community both the results of the conversation and actions taken takes time. It will take an even longer time for notice of this work to spread citywide. An old advertising aphorism is that customers need to see an ad seven times before they will make a purchase. Similarly, residents who have had neutral or even negative experiences with city government will need repeated exposure to an institution that listens before they trust the commitment.

The follow-up to the civic conversation is vital. Sending residents an email or text message with a report of the meeting results and subsequent updates on the issue they care about is well within the capabilities of most organizations' communications staff. Maintaining the bulk communication lists needed for this is a specialty available even in small municipalities. If progress stalls or the administration decides to incorporate the issue into other legislative priorities, people still want to know. Communicating this information treats them with respect and provides an opportunity to explain the administration's perspectives.

> Communicative and deliberative approaches work well as
> ideals and evaluative yardsticks for decision making, but they
> are quite defenceless in the face of power.
> (Flyvbjerg et al., 2003, p. 7)

The quote from economist and geographer Bent Flyvbjerg illustrates a key challenge in this kind of work. Studies show that for conversations to be effective, everyone involved needs to be committed to the process, which involves participating in the cycles of listening, thinking, and speaking equitably on all sides (Dubberly & Pangaro, 2009; Scharmer, 2009; Bohm, 1991). While power imbalances are hard to avoid, they can be lessened if those with power choose not to use it or if they pay attention to the community's needs and desires. Flyvbjerg points out a different issue, though: when people work around the system of discussion and decision-making, it can undermine the process. Deliberative approaches only work if the government is open to considering the input it receives. If powerful leaders or groups try to disrupt the process, it can become vulnerable to manipulation.

And powerful groups will try to disrupt the process. During the work of the Pittsburgh's Affordable Housing Task Force, our meetings were sites for protest by community groups. We were contacted by developers and real estate groups with various requests, and our meetings were attended by people with a variety of real estate-related special interests who hoped to influence the outcomes. City councilpersons reported that real estate developers and business associations reached out to them attempting to short-circuit the public comment process, and one protest group produced stickers for meeting attendees to attach to the exit survey we designed—in a sense a material "hacking" of the survey.

The commitment to civic conversation is its own reward. A responsive government that steers its ship in response to the needs of a broad constituency is a government that aspires to be just and responsive. By prioritizing open dialog and ensuring that residents remain informed and engaged, the government demonstrates its dedication to transparency and accountability. This process not only strengthens bonds, but builds a culture of active participation, a culture where residents will show up for public conversations because they know that they will be heard.

COMPRESSION

Structures that attempt to reduce the richness of civic conversations to principles or algorithms miss the point. The evaluative structures must appreciate the inherent complexity and irreducibility of these dialogues. These events are a site where values are surfaced and have the capacity to restructure a model of the system that evoked the conversation. It is not the chain of reporting that does the work of restructuring, however, but the richness of the heterogeneous experiences of the participants and the activity that is catalyzed by these events. As no preflight checklist can ever capture the vast world of potential events that could happen within an aircraft, no post-event survey can adequately provide a format to capture the richness of the conversation event.

In fact, the data of these events, in all their richness, are transitory. The experience of the event exists for the participants and the moderators, then passes into memory, where it becomes a part of the biological elements of the organisms. The imperfect memories of each participant are where the true data of the conversation live. The output gathered on surveys, in notes, even in video is just one kind of representation of the conversation event. The limitations of the conversation are that it is an event in the context of a larger process. While the conversation may be dramatic and compelling, much of the work is in the implementation or translating participants' statements of value into a plan for policymaking—or, in other projects, a plan for poured concrete, setback regulations, or a program to create and ensure the continued existence of affordable housing. It must be carried through with intention, diligence, and an ethic of materializing the charge of values.

Even when planned carefully, civic conversations are contingently contingent. It may be frustrating to find that audiences and city officials are looking for actionable results instead of a replete recounting of the specifics. But it's in the specifics and rich and nuanced detail that the true value of design-based thinking lies. As Michael Polanyi famously said, we "know more than we can tell." Mimi Onuoha, in her talk at the SPAN conference in Pittsburgh, said researchers prefer to collect data that fit their collection methods. To add to that, systems are biased toward data that fit how they're set up to work. So, while it's tempting to reduce these conversations to lists of ranked preferences, recommendations, guidelines, or an executive summary, that approach misses the real essence. These conversations bring out underlying values, uncover hidden worlds, and have the power to reshape how systems work.

Understanding the issue, the local context of the issue, and the rhizomatic tendrils of that issue that extend throughout the community allows event designers to invite people to participate in conversation. What is of key importance is engaging the network of people that exists around the issue. Even if other elements of the event fail, something useful will emerge if organizers can bring to the room earnest people who represent a complex and diverse group and who are willing to engage around the issue.

CIVIC CONVERSATIONS ARE INHERENTLY LOCAL AND PLACE-BASED

Municipal governments remain one of the few place-based institutions with the power to bring people together in an era dominated by the internet and transactional communities. While online networks create relationships that are that are far-flung and time-shifted, municipal governments operate in a world that is circumscribed by the local city limits, imminently material and geographic, and bound up with concerns of provisioning to the needs of community members within a particular geographic region. Civic conversations are rooted in this physical and geographic context, addressing the immediate concerns of community members.

In the neighborhoods of decades past, under a set of social structures that were more place-based, where relations were structured principally around proximity, matters of concern might have been encountered at the workplace, in the parent-teacher association, again at the bakery or the greengrocers, and again at church. This suite of contiguous but independent institutions engendered more replete relationships based upon spatial proximity. Essentially, people worked, participated in religious and civic life, and engaged with the schools near the neighborhoods where they lived. However, this replete geographically based network has been altered fundamentally, as people identify and spend more and more of their time participating in social networks that are more transactional (Castells 2012).

Further, from observations in this fieldwork, supplemented by evidence developed by Foa & Mounk (2016) and the US Senate Joint Economic Committee Report on Associational Life in the US (2017), and Robert Putnam's landmark *Bowling Alone* (2000) I argue that residents have lost some of the civic literacy that associational life served to exercise and reinforce. Yet, it is within this context that the municipal government must operate. To catalyze these conversations, municipal government is the key, interested actor who can take steps to scaffold civic participation even in the face of the decline of these other institutions.

While this middle tier of social relations has begun to deconsolidate due (in part) to the organization of new types of social relation, design can serve to reshape democracy to be more accommodating to participants, as well as support people to reconnect with the local. Frameworks like the one supplied in this book can help designers, city governments, and organizations for social good begin to take these steps.

CONTRIBUTIONS TO DESIGNERLY KNOWLEDGE

Reframing the role of designers in civic meetings is the key first step. Designers must lead these events with an awareness of cultural contexts and content. Their professional practice and understanding of the balance between advocacy and communication can keep projects on track amidst conflicting priorities. Designers apply their knowledge to structuring environments and experiences, from document design and table choice to facilitating and engaging community members in discussions.

For designers, reframing the role of the designer in these meetings is a significant step. Because the cultural contexts and cultural content is a significant component of this practice, it is essential for contextually aware designers to lead the development of these events. From undergraduate education in designing for personas, designers have long been trained to pay attention to the needs and languages of diverse groups. Further, from experience in professional practice, designers tacitly understand the difference between advocacy and communication. Bringing that understanding helps to keep the project on a balanced track in the face of multiple, conflicting priorities. Through these conversation events, designers gain the opportunity to apply designerly understandings of structuring the material environment to support a set of behaviors: at the basest level of the supporting document design and table choice, at the mid-level of choice of location and design of participant experience, and at the highest level of engaging the community systems.

Ultimately, what designers gain from the experience accumulated in this book is access to a set of memories generated by an ongoing design conversation with the systems of cities. This work argues that those memories and the patterns that those memories constitute comprise a set of strategies for approaching similar challenges in the future.

The designer's power in these events is a power of noticing. Noticing during the development of a deliberative community forum allows the designer to shape the discourse to be more inclusive. Further, a designer coming to a robust understanding of the array of evaluative models lends a rigor to the design work and provides a metric against which experiences can be critiqued.

When people come to a civic or public conversation bearing their matters of concern, the conversation has the potential to be a veritable potluck of matters. Through framing the process with scaffolding documents, framing the experience as a search for what neighbors need to discover about this problem, the designer has the opportunity to help people organize their matters of concern and understand them in the light of the concerns of their neighbors. Ultimately, these meetings represent the potential for opening neighbors' worlds to other worlds through disclosive conversation. The designer is part of the process to design the physical environment, but also to shape the social environment toward inclusive discourse that evokes participants' lived experiences. Through considered research, and through engagement in the network of stakeholders that surrounds these issues, designers play an important role that is not taken up by other actors.

The process of the conversation is bigger than simply having a conversation. And really, the meetings where these conversations are resident are not opportunities for design in the sense that we can design branding or infographics. These meetings and the conversations that they contain are a way to test how effectively designers can organize human activity.

Public conversations are a powerful site for knowledge creation and change. The types, sites and methods of conversation are designed and designable. This design work operates across many levels, from the visual design of paper or digital documents, to the arrangement of furniture in the space, to the engagement of the network of stakeholders queried to shape the discourse, to the communities of participants who attend and share their particular wisdom. This work reaches out, affecting the material environment of the city, the processes of policymaking, and the needs of communities. Knowing stories of the landscape of conversation in public life offers some direction to guideposts on the journey. With these cases and types as a guide, designing for conversation and facilitation you may avoid some of the problems I faced in my early work.

Conversations are one way that we as humans can coordinate and do things together. Conversations show us our differences, and conversations are the threads of our solidarity. In the United States, our founding government document, the US Constitution begins with the text *We the people...*
A conversation can only be had when there is *we*. In public life conversation is the most foundational and fundamental act that organizes our democracy. Conversation is a practice we engage in, of being with, listening to, and caring for another. And the system of conversation, in turn, engages back. To design for conversation is to design the very thing that reflects our best qualities.

INDEX

R

resilience 28–30, 32, 107, 109, 157
Ricketts, Delanie 145
Rittel, Horst 10, 68–70, 87, 108
Rockefeller Foundation 28
role-play 25, 30–32, 124

S

Sanders, Bernie 122
Sanders, Elizabeth B.-N. 168
satisficing 68
scenarios 25, 28–29, 31–32,
        69–71, 74, 154, 155, 177
Schmidt, Peter 150–152
Schön, Donald 10, 115
Searle, John 48
see ludic space 126–127
sense-making 10, 74, 118, 181
service design 89
Shostack, Lynn 93
Shove, Elizabeth 112
Simon, Herbert 36, 68–69
situation rooms 101, 116–18
Solomon, Robert 47, 115–116
speech acts 48
Spinosa, Charles 46, 85,
        155–156, 174, 181
Suber, Peter 129, 130, 131
Suchman, Lucy 11, 123
surfacing conversation 18, 22–28,
        30, 32, 37, 154

T

table facilitator 91, 95, 99, 102, 135, 153
tacit knowledge 166, 173, 174
thematic analysis 172
things 8, 11, 16–19, 46, 61, 78, 89, 99,
        111, 112, 119, 123–124, 133, 138,
        140, 144–148, 150, 153, 167, 182,
        191
Traganou, Jilly 142
Trivial Pursuit 123, 124
trust 37, 42, 46, 47, 50, 71, 92, 99, 136,
        165, 183, 185

U

US Veteran's Administration 16, 56,
        102, 181

V

veterans 56, 102, 114, 122, 181
Viewpoints 155

W

Wade, Helen 140
wicked problems 10, 69, 71
Winograd, Terry 11, 78, 118
WQED 22, 176

Y

Young, Iris Marion 14, 109, 155

BIBLIOGRAPHY

BIBLIOGRAPHY

Introduction

Arendt, H. (1998). *The human condition* (2nd ed). University of Chicago Press.

Bohm, D. (1996). *On dialogue* (L. Nichol, Ed.). Routledge.

Burkhalter, S., Gastil, J., & Kelshaw, T. (2002). A Conceptual Definition and Theoretical Model of Public Deliberation in Small Face-to-Face Groups. *Communication Theory*, *12*(4), 398–422. https://doi.org/10.1111/j.1468-2885.2002.tb00276.x

Flores, F. (2012). *Conversations For Action and Collected Essays: Instilling A Culture of Commitment in Our Working Relationships* (M. F. Letelier, Ed.). CreateSpace Independent Publishing Platform.

Latour, B. (2004). Why Has Critique Run out of Steam? From Matters of Fact to Matters of Concern. *Critical Inquiry*, *30*(2), 225–248. https://doi.org/10.1086/421123

Nabatchi, T., Gastil, J., Weiksner, G. M., & Leighninger, M. (Eds.). (2012). *Democracy in motion: Evaluating the practice and impact of deliberative civic engagement*. Oxford University Press.

Nixon, R. (2014). *Six crises*. Simon & Schuster.

Pask, G. (1987, November 30). *Conversation & Support*. Research Programme Ondersteuning Overleving & Cultuur (OOC), University of Amsterdam. http://www.pangaro.com/pask/pask%20conversation%20and%20support%201987.pdf

Schön, D. A. (1983). *The reflective practitioner: How professionals think in action*. Basic Books.

Suchman, L. (1993). Do categories have politics?: The language/action perspective reconsidered. *Computer Supported Cooperative Work (CSCW)*, *2*(3), 177–190. https://doi.org/10.1007/BF00749015

Winograd, T. (1987). A Language/Action Perspective on the Design of Cooperative Work. *Human–Computer Interaction*, *3*(1), 3–30. https://doi.org/10.1207/s15327051hci0301_2

Winograd, T., & Flores, F. (1986). *Understanding computers and cognition: A new foundation f or design*. Ablex Pub. Corp.

Woolgar, S., & Suchman, L. A. (1989). Plans and Situated Actions: The Problem of Human Machine Communication. *Contemporary Sociology*, *18*(3), 414. https://doi.org/10.2307/2073874

Young, I. M. (2000). *Inclusion and democracy*. Oxford University Press.

Chapter 1

De Bono, E. (1999). *Six thinking hats* (1st Back Bay pbk. ed., rev.updated). Back Bay Books.

Hayek, F. A. (1945). The Use of Knowledge in Society. *The American Economic Review*, *35*(4), 519–530.

Chapter 2

Austin, J. L. (1962). *How to do things with words*. Harvard University Press.

Grice, H. P. (1989). Logic and Conversation. In *Studies in the way of words*. Harvard University Press.

Searle, J. R. (1980). Minds, brains, and programs. *Behavioral and Brain Sciences*, *3*(3), 417–424. https://doi.org/10.1017/S0140525X00005756

Spinosa, C., Flores, F., & Dreyfus, H. L. (1997). *Disclosing new worlds: Entrepreneurship, democratic action, and the cultivation of solidarity*. MIT Press.

Chapter 3

Centers for Disease Control and Prevention. (n.d.). *WISQARS National Violent Death Reporting System* [Dataset]. Retrieved July 13, 2024, from https://wisqars.cdc.gov/nvdrs

De Domenico, G. S. (1995). *Sand Tray World Play: A comprehensive guide to the use of the sand tray in psychotherapeutic and transformational settings*. Vision Quest Images.

DeSilver, D. (2013, May 24). Suicides account for most gun deaths. *Pew Research Center*. https://www.pewresearch.org/short-reads/2013/05/24/suicides-account-for-most-gun-deaths/

Hemenway, D., & Miller, M. (2013). Public Health Approach to the Prevention of Gun Violence. *New England Journal of Medicine*, *368*(21), 2033–2035. https://doi.org/10.1056/NEJMsb1302631

Miller, M., & Hemenway, D. (1999). The relationship between firearms and suicide. *Aggression and Violent Behavior*, *4*(1), 59–75. https://doi.org/10.1016/S1359-1789(97)00057-8

Schadler, G., & De Domenico, G. S. (2012). Sandtray-Worldplay for people who experience chronic mental illness. *International Journal of Play Therapy*, *21*(2), 87–99. https://doi.org/10.1037/a0027192

Stone, D., Patton, B., & Heen, S. (2010). *Difficult conversations: How to discuss what matters most; [updated with answers to the 10 most frequently asked questions about difficult conversations]* (2. ed., 10. anniversary ed., now updated with a new chapter). Penguin Books.

Chapter 4

Crompton, T. (2008). *Weathercocks and signposts: The environment movement at a crossroads* (p. 40). WWF-UK. http://assets.wwf.org.uk/downloads/weathercocks_report2.pdf

Doblin, J. (1987). A short grandiose theory of design. *STA Design Journal*.

Funtowicz, S. O., & Ravetz, J. R. (1993). Science for the post-normal age. *Futures*, *25*(7), 739–755. https://doi.org/10.1016/0016-3287(93)90022-L

Klein, G. A. (2017). *Sources of power: How people make decisions* (20th Anniversary Edition). MIT Press.

Kunreuther, H., Meyer, R., Zeckhauser, R., Slovic, P., Schwartz, B., Schade, C., Luce, M. F., Lippman, S., Krantz, D., Kahn, B., & Hogarth, R. (2002). High Stakes Decision Making: Normative, Descriptive and Prescriptive Considerations. *Marketing Letters*, *13*(3), 259–268. https://doi.org/10.1023/A:1020287225409

Lakoff, G. (2010). Why it Matters How We Frame the Environment. *Environmental Communication*, *4*(1), 70–81. https://doi.org/10.1080/17524030903529749

Lederach, J. P. (1997). *Building peace: Sustainable reconciliation in divided societies*. United States Institute of Peace Press.

Maiese, M. (2003). Midlevel Actors. In G. Burgess & H. J. Burgess (Eds.), *Beyond Intractability*. Conflict Information Consortium. http://www.beyondintractability.org/essay/midlevel-ngos-gos

Quist, J. (2007). *Backcasting for a sustainable future: The impact after 10 years*. Eburon.

Rittel, H. W. J. (1972). On the planning crisis: Systems analysis of the "first and second generations." *Bedriftsøkonomen*, *8*, 390–396.

Rittel, H. W. J., & Webber, M. M. (1973). Dilemmas in a general theory of planning. *Policy Sciences*, *4*(2), 155–169. https://doi.org/10.1007/BF01405730

Ross, S. A. (1973). The Economic Theory of Agency: The Principal's Problem. *American Economic Review*, *63*(2), 134–139.

Sheridan, S. L., Harris, R. P., & Woolf, S. H. (2004). Shared decision making about screening and chemoprevention. *American Journal of Preventive Medicine*, *26*(1), 56–66. https://doi.org/10.1016/j.amepre.2003.09.011

Simon, H. A. (1996). *The sciences of the artificial* (3rd ed). MIT Press.

Weinstein, N. D., Kolb, K., & Goldstein, B. D. (1996). Using time intervals between expected events to communicate risk magnitudes. *Risk Analysis: An Official Publication of the Society for Risk Analysis*, *16*(3), 305–308.

Winograd, T., & Flores, F. (1986). *Understanding computers and cognition: A new foundation for design*. Ablex Pub. Corp.

Chapter 5

Argyris, C. (2012). *Organizational traps: Leadership, culture, organizational design* (1. publ. in paperback). Oxford Univ. Press.

Arnstein, S. R. (1969). A Ladder Of Citizen Participation. *Journal of the American Institute of Planners*, *35*(4), 216–224. https://doi.org/10.1080/01944366908977225

Boyer, B., & Hill, D. (2013). *Brickstarter* (R. Hyde, Ed.). Sitra. https://media.sitra.fi/2017/02/24045108/Brickstarter.pdf

Certeau, M. de. (1984). *The practice of everyday life. 1: …* (2. print). Univ. of California Press.

Conklin, E. J. (2006). *Dialogue mapping: Building shared understanding of wicked problems*. Wiley.

Dubberly, H., Esmonde, P., Geoghegan, M., & Pangaro, P. (2002). Notes on the Role of Leadership & Language in Regenerating Organizations. In *Driving Desired Futures: Turning Design Thinking into Real Innovation*. Sun Microsystems.

Dweck, C. S. (2008). Can Personality Be Changed?: The Role of Beliefs in Personality and Change. *Current Directions in Psychological Science*, *17*(6), 391–394.

Fishkin, J. S. (1991). *Democracy and deliberation: New directions for democratic reform*. Yale Univ. Press.

Fishkin, J. S., & Luskin, R. C. (2005). Experimenting with a Democratic Ideal: Deliberative Polling and Public Opinion. *Acta Politica*, *40*(3), 284–298. https://doi.org/10.1057/palgrave.ap.5500121

Foa, R. S., & Mounk, Y. (2016). The Democratic Disconnect. *Journal of Democracy, 27*(3), 5–17. https://doi.org/10.1353/jod.2016.0049

Glanville, R. (2007). Try again. Fail again. Fail better: The cybernetics in design and the design in cybernetics. *Kybernetes, 36*(9/10), 1173–1206. https://doi.org/10.1108/03684920710827238

Jenssen, S. (2008). Deliberative Democracy in Practice. *Acta Politica, 43*(1), 71–92. https://doi.org/10.1057/palgrave.ap.5500208

Kunz, W., & Rittel, H. W. J. (1970). *Issues as elements of information systems* (p. 9). http://citeseerx.ist.psu.edu/viewdoc/download?doi=10.1.1.134.1741&rep=rep1&type=pdf

Lévi-Strauss, C. (1966). *The savage mind*. Weidenfeld and Nicolson Ltd.

Max-Neef, M. A., Elizalde, A., & Hopenhayn, M. (1991). *Human scale development: Conception, application and further reflections*. The Apex Press.

Ravetz, J. (1999). Editorial: What is post-normal science? *Futures, 31*(7), 647–653. https://doi.org/10.1016/S0016-3287(99)00024-5

Rittel, H. W. J., & Webber, M. M. (1973). Dilemmas in a general theory of planning. *Policy Sciences, 4*(2), 155–169. https://doi.org/10.1007/BF01405730

Shostack, G. L. (1984, January 1). Designing Services That Deliver. *Harvard Business Review*. https://hbr.org/1984/01/designing-services-that-deliver

Spinosa, C., Flores, F., & Dreyfus, H. L. (1997). *Disclosing new worlds: Entrepreneurship, democratic action, and the cultivation of solidarity*. MIT Press.

Wenger, E. (1998). *Communities of Practice: Learning, Meaning, and Identity*. Cambridge University Press.

Young, I. M. (2000). *Inclusion and democracy*. Oxford University Press.

Chapter 6

Akrich, M. (1992). The De-Scription of Technical Objects. In W. E. Bijker & J. Law (Eds.), *Shaping technology/building society: Studies in sociotechnical change* (pp. 205–224). MIT Press.

BoardGameGeek. (n.d.). *1000 Blank White Cards*. BoardGameGeek. Retrieved March 30, 2018, from https://boardgamegeek.com/boardgame/4550/1000-blank-white-cards

Churchill, W. (1943). House of Commons Rebuilding, HC Deb 28 October 1943 vol 393 cc403-73. In *Hansard Millbank Systems*. https://doi.org/10.1016/S0140-6736(02)99717-5

Collaboration IPDAS. (2005). *IPDAS 2005: Criteria for Judging the Quality of Patient Decision Aids*. The International Patient Decision Aid Standards (IPDAS) Collaboration. http://ipdas.ohri.ca/IPDAS_checklist.pdf

Common Practice. (2016). *My Gift of Grace*. Common Practice LLC.

Culmsee, P., & Awati, K. (2012). Towards a holding environment: Building shared understanding and commitment in projects. *International Journal of Managing Projects in Business, 5*(3), 528–548. https://doi.org/10.1108/17538371211235353

Delinikolas, D., DeSoto, P., & Dragona, D. (2013, May 29). Mapping the Urban Commons. A new representation system for cities through the lenses of the commons. *Hybrid City*. http://www.academia.edu/3886909/ Mapping_the_Urban_Commons._A_new_representation_system_for_cities_through_the_lenses_of_the_commons

Dewey, J. (1958). *Art as experience*. Capricorn Books, G. P. Putnam's Sons.

Donaldson, L. E. (1998). Writing the talking stick Alphabetic Literacy as Colonial Technology and Postcolonial Appropriation. *American Indian Quarterly; Lincoln*, *22*(1/2), 46–62.

Ertel, C., & Solomon, L. K. (2014). *Moments of impact: How to design strategic conversations that accelerate change*. Simon & Schuster.

Gomart, E., & Hajer, M. (2003). Is that politics? In B. Joerges & H. Nowotny (Eds.), *Social Studies of Science and Technology: Looking Back, Ahead* (pp. 33–61). Springer Netherlands. http://www.springer.com/gp/book/9781402014819

Harrison, S., & Dourish, P. (1996). Re-place-ing Space: The Roles of Place and Space in Collaborative Systems. *Proceedings of the 1996 ACM Conference on Computer Supported Cooperative Work*, 67–76. https://doi.org/10.1145/240080.240193

Hofstadter, D. R. (1985). *Metamagical themas: Questing for the essence of mind and pattern*. Basic Books.

Houde, S., & Hill, C. (1997). What do Prototypes Prototype? In *Handbook of Human-Computer Interaction* (pp. 367–381). Elsevier. https://doi.org/10.1016/B978-044481862-1/50082-0

Huizinga, J. (1950). *Homo Ludens: A Study of the Play-Element in Culture*. The Beacon Press.

Illich, I. (1973). *Tools for conviviality* (1st ed.). Harper & Row.

Jelsma, J. (2003). Innovating for Sustainability: Involving Users, Politics and Technology. *Innovation: The European Journal of Social Science Research*, *16*(2), 103–116. https://doi.org/10.1080/13511610304520

Kegan, R. (2001). *The evolving self: Problem and process in human development*. Harvard University Press.

Knockwood, I., & Thomas, G. (1992). *Out of the Depths: The Experiences of Mi'kmaw Children at the Indian Residential School at Shubenacadie, Nova Scotia*. Roseway Publishing Ltd.

Lakoff, G. (2010). Why it Matters How We Frame the Environment. *Environmental Communication*, *4*(1), 70–81. https://doi.org/10.1080/17524030903529749

Landgren, J., & Bergstrand, F. (2016). Work Practice in Situation Rooms – An Ethnographic Study of Emergency Response Work in Governmental Organizations. In P. Díaz, N. Bellamine Ben Saoud, J. Dugdale, & C. Hanachi (Eds.), *Information Systems for Crisis Response and Management in Mediterranean Countries* (Vol. 265, pp. 157–171). Springer International Publishing. https://doi.org/10.1007/978-3-319-47093-1_14

Latour, B. (1996). On Interobjectivity. *Mind, Culture, and Activity*, *3*(4), 228–245. https://doi.org/10.1207/s15327884mca0304_2

Marres, N. (2012). *Material Participation: Technology, the Environment and Everyday Publics*. Palgrave Macmillan. https://doi.org/10.1057/9781137029669

Meadows, D. (1999). *Leverage Points: Places to Intervene in a System*. The Sustainability Institute. http://www.donellameadows.org/wp-content/userfiles/Leverage_Points.pdf

Merica, D. (2015, August 10). *Black Lives Matter protesters shut down Sanders event in Seattle*. CNN Politics. https://www.cnn.com/2015/08/08/politics/bernie-sanders-black-lives-matter-protesters/index.html

Morehead, A. H., Mott-Smith, G., & Morehead, P. D. (2001). *Hoyle's rules of games: Descriptions of indoor games of skill and chance, with advice on skillful play: based on the foundations laid down by Edmond Hoyle, 1672-1769* (E. Hoyle, Ed.; 3rd rev. & updated ed). Plume.

Murphy, D. (2015, August 11). *Trump to Black Lives Matter: I won't give up my microphone*. NY Daily News. http://www.nydailynews.com/news/politics/trump-black-lives-matter-won-give-microphone-article-1.2322496

Parlett, D. S. (1999). *The Oxford history of board games*. Oxford University Press.

Ruder, N., Nakano, K., & Aeschlimann, J. (2017). *The GA handbook: A practical guide to the United Nations General Assembly* (J. Aeschlimann & M. Regan, Eds.; 2 ed). Permanent Mission of Switzerland to the United Nations.

Salen, K., & Zimmerman, E. (2003). *Rules of play: Game design fundamentals*. MIT Press.

Schön, D. A. (1984). Problems, frames and perspectives on designing. *Design Studies, 5*(3), 132–136. https://doi.org/10.1016/0142-694X(84)90002-4

Shove, E., Pantzar, M., & Watson, M. (2012). *The Dynamics of Social Practice: Everyday Life and How it Changes*. SAGE Publications Ltd. https://doi.org/10.4135/9781446250655

Spinosa, C., Flores, F., & Dreyfus, H. L. (1997). *Disclosing new worlds: Entrepreneurship, democratic action, and the cultivation of solidarity*. MIT Press.

Suber, P. (1990). *The paradox of self-amendment: A study of law, logic, omnipotence, and change*. Peter Lang International Academic Publishers. https://dash.harvard.edu/handle/1/23674879

Uchida, M. (1989). *Golden Axe* [Arcade console]. Sega.

Winograd, T., & Flores, F. (1986). *Understanding computers and cognition: A new foundation for design*. Ablex Pub. Corp.

Chapter 7

Arnold, M. (2016a). An introduction to systemic structural constellations. In *Systemic Structural Constellations and Sustainability in Academia: A New Method for Sustainable Higher Education* (pp. 21–29). Routledge.

Arnold, M. (2016b). Methodical reflections on systemic constellations. In *Systemic Structural Constellations and Sustainability in Academia: A New Method for Sustainable Higher Education* (pp. 35–38). Routledge.

Arnold, M., & Fischer, A. (2018). *Systemic structural constellations in academia facilitating transformation processes towards sustainability*. 15.

Barrett, F. J. (2017). Creativity and Improvisation in Jazz and Organizations: Implications for Organizational Learning. In S. Minahan & J. Wolfram Cox (Eds.), *The Aesthetic Turn in Management* (1st ed.). Routledge. https://doi.org/10.4324/9781351147965

Bogart, A., & Landau, T. (2012). *The Viewpoints Book: A Practical Guide to Viewpoints and Composition*. Theatre Communications Group.

Brooks, D. (2016, October 7). Letter of Complaint: Cards Against Humanity. *The New York Times*. https://www.nytimes.com/2016/10/07/magazine/letter-of-complaint-cards-against-humanity.html

Chueng-Nainby, P., Woodcock, A., & McDonagh, D. (2016, June 27). *Mobility as Empowerment: Co-Design with Communities as Empathic Service Innovation*. DRS 2016: Design + Research + Society: Future-Focused Thinking, Brighton, UK. https://static1.squarespace.com/static/55ca3eafe4b05bb65abd54ff/t/57378a2c4d088e9a0cc37ac6/1463257647352/Chueng+Nainby-Mobility+as+Empowerment-DRS+Workshop.pdf

Ciliotta Chehade, E., & Arnold Mages, M. (2022). Systems for Innovation: Towards a model of requisite variety through intercultural conversations. *Proceedings of Relating Systems Thinking and Design*. RSD11, Brighton, UK. https://rsdsymposium.org/achieving-requisite-variety-through-intercultural-conversations

Cocker, J. (2010, November 7). *BBC - Jarvis Cocker's Sunday Service: Jarvis Talks to Brian Eno about Creative Strategy*. BBC Radio 6.
http://www.bbc.co.uk/blogs/jarviscocker/2010/11/jarvis-talks-to-brian-eno-abou.shtml

Cohen, D. B. (2006). "Family Constellations": An Innovative Systemic Phenomenological Group Process From Germany. *The Family Journal*, *14*(3), 226–233.
https://doi.org/10.1177/1066480706287279

Collins, H. M. (2000). Four Kinds of Knowledge, Two (or Maybe Three) Kinds of Embodiment, and the Question of Artificial Intelligence. In *Essays in honor of Hubert L. Dreyfus. 2: Heidegger, coping, and cognitive science / ed. By Mark A. Wrathall* (pp. 179–196). MIT.

Crowley, G. J. (2011). Building Trust through Inclusion: Reflections on the Practice of Deliberative Democracy. In R. Cavalier (Ed.), *Approaching Deliberative Democracy: Theory and Practice* (pp. 179–197). Carnegie Mellon University Press.

Dean, P., Lees, M., & Smith, Q. (2015, May 7). Review: Cards Against Humanity » Shut Up & Sit Down [Blog]. *Shut Up & Sit Down*.
https://www.shutupandsitdown.com/review-cards-against-humanity/

Dillon, J., Dranove, D., Halpern, E., Hantoot, B., Munk, D., Pinsof, D., Temkin, M., & Weinstein, E. (2017). *Cards against humanity* (1.7). Cards Against Humanity, LLC.

Eno, B., & Schmidt, P. (2001). *Oblique strategies: Over one hundred worthwhile dilemmas* (5th ed.). [The Authors].

Hagberg, G. L. (2014). *Ensemble Improvisation, Collective Intention, and Group Attention* (G. E. Lewis & B. Piekut, Eds.; Vol. 1). Oxford University Press.
https://doi.org/10.1093/oxfordhb/9780195370935.013.011

Harrison, S., & Dourish, P. (1996). Re-place-ing Space: The Roles of Place and Space in Collaborative Systems. *Proceedings of the 1996 ACM Conference on Computer Supported Cooperative Work*, 67–76.
https://doi.org/10.1145/240080.240193

Mulder-Nijkamp, M., & Chueng-Nainby, P. (2015, July 22). *Collective Brand Imagery Weave: Connecting Brand Values to Product Characteristics Using Physical Complex Installation*.
https://doi.org/10.13140/RG.2.1.2316.6883

Nagel, T. (1974). What is it like to be a bat? *The Philosophical Review*, *83*(4), 435–450.

Neely, S., & Arnold Mages, M. (2024). A Gradient of Unisons: The Emergent Superunit in Collective Action. *Design Issues*, *40*(2), 42–55. https://doi.org/10.1162/desi_a_00754

Policy Lab. (2015, July 10). *Cards toolkit to help generate ideas and develop your policy project in an agile way—Policy Lab* [Blog]. Policy Lab. https://openpolicy.blog.gov.uk/2015/07/10/cards-toolkit-to-help-generate-ideas-and-develop-your-policy-project-in-an-agile-way/

Ricketts, D., & Lockton, D. (2019). Mental landscapes: Externalizing mental models through metaphors. *Interactions*, *26*(2), 86–90. https://doi.org/10.1145/3301653

Scholtens, S., Petroll, C., Rivas, C., Fleer, J., & Konkolÿ Thege, B. (2021). Systemic constellations applied in organisations: A systematic review. *Gruppe. Interaktion. Organisation. Zeitschrift Für Angewandte Organisationspsychologie (GIO)*, *52*(3), 537–550.
https://doi.org/10.1007/s11612-021-00592-8

Snyder-Young, D., Arnold Mages, M., Bhargava, R., Carr, J., Perovich, L., Talmadge, V., Wason, O., Zellner, M., C-Dina, A., Birnholz, R., Brockett, H., D'Ascoli, E., Holt, D., Love, S., & Belliveau, G. (2024). Viewpoints/Points of View: Building a Transdisciplinary Data Theatre Collaboration in Six Scenes. *Arts*, *13*(1), 37. https://doi.org/10.3390/arts13010037

Spinosa, C., Flores, F., & Dreyfus, H. L. (1997). *Disclosing new worlds: Entrepreneurship, democratic action, and the cultivation of solidarity*. MIT Press.

Strmic-Pawl, H. V., & Wilson, R. (2016). Equal Opportunity Racism? Review of Cards Against Humanity, created by Josh Dillon, Daniel Dranove, Eli Halpern, Ben Hantoot, David Munk, David Pinsof, Max Temkin, and Eliot Weinstein, distributed by Cards Against Humanity LLC. *Humanity & Society*, *40*(3), 361–364. https://doi.org/10.1177/0160597616653154

Wade, H. (2004). Systemic working: The constellations approach. *Industrial and Commercial Training*, *36*(5), 194–199. https://doi.org/10.1108/00197850410548576

Chapter 8

Ashby, W. R. (1956). *An introduction to cybernetics*. Chapman & Hall : Methuen.

Burgess, M. M. (2014). From 'trust us' to participatory governance: Deliberative publics and science policy. *Public Understanding of Science*, *23*(1), 48–52. https://doi.org/10.1177/0963662512472160

Charmaz, K. (2014). *Constructing grounded theory* (2nd edition). SAGE.

Christensen, C. L. (2017, February 26). Indivisible Pittsburgh Will Destroy Itself. *Huffington Post*. https://www.huffingtonpost.com/entry/indivisible-pittsburgh-will-destroy-itself_us_58b205ede4b02f3f81e4484b

Ehn, P. (2008). Participation in Design Things. *Proceedings of the Tenth Anniversary Conference on Participatory Design 2008*, 92–101. http://dl.acm.org/citation.cfm?id=1795234.1795248

Gastil, J., Knobloch, K., & Kelly, M. (2012). Evaluating Deliberative Public Events and Projects. In T. Nabatchi, J. Gastil, M. Leighninger, & G. M. Weiksner (Eds.), *Democracy in Motion* (pp. 205–228). Oxford University Press. https://doi.org/10.1093/acprof:oso/9780199899265.003.0010

Guba, E. G., & Lincoln, Y. S. (1989). *Fourth generation evaluation*. Sage Publications.

Nalbandian, J. (1994). Reflections of a "Pracademic" on the Logic of Politics and Administration. *Public Administration Review*, *54*(6), 531–536. https://doi.org/10.2307/976672

Polanyi, M. (2009). *The tacit dimension*. University of Chicago Press.

Sanders, E. B.-N., & Westerlund, B. (2011). Experiencing, Exploring and Experimenting in and with Co-Design Spaces. *Nordes*, *0*(4). http://www.nordes.org/opj/index.php/n13/article/view/110

Secko, D. M., Preto, N., Niemeyer, S., & Burgess, M. M. (2009). Informed consent in biobank research: A deliberative approach to the debate. *Social Science & Medicine*, *68*(4), 781–789. https://doi.org/10.1016/j.socscimed.2008.11.020

Spinosa, C., Flores, F., & Dreyfus, H. L. (1997). *Disclosing new worlds: Entrepreneurship, democratic action, and the cultivation of solidarity*. MIT Press.

Stalvey, L. M. (1989). *The education of a WASP*. University of Wisconsin Press.

Chapter 9

Bohm, D., Factor, D., & Garrett, P. (1991). *Dialogue—A proposal*. David Bohm. http://www.david-bohm.net/dialogue/dialogue_proposal.html

Castells, M. (2012). *Networks of outrage and hope: Social movements in the Internet Age*. Polity Press.

Costanza-Chock, S. (2020). *Design justice: Community-led practices to build the worlds we need*. The MIT Press.

Dubberly, H., & Pangaro, P. (2009). What is conversation, and how can we design for it? *Interactions*, *16*(4), 22. https://doi.org/10.1145/1551986.1551991

Flyvbjerg, B., Bruzelius, N., & Rothengatter, W. (2003). The megaprojects paradox. In *Megaprojects and risk: An anatomy of ambition*. Cambridge University Press.

Foa, R. S., & Mounk, Y. (2016). The Democratic Disconnect. *Journal of Democracy*, *27*(3), 5–17. https://doi.org/10.1353/jod.2016.0049

Korzybski, A. (2005). *Science and sanity: An introduction to non-Aristotelian systems and general semantics* (5. ed., 3. print). Inst. of General Semantics.

Mason, J. (2002). *Researching your own practice: The discipline of noticing*. Routledge.

Noel, L.-A. (2023). *Design Social Change: Take action, work toward equity, and challenge the status quo* (First edition). Ten Speed Press.

Onuoha, M. (2017, September 15). *Implications of Data Collection*. SPAN 2017 Pittsburgh, Google Pittsburgh, 6425 Living Pl Pittsburgh, PA 15206. https://www.youtube.com/watch?v=0AhuqZQKnvE&feature=youtu.be&t=2h55m20s

Polanyi, M. (2009). *The tacit dimension*. University of Chicago Press.

Putnam, R. D. (2000). *Bowling alone: The collapse and revival of American community*. Simon & Schuster.

Scharmer, C. O. (2009). *Theory U leading from the future as it emerges: The social technology of presencing*. Berrett-Koehler Publishers. http://www.books24x7.com/marc.asp?bookid=42600

Spinosa, C., Flores, F., & Dreyfus, H. L. (1997). *Disclosing new worlds: Entrepreneurship, democratic action, and the cultivation of solidarity*. MIT Press.

Vice Chairman's Staff of the Joint Economic Committee. (2017). *What We Do Together: The State of Associational Life in America* (p. 81). https://www.lee.senate.gov/public/_cache/files/b5f224ce-98f7-40f6-a814-8602696714d8/what-we-do-together.pdf

ABOUT THE AUTHOR

Michael Arnold Mages, PhD, has designed to facilitate people having better conversations for over two decades. He teaches in the department of Art + Design and the College of Arts, Media, and Design at Northeastern University, and is a researcher and core faculty in Northeastern's Center for Design.

His research supports people in civic and healthcare contexts, and his research has been supported by the Heinz Endowments, and the National Institutes of Health, among others. He has written numerous articles and taught and lectured internationally.